THE JOB SEARCH SOLUTION

The Ultimate System for Finding a Great Job Now!

SECOND EDITION

TONY BESHARA

AMACOM

American Management Association

New York • Atlanta • Brussels • Chicago • Mexico City • San Francisco
Shanghai • Tokyo • Toronto • Washington, D.C.

Bulk discounts available. For details visit:
www.amacombooks.org/go/specialsales
Or contact special sales:
Phone: 800-250-5308
Email: specialsls@amanet.org
View all the AMACOM titles at: www.amacombooks.org

This publication is designed to provide accurate and authoritative information in regard to the subject matter covered. It is sold with the understanding that the publisher is not engaged in rendering legal, accounting, or other professional service. If legal advice or other expert assistance is required, the services of a competent professional person should be sought.

Portions of this second edition also appear in Tony Beshara's books *Unbeatable Résumés* and *Acing the Interview*.

Library of Congress Cataloging-in-Publication Data
Beshara, Tony, 1948-
    The job search solution : the ultimate system for finding a great job now! / Tony Beshara. — 2nd ed.
        p. cm.
    Includes bibliographical references and index.
    ISBN-13: 978-0-8144-1799-7
    ISBN-10: 0-8144-1799-X
  1. Job hunting.   2 Job hunting—Psychological aspects.   3. Employment interviewing.   4. Self-presentation.
I. Title.
    HF5382.7.B472 2012
    650.14—dc23   2011033265

About AMA
American Management Association (www.amanet.org) is a world leader in talent development, advancing the skills of individuals to drive business success. Our mission is to support the goals of individuals and organizations through a complete range of products and services, including classroom and virtual seminars, webcasts, webinars, podcasts, conferences, corporate and government solutions, business books, and research. AMA's approach to improving performance combines experiential learning—learning through doing—with opportunities for ongoing professional growth at every step of one's career journey.

Printing number
10 9 8 7 6 5 4 3 2 1

Contents

Dedicated to God's greatest blessings,
My wonderful wife and best friend, Chrissy, and our family.

Acknowledgments

Greatest thanks go to Chrissy for her prayers, time, and spiritual support. A great deal of thanks go to the "team" at AMACOM: Ellen, Erika, Carole, Kama, and Barry . . . you all are the best! Thanks also go to Pam Williams, who kept these chapters straight revision after revision; to Susan Bartosh, who carefully proofed the manuscript; and to Vernelle Fugitt for her research. Thanks to Phil McGraw, his organization, and their spirit of service. And a special thanks to the thousands of candidates and hiring authorities I have worked with over the years who contributed to this book's contents.

Preface

THIS LETTER, written to me in September of 2009, during the worst recession since the Great Depression of 1933, is from a woman who lives in Detroit, Michigan. At the time she wrote it, the unemployment rate in Detroit was 13 percent. She had worked for a number of years for GM and, along with thousands of others, was laid off.

September 10, 2009

Tony,

Thank you for all of your guidance and support during this phase in my employment. I know that if we had not crossed paths, I would not be traveling my new, prosperous, and much brighter path.

I began my job search six months before I learned of my layoff. I registered with two large job boards, visited numerous company websites, and enlisted the services of three recruiters.

Given the current economic state of Detroit, I decided to form my own business and offer my services to companies who were reluctant to hire new employees. I attended numerous networking events weekly. I also attended conferences and seminars where my target clients would gather. Though I picked up some clients, it was not enough to cover my cost of living and my outlook on employment grew very dim.

After my formal layoff and slow business growth, I actively searched for jobs for nearly six months. I then found your books and your program. Through them, I learned about numerous unconventional ways to find work. Each week I networked, cold called, and even walked through the front doors of local businesses looking for work. I followed your system.

Your advice to call everyone I knew, including family, friends, former coworkers, and even their associates, was invaluable. What was just as important was

---

that you taught me what to say. After making a list, I called someone whom I had met only twice and explained my employment situation. Even though she was not in any position to offer me employment she did offer to speak with me and, as I learned from *The Job Search Solution*, any opportunity to present yourself is an interview.

Over a year earlier, she lost an employee and really had not considered filling the position. I followed the scripts that you provided and within the first 10 minutes of meeting me, she knew I would be a great candidate if she ever decided to open the position up. I followed up the next day with a thank you and the employer asked if I would like to further discuss the vacancy in her practice. For my second "meeting/interview," following the instructions of *The Job Search Solution*, I created a simple presentation about why I should be hired. That meeting was concluded by asking me to decide what an equitable rate would be for me to join the firm.

I now earn a considerable amount more than my previous automotive employer compensated me and work under much more desirable conditions. I know I would have never found this career if I had not learned and followed the methods given by you in *The Job Search Solution*. I learned how to get the job of my dreams in the down economy of the Motor City. Your advice motivated me to not give up. It was by faith, following your instructions "exactly" the way you recommend, as well as remaining positive that I now have the job of my dreams!

With Warmest Regards,
Shaniece Bennett

Shaniece is very kind. Of all of the letters, emails, and notes I've received over the years, this one is probably the most meaningful. This woman had been laid off by General Motors at the height of the recession in a city with 13 percent unemployment and she found another job. As any good coach would tell you, no matter how good his strategy is and how good the plays he calls are, the "players" still have to execute. Shaniece executed flawlessly. She practiced the techniques that I wrote about and followed the instructions to a T.

The message is simple. I'm not guaranteeing that it's easy, but it is simple. If you follow the instructions in the process that I recommend in this book, you have a very good chance of getting a job.

Introduction

SINCE WRITING THE FIRST EDITION of *The Job Search Solution* in 2006, I've received thousands of letters, emails, and phone calls thanking me for the advice I provided people in their job search.

I'm proud of the fact that this is one of the few job search books written by somebody who's actually in the trenches, finding people jobs on a daily basis. What I write about is not theoretical. It is advice that comes from experience. Since 1973, I've personally found more than 8,500 people jobs—*one candidate at a time and one job opportunity at a time.*

I'm on the phone an average of six hours a day, speaking with candidates and employers. I've interviewed more than 25,000 candidates face-to-face and I've worked with more than 22,000 different companies and individuals in those companies, many of whom have hired candidates from me. I've also been personally involved in more than 50,000 interviewing "cycles" where my candidate did not get hired, or the hiring authority, after interviewing, did nothing at all—which happens 20 percent of the time.

I have placed people in almost every kind of position, from accountants, salespeople, and attorneys to CFOs, CEOs, IT professionals, hourly workers, mechanics, mathematicians, engineers, machinists, sheet metalworkers, and chemists—in short, from entry-level to the board room. I've seen just about everything you can imagine in the interviewing and hiring process, and probably some things you can't imagine.

The firm I own, Babich & Associates, has been in business since 1952. We're the oldest placement and recruitment firm in the Southwest and one of the largest. Since its founding, my firm has helped more than 120,000 people find jobs. We have developed a system for finding people new jobs and new careers. I've imparted the *system* that we have developed in this book. This is real-world stuff.

Recessions and Getting a Job

I have experienced six recessions since I've been in this profession. Every one of them has been different and has had a different impact on business and the job search environment. Ironically, when I first got into this profession in 1973, it was the beginning of an economic recession. The most recent recession has been the worst one since the 1930s. Employment recessions can be national, regional, statewide, or community-based. If you've been out of work for five or six months or more, it's a recession to you.

The employment market is a bit different every time we crawl out of one of these recessions. Digging out of this one is going to take a while. This fact has a decided impact on what hiring authorities and companies look for when they go to hire people. Being in the trenches every day, listening to business owners, managers, everyone from CEOs down to the first-line production managers, I hear exactly what goes on in the minds and hearts of front-line business managers. I impart that knowledge in this book.

Looking for a job is harder to do during a recession and equally hard as we come out of one. If you're searching for a job, you need to be aware of how hiring authorities and business managers think. The bottom line is that they are uncertain. Uncertainty leads to doubt and doubt leads to fear. Even as we come out of this recession, doubt, uncertainty and fear will be part of America's business environment for years to come. This business condition affects your job search. You need to know that the hiring authority who is interviewing you is worried about making a mistake in hiring. He or she is looking for as many reasons *not* to hire you as reasons *to* hire you. I will teach you how to deal with this.

Babble and Misguided Advice

Unfortunately, most of the stuff published about finding a job is written by people who might be sincere, but who are résumé writers, career authors, counselors, career coaches, advisers, or just people who found a few jobs in their career. Most of the advice given ranges anywhere from misguided to pure junk. The biggest problem with advice about looking for a job is that most everyone has an opinion or an idea about what works. Being married doesn't make any of us an expert on marriage and certainly doesn't qualify us to give marriage advice. Most people don't know what they don't know.

Google "how to find a job" and you will get advice like "networking is the only way to go" (which is really one way, but not the only way); "find a job online" (which is hardly ever successful); uncover the "hidden job market" (there is no such thing); and a career coach's recommendation that you should go into an interview letting the hiring authority know that, "I'm not really looking for a job—I'm investigating companies." (Oh, brother, that approach sure won't get you hired.)

A fellow "executive recruiter" gave the ridiculous advice of "don't worry about practicing interviewing or answering interviewing questions—let it come naturally." That's like telling a basketball player that he doesn't need to worry about practicing, he can compete against LeBron James or Dirk Nowitzki by just relying on his natural ability. One "authority" told the readers that it was best to be last in the interviewing lineup, and another said it was best to be first. (The real truth is that they're both right, *depending on the situation*.) Another job search writer told readers that they should get one job offer for every six interviews. (Are you kidding me!) And, alas, a top author (who doesn't find people jobs but writes about it) advised readers that the best way to find a job is to "target" the top ten companies you'd like to work for and pursue them. It doesn't seem to matter if those firms are hiring or laying off or if what they do has nothing to do with what you do—apply anyhow. (Is this guy nuts?)

I don't know where people come up with this stuff, but I hear it every day. Some of it actually defies common sense, like the existence of a "hidden job market" or saying, "I'm not really looking for a job." The only authorities worth listening to are those who are actually *finding* people jobs on a daily basis.

My System

What I'm laying out for you in this book is a systematic approach to finding a job. You will notice that I emphasize, as John Wooden taught, that if you focus on the process you don't have to worry about the result. If you correctly manage the process of getting a job, you will eventually successfully find one.

You will learn a systematic approach to getting interviews, performing well on those interviews, following up on those interviews, and managing the process to actually get an offer and go to work. The process is very simple, but it isn't easy—in fact, it's very hard. As with all systems, there is an *artistic* side of the equation. The "formula" of the system will work only with an "artistic" performance in getting interviews, performing well in interviews, performing well on follow-up interviews, and handling negotiation. I can teach you what to say, but I can't teach you to say it with sincerity, feeling, empathy, and confidence. That takes practice.

I've always been amazed that in my personal practice I can teach two different candidates the same thing. One will go through the process with a stellar performance and negotiate an offer beyond what the hiring authority said the company would pay. The other, who is equally as good a candidate, will get exactly the same information and won't get beyond the first 15 minutes of an initial interview. That's where the art and practice come in.

Is My Sell-Yourself Approach Too Aggressive?

There are some critics and reviewers of the first edition of *The Job Search Solution* who claim that what I advised was just too aggressive for them—that I was just a salesman advising sales techniques and scripts. They are absolutely right! Getting a job in today's market—or in any market—requires selling yourself better than any other candidate. What I teach *is* aggressive. It is sales. It is only pushy, however, if you don't use the scripts in the right way.

If you don't practice what I teach and communicate humility and sincerity in your presentations and during the process, you will come across as *pushy* and you won't get to first base. It takes practice. If you *sell* yourself with the attitude that you are more in-terested in what you will *get* from someone rather than what you can *do* for them, you will come across as pushy. If you use what I teach in an obnoxious, egotistical manner, none of it will work. If you present yourself in an "I'm interested in helping you get what you want and in the process, get what I want" way, you'll be in great shape. It's all a matter of attitude.

Don't confuse pride with arrogance. Presenting yourself with confidence is differ-ent from being obnoxious. Some critics claim that the techniques I teach are too ag-gressive for them, that they know a *better* way. That's wonderful! If what I teach is too aggressive for you, if you're uncomfortable with it, don't use it or modify it to your personal style. If you've been successful in finding a job a different way, God bless you. The system I teach is not the *only* way to find a job. I'm simply presenting a system and process that has helped thousands of people find a job. The techniques are proven and, if done the right way, really work. They get positive results.

Guarantee

If you buy this book and it doesn't help you, send it to me with your name and address and I'll either send you your money back or give the price of the book to charity in your name. Just choose one of the options.

1   The Emotional and Psychological Dimensions of Finding a Job

NEXT TO THE DEATH OF A SPOUSE, child, or parent, the fourth most emotional thing we do (tied with divorce) is look for a job. No matter what anybody tells you, changing jobs (and the difficulties in doing so) can be an emotionally debilitating experience for anyone; and certainly it's difficult for the other important people in your life: spouse, relatives, friends—in short, any significant people who touch your life.

The last five or six years have made things even more difficult. We've experienced a major recession and unemployment levels recently have hovered close to 10 percent nationally and as high as 12 or 13 percent in some parts of the country. At the time of this writing there are 15 million Americans who are jobless. This doesn't include those who are working part time but would prefer to work full time. Nor does it include a record 1.3 million who are too discouraged even to look for work.

Among other benefits, our jobs give us a sense of belonging, a sense of contributing to a group or a society, and mostly offer us a great sense of personal growth. Our jobs make us feel productive and useful. We describe ourselves in terms of work and what we do, and we identify with that work. In fact, a large part of our identities and self-respect are dependent on our jobs. The sudden loss of employment or feelings of dissatisfaction with our job can cause great disruption in our lives. These changes can reorder our priorities and have a tendency to damage our self-esteem.

In the past, we associated the emotional strain of looking for a job with people who were unemployed. But the erratic state of the current economy and the state of business in the United States can cause even those who have a job to be worried about it on a daily basis—which can create more strain. We read about companies scaling back their workforces and/or shying away from adding employees. We see our peers, neighbors, friends, and relatives either being laid off or living with the threat of being laid off. So, even if we have a job, we are scared.

It is said that as many as 52 percent of people employed in the United States would like to leave their current jobs. Maintaining a job that you really don't like is as difficult as finding a job when you don't have one. A study done for *The Conference Board Review* revealed that as many as two-thirds of U.S. employees are either actively looking for a new job or merely going through the motions at their current jobs.

This kind of emotional state is called the *psychological recession*. In this condition, people feel worried about the present and even more pessimistic about the future. This is especially relevant in the business world, because chronically fearful people are too exhausted to be creative and innovative. They expect the worst to happen, so they see no reason to give their all at work.

Acknowledge Your Emotions

> *"It's a recession when your neighbor loses his job; it's a depression when you lose yours."*
>
> —PRESIDENT HARRY S. TRUMAN

The loss of a job is accompanied by just about every negative emotion that a person can experience. That is why, on the emotional severity scale, losing a job ranks close behind the death of a loved one. In fact, the death of a spouse and loss of a job are the two life events that are considered to be emotionally devastating for the longest period of time. The solution is not to deny that you're going to experience these emotions, but to figure out how you're going to minimize them so they have the least effect on you, your psyche, and your ability to go out and find a new job.

> "My sister gave me your book in 2008. I didn't need a job then. This job search has been the most emotionally trying experience I've ever known. You were right."
> —Tonya S., St. Louis, Missouri

People often underestimate the challenge of looking for a new job and the negative emotions connected with that effort. I can't tell you the number of hiring authorities I've worked with over the years who have told me they weren't interested in interviewing candidates who are not currently employed. Their opinion is that, if someone is out of work, there must be something wrong with the individual. But when these people find themselves out of work as well, their view of people without jobs changes overnight.

The probability today of anyone either being out of work or being fearful about losing his or her job is about twice what it was as little as ten years ago. I explain this phenomenon in the next chapter, but, in short, it's because business operations—and therefore jobs—are much more erratic than they've ever been. And it isn't going to get any better in the near future.

Looking for a job is an emotional roller-coaster. As you get over the fears and insecurities of *having* to look for a job, you nevertheless go through the same emotions while *actually looking* for one. These emotions carry over into the interviewing and job-finding process. Your hopes will be dashed. Your ego will be assaulted. You will be lied to. You will feel strung out by the process—encouraged, then deflated. We address the causes of these frustrations in a subsequent chapter. Just be ready for the emotional strain.

* * *

Similarly, if you think having a job while you're looking for a new one is emotionally or psychologically easy, think again. Even if you like your job but need to change for one reason or another, being employed while looking for a new job is only slightly more comforting than being out of work and looking for a job. The stress you'll feel from trying to find a new job (which is a job in itself) while also performing your best at the present job is often *more* difficult than simply devoting all your efforts to finding a job.

An erratic economy can make this job-hunting experience even more emotionally challenging. When the employment picture is uncertain, thousands of other people are out of work, too, or are looking for new jobs while they worry about their present ones. You are going through emotionally difficult times, but so are many others. The quick and unexpected downsizings, layoffs, and firings occur on a regular basis. Many candidates (whose companies are downsizing) get assurances on a Friday that their jobs are not in jeopardy, but then on Monday they are told they are being laid off! You can't do much about the poor economy. You can, however, control how you react to it.

Get Over It—Life Isn't Fair

Expect mood swings and physical changes that stress your body. However, the sooner you get over all these emotions and put them in perspective, the better off you are going to be. People who can process their emotions by analyzing them will deal more constructively with the grief that accompanies a job loss. That is, people who express their grief get over it faster. And the faster you deal with all your negative emotions, the faster you will gain perspective on your situation and move on to finding a new job.

EXERCISE: EXPRESS YOUR FEELINGS IN DETAIL

Please, please, please, don't overlook this exercise. Take a few minutes to write down the feelings and thoughts you have about each of the following. Soon, you'll be empowered to put these emotions into their proper perspective and be able to move on. Remember, you're not going to ignore these feelings or try to deny them. You're going to delve into them so deeply that you'll understand them, see them as distractions, and release them from your mind.

Try to answer the following questions:

- How were you *frustrated* in your previous or current employment?

- What were the *disappointments* you had with the job or company you left or are now experiencing in your current employment?

- Did you lose or are you losing *self-esteem*? How?

- Were you *shocked* at being laid off, fired, or forced to look for a new job?

- Who is to *blame* for your having to look for a new job? Describe the situation in detail.

- Describe your *disillusionment* with the entire situation. How did it come about?

- Describe the *shame* you feel in needing to look for a new job. Describe what other people will think and say about you, about your having to find a new job, about your being fired or laid off, and so forth.

- Do you feel *isolated* by having to look for a new job? Can other people really understand?

- Are you *denying* any of the things or situations that happened? Can you describe them clearly, even if emotionally?

- Do you feel *guilty* about what happened in losing your job or the reason you need to look for a new one? Is there anything you could have done to prevent the situation?

- Whom do you feel *hostile* toward, if anyone? Why do they deserve your hostility?

Now, for some longer items:

1. Complete this sentence: I am *angry* because: *America Job System is Messed up! Period*

   (Really go into an in-depth explanation as to why you're angry. Be as angry as you want to be; write as long as you would like.)

2. Describe the *depressed feelings* you might have about the situation. Do you feel sad, empty, or fatigued about it? How does "poor you" feel about this whole thing? How do you describe "poor you"? Mention details: _____

   _____

3.　Describe, if it applies, how *unfair* the entire situation is. Mention details: _____

_____

_____

4.　Write down all the things that make you *fearful* about this situation. Be as detailed as you need to describe exactly what you are afraid of—even ridiculous fears: _____

_____

_____

After you have written out your explanations in detail, read them at least three times, preferably out loud. I want you to really feel every one of the emotions that you're experiencing. It is important to focus on and *deeply appreciate* every feeling you have had, even if this isn't a pleasant experience. Read the answer to each question, then ask yourself aloud: "Can I let this feeling go?" Then, "Do I want to let this feeling go?" Do not be surprised if your answers are no. It is not uncommon to want to hold on to these feelings during the "grieving" period. The important thing is to feel these emotions repeatedly until you genuinely, sincerely feel that you have let them go.

Realize that you may never let go of all of these emotions—you may never eliminate them completely from your emotional memory. The objective here is not to eliminate them altogether, but to minimize their impact on you. You want to move forward toward a positive emotional state so as to interview well and attain a new job. Use this exercise three or four times at one sitting, and do two or three sittings a day until the emotions are neutralized.

There are two variations on this exercise. The first is to use a tape recorder and record an audio version of your emotional responses instead of writing them down. Then listen to the tape to recapture the emotions before you release them. The other variation is to discuss the responses, after you have written them, with a loving spouse, empathetic friend, or coach. Ask that person to just listen nonjudgmentally, thereby helping you clarify your feelings, no matter what how negative they are.

Visualize Your Feelings

Another way to deal with the mixed feelings of job loss and job stress is to visualize them. Close your eyes and "see" the exercise questions. This is a lot like playing a movie of your frustrations, disappointments, loss of self-esteem, shock, and so on—picturing the scene in your mind, with you as the central character. Think close-ups and in color. Try to make the picture as detailed as possible. As you run that movie in your mind, at a certain point change it to black-and-white and project it as far out in front of you as possible, until it becomes a speck in the distance. Your negative emotions will travel away with that image as it disappears from sight. *Doing this kind of exercise, over and over, neutralizes the emotion that is associated with being up close, in color, and involved in the picture itself.*

Of all the things you can do to put your emotions in perspective, writing your feelings down in detail and visualizing them are the most effective. Dealing with anger and fear in an honest, forthright, and detailed manner will help relieve the acidity of the emotions.

Getting Started

> *"Action conquers fear."*
>
> —Peter Nivio Zarlenga, *The Orator*

The greatest antidote for these psychological "poisons" is to take massive, massive action. The problem is that most people don't know exactly where to begin. That's what this book is all about.

There is so much junk advice and "noise" out there about how to find a job that even reading it all can get confusing and be depressing. But, hold on. . . . We're going to make it real simple—not easy, but simple.

2 Be Ready for the Crazy, Chaotic World of Trying to Get Hired

IF YOU GET THE MESSAGE OF THIS CHAPTER, the expectations you have about your job search will change. Most people believe that they are going to be interviewed and hired by astute, competent leaders with great business acumen, who make logical, thoughtful, timely, commonsensical, intelligent decisions. After all, they are interviewing you—or should be, anyhow. Right? Wrong!

Having interviewed more than 25,000 candidates, face-to-face, since 1973, I'm always amazed that people looking for a job think that those people who run companies in the United States really know what they're doing when it comes to business matters and especially hiring. Most people recognize that this is not the case with the companies they are now working for or have worked for in the past. But all of a sudden, when they become *candidates* for employment and begin looking for a new job, they think that all those other companies in America are being managed by astute leaders who have great business sense.

> "Most of the companies I have worked for were run by the seat of their pants. I don't know why I thought it would be different when I looked for a job. In the past two weeks I had one employer tell me he was going to hire me, then didn't; and one company that said on a Friday that they were going to get me an offer letter on Monday. Then the company was sold over the weekend and all hiring was off. Businesses are so goofy." —Mark S., *The Job Search Solution* radio caller

Some Statistics on the Nature of Employers

As of 2010, there were 7.5 million businesses in the United States with employees and 27.5 million businesses without employees. Almost all of the businesses (99.9 percent) with employees have fewer than 500 employees and 98 percent of them employ fewer than a hundred people. In fact, the average number of employees in those 7.5 million businesses with employees is sixteen. Back in the year 2000, that figure was the same—sixteen.

The Bureau of Labor Statistics (BLS) indicates that between December 2000 and November 2008, the monthly turnover rate for U.S. companies was 3.3 percent. In 2010, the monthly hire-and-separation rate of employees and American companies, according to the BLS, was 3.2 and 3.1 percent, respectively. The point is that we are a nation of small companies, with 3 percent of our employees coming and going on a monthly basis. And some of these statistics reflect the situation before the present recession hit, with the unemployment rate now 9.8 percent. As I mentioned above, most people, for some reason, think that the majority of businesses in the United States are run with great business acumen and have a solid system of doing business. For job seekers, that translates into the misguided perception that their résumé is going to fall into the hands of intelligent people who are going to read it, who have the authority to hire, and who will bring them in for an interview.

Ironically, most of us know, in our hearts and minds, how messy, sloppy, and unorganized most businesses are. But for some reason, we imagine that when these people have the opportunity to interview us, things are going to change.

The average job in the United States lasts two-and-a-half to three years. Even at the C-suite level, there is little stability. Every year since 2007, the average CFO's tenure at the Fortune 500 and S&P 500 companies has been three years.

In 1975, the average company in the United States was fifty-eight years old. In 2011, the average company was fifteen years old. That is a drastic difference. If we stop and think about it, most of us should know in our hearts how erratic the nature of business is.

Even very large companies make poor business decisions and teeter on insolvency. All we need to do is look at the automotive firms and the major banks that, at one time, were model businesses; then, they had to be bailed out by the public. Business success, even survival, is much more of an imprecise science than most of us would want to admit.

Recent books like *Outliers* by Malcolm Gladwell, *Talent Is Overrated* by Geoff Colvin, and *The Talent Code* by Daniel Coyle reveal that, while hard work is certainly necessary, a great deal of good fortune also is behind both individual and business success. We have a tendency to look at successful businesses and successful people and think that they have magic potions and dazzling talent. Our own egos deceive us into believing that, when we are successful also, it is mostly due to our "dazzling brilliance," not that we take advantage of good circumstances when we encounter them.

Bill Gates summed it all up well: "Success is a lousy teacher; it seduces intelligent people into thinking they can't lose."

One study, written by Akbar Sadeghi for the Bureau of Labor Statistics, estimated that, in 2006, more than 70,000 businesses were established *every month* in the United States, and that more than 60,000 closed down *every month*. The same study attributed the creation of more than 300,000 new jobs per month to the birth of these firms, as well as more than 250,000 job losses from the deaths of those other firms. And that was in 2006, when the economy was stronger.

Another more conservative study by the U.S. Department of Commerce estimated that, in 2008, there were 627,200 new firms that began operation in the United States—and 639,146 firms that closed or went bankrupt that same year.

Once the recession was well under way in 2009, according to the BLS, there were 58,461 business establishments started every month in the United States, but there were 76,833 business establishments that went away. In that same period, there were 279,166 jobs per month created in the United States, while 237,083 jobs per month were lost.

The U.S. Department of Commerce states that seven out of ten new employer firms last at least two years, and about half of those survive five years. It is obvious though, that at the time of this writing, with unemployment at more than 9 percent, the rate of new jobs is not increasing. In fact, many businesses seem to be contracting. A recent confidence survey conducted by *Resources for Entrepreneurs* found that 61 percent of small-business owners do not expect the economy to fully recover until 2012 or later.

I'm not trying to overwhelm you or scare with all these numbers. I'm just trying to give you a realistic view of the overall employment picture. It's crazy!

People Who Manage Are Like the Rest of Us

To make matters even more complicated, the challenges of *enlarged ego*s and greed are often overlooked, or not even recognized, in most U.S. businesses. We certainly realize the destructive activities of Bernard Madoff, Raj Rajaratnam, and others like them because of the massive impact they have had on so many other people's lives. There are, however, countless other people managing and running businesses in the United States with the same enlarged egos and greed as these people had. The number of people whom these lesser known individuals impact isn't as great as the high-profile characters, but their actions can be just as devastating to the few who need to work for them or are their customers or clients.

When you come down to it, the people who manage most businesses in the United States are downright goofy, just as Mark, the radio caller, said. It is amazing that as many of them last as long as they do—and even make money in spite of themselves.

I have personally dealt with more than 23,000 different hiring authorities since 1973. I am convinced that most businesses in the United States model themselves after the people who run them. That is, people run their businesses not much differently from how they run their personal lives. Self-centeredness, greed, ego, lack of common sense, and general overall inflation of one's business acumen are more the norm than most of us would admit.

Most businesses are started and run by "technicians." These are people who are good at a particular skill, such as engineering, accounting, or sales. They think that because they are good at what they do, they can start or run a business or even run somebody else's business (that is, manage). Odds are, you've worked for these kinds of people before. They are good at what they do, but they are not really good "people people" and sometimes are awful at managing a successful business.

Most businesspeople are unrealistic. For example, they often overestimate their capability in dealing with a varying economy. One report estimated that 42 percent of small-business owners expected to increase wages during 2010. Now, we know that, except in small pockets of business, wages did not increase in 2010. In fact, the National Association for Business Economics released a survey at the beginning of 2010 reporting that 37 percent of queried firms planned to hire people in the next six months. Yet at the end of 2010, that hiring did not happen. The businesspeople were doing some wishful thinking.

Indeed, many of us see our own narrow slice of the economic pie in overly optimistic terms. We kid ourselves about the future and about our increased hiring. We hope the future will be better. Even supposed authorities promote this delusion. One popular job-hunting author recently wrote that companies assess their needs twelve months in advance. Oh, brother! The truth is that 99 percent of the businesses in the United States don't have that kind of vision. They never had, and they never will.

Let's get real. Recovery from each recession the United States has experienced has taken longer than the ones that went before. According to a recent study by the Mc-Kinsey Global Institute, for the recessions occuring after World War II and before 1990, employment recovered to its prerecession level within about six months after the end of the recessions. The recovery, however, after the 1990-91 recession took 15 months. After the 2001 recession it took 39 months. And McKinsey concluded it will take 60 months to recover after this recent recession.

And there are other factors. Nonfarm productivity has gone up nearly 7 percent from 2009 to 2010 and the cost of labor has gone down 6 percent. In fact, the last three quarters of 2009 represented the most rapidly increasing productivity in half a century, reaching a 7.4 percent annual rate. Some will say that this is due to technology. But it also is because employers are pushing their present employees harder and employees are reluctant to leave because it's so difficult to find another job. There are fewer jobs and more people are seeking them.

The Economic Policy Institute reported on February 6, 2011, "Aside from today's muddled picture, one thing is crystal clear: the U.S. labor market started 2011 with half a million fewer jobs than it had eleven years ago, in January 2000, though the labor force has grown by nearly 11 million workers since then. Today's numbers are a testament to both the enormity of the current labor market crisis plus the very weak jobs growth."

On top of this, companies have "unhappy" employees. The Conference Board reported in early 2011 that 61 percent of workers under the age of twenty-five were not happy with their jobs, and less than 45 percent of workers between the ages of forty-five and fifty-four were satisfied with their jobs. So, the hiring authority who is potentially going to interview you—unless he or she is the owner of the company—probably doesn't like his or her job any more than you like yours and is simply operating out of fear of loss rather than vision of gain.

When the people running a business are fearful about what is going to happen, it makes things difficult for the hiring authority, but even more difficult for the candidate. Hiring authorities can't afford to make a mistake. They perceive that there are hoards of candidates to choose from—and there are. They tell themselves and each other that they can't afford to hire anyone but the "perfect" candidate, so they are going to keep looking until they find that person. They may not even know if one of those candidates exists, but, by goodness, they need to find him or her.

Why is this important for you to know? Because if you are like most candidates, you think that you are going to be considered and evaluated by intelligent businesspeople who have a genuine sense of appreciation for what you can do for their company. You think a great hiring authority is personally anxious to interview and hire you.

If you assume that the "right people" are reviewing your résumé and thinking about interviewing you, you need to think again. I have been a professional recruiter since 1973. Here's what I have found:

- Thirty percent of "job openings" are never filled. Companies change their mind about hiring, postpone the hiring, or simply divide the job among existing employees.

- Sixty percent of the résumés received for a particular opening are never reviewed by the hiring authority.

- Seventy percent of the résumés received for a particular opening are reviewed by a third-party person—that is, Human Resources (HR), an internal recruiter, or some administrative person—who may or may not be qualified to interview any future employee. (A few years ago, we got a call from the CEO of a $40 million manufacturing company. He stated that he needed to hire a controller and that his daughter was going to do the initial interviewing—while she was home from college over Christmas break.)

- Sixty percent of the third-party people who *review* a résumé have no direct experience with the job they are recruiting for. They are going by information that is given to them by someone else.

- Fifty percent of position searches that companies do will have to be started over at least once; 25 percent of them will have to start over two times or more.

- Most people think companies take thirty to sixty days to fill vacancies. The average is more like 150 to 180 days.

- Forty percent of the résumés that are "opened" to be read are deleted because the reader can't tell immediately what the person has done, whom they have worked for, and how successful they have been in that position.

- The people who are reading the résumés are fearful for their own jobs.

On top of all of this, there are at least 100 résumés received for every job posted to the public. Even if a hiring authority decides to read *all* of them him or herself, the odds of yours reaching the top of the pile aren't great.

Hiring Is Mostly an Emotional Decision

It is important to learn early that the most qualified candidate for a job often is not the one who gets hired. The primary reasons people are *interviewed* are different from the primary reasons they are *hired*. In short, there's a big difference between the candidate's qualifications and his or her ability to get hired. People are often hired, or not hired, for all kinds of reasons that have nothing to do with the job, the company, or their qualifications. Over the years I've seen people get hired for all sorts of crazy reasons:

- They were from the same school as the hiring authority.

- They were young and theoretically had more energy.

- They were older and the hiring authority felt that older people are more committed.

- They were average performers and so they wouldn't "show up" anyone else in the department.

- They had no experience in the business and therefore wouldn't have acquired any "bad habits."

I could go on and on with things that you would laugh at or, in some cases, cry about. But I guarantee you that your qualifications are just part of the decision to hire or not to hire.

No hiring authority is ever going to admit that he or she hired someone who couldn't do the job. Just remember that the primary reason certain people are hired usually doesn't have anywhere as much to do with their qualifications as it does with their *perceived ability* to do the job—plus their ability to interview well and convince the hiring authority that they're the best persons for the job.

Remember these points:

- Hiring authorities and their companies are just as fearful of making a mistake in hiring as they are concerned about hiring the right person.

- The only thing hiring authorities really care about is finding someone to do the job. They won't give a darn about you as a candidate—your feelings, your preference, or how you prefer to be treated.

- Expect lies and confusion. Companies are going to tell you that they are going to call you back, that they are very interested in you as a candidate, that you would be excellent for the job—blah, blah, blah. Then you will never hear from them again.

- Many interviewing authorities, such as third-party screeners, people in the Human Resources department, or anyone involved in the hiring who is responsible for the evaluation of candidates but who doesn't actually have authority, will complicate the process.

- Expect politics to be involved. From the board of directors down to the cleaning crew, when people are involved it's political. As hiring is a personal reflection of many people in the organization, the process itself is political. Candidates will often become pawns in the politics of the company.

- The hiring authorities have inflated opinions of themselves and their companies. They tend to think that, if they have a job opening, it's the only one in town and "everyone would love to work here."

- Ignorance about hiring abounds. The hiring authorities know that someone must be hired, but they often don't know how to go about doing it.

- The organizations that will be interviewing you are going to change their minds daily, weekly, or monthly. They will tell you that they need to hire someone today, and four weeks later they will tell you the same thing.

- Finding a job is one of your highest priorities. In spite of what he or she tells you, don't believe a word any hiring authority says until the individual acts as though it is a high priority also.

- Ten to 15 percent of the time companies who say they want to hire a new person promote from within. You might ask, "Why would organizations interview external candidates if they are probably going to hire from within?" Well, the answer is pretty simple: Nobody wants to look bad. They want to appear as though they have surveyed the market, done their research, and hired the most qualified candidate.

- The interviewing and hiring process sometimes becomes so convoluted that the organization stops interviewing, reorganizes, and hires no one. I estimate this happens at least 30 percent of the time.

It is easy to get discouraged in your job search when you see this vision of this reality. But it is better to be aware of what really goes on than to be living a delusion and be disappointed.

3 Control the Process by Taking Massive Action Now!

HOPE IS A VIRTUE . . . NOT A STRATEGY! You can't hope and wish your way to a job. You have to develop a plan and a strategy of action.

Action is power! But when you're looking for a job, especially in a difficult job market, only massive action will get you the results that you need. What do I mean by massive action? It's simple: Expect it to be harder to get interviews. Be prepared to interview more times than you ever imagined. Know that you must perform better in an interview than you ever have imagined. You need to sell yourself harder than you ever thought you would. And your job search is going to take longer than you ever imagined.

This is a numbers game, pure and simple. The ability to find a job today depends on the number of interviews you can get. How you go about getting those interviews is complicated, though. That's why the majority of this book is devoted to this process.

It's all *numbers, numbers, numbers*! Numbers of contacts; numbers of friends; numbers of phone calls; numbers of face-to-face interviews with people who may or may not have job opportunities; numbers of first, second, third, fourth, and fifth interviews with anyone able to hire you. These are all necessary for you to find even a reasonable job opportunity in today's economy.

You are going to be depressed, dejected, rejected, refused, denied, forgotten, ignored, lied to, storied to, insulted, emotionally stomped on, messed with, postponed, forgotten on hold, eliminated, jilted, and conspired against. And after all that abuse, you are going to have to get up and run the risk of its happening again.

The reality: There are hordes of well-qualified candidates out there who are every bit as good as you—some even better—and they are competing for the same job you want. The difference between you and them can be your determination, your willingness to take massive amounts of action. You are going to interview at more places, you are going to sell yourself better than your competition, and you are going to have more job offers than anyone else.

When I wrote about this attack method in the first edition of *The Job Search Solution*, I got tons of emails and even phone calls from readers who claimed I was the only author who explained how difficult it was going to be to look for a job—and how they didn't believe me at first. But they wrote and expressed their gratitude for the advice, telling me about how right I was. So, you can believe me now or believe me later. You had best prepare for a real challenge.

The Process

> *"Do what you do best and the score takes care of itself."*
> —John Wooden, famous UCLA basketball coach

This concept of a "process" was the most remarked-about idea from the first edition of *The Job Search Solution*. It was a great "aha moment" for most readers. A tremendous number of people commented that, once they "got" this concept, they adopted a totally different outlook on seeking a job. The following story will illustrate their experience:

A young but earnest Zen student approached his Zen master. He asked, "Master, if I work very hard and diligently, how long will it take me to reach the goal of enlightenment and the way of Zen?" The master thought about it for a while and then replied to the students, "Ten years, my son."

So the student then said, "But Master, what if I work very, very hard and diligently, and I really apply myself to learn fast—how long will it take to reach the goal?" The Zen master thought a moment and then replied, "If you work very, very hard and apply yourself, it will take you twenty years, my son."

The student once again asked, "Master, if I really work at it, harder than I have ever done anything before, and devote my whole life to it, then how long will it take me to reach the goal?" The master pondered the question and said, "My son, if you do as you say, it should take you thirty years." The student, with a look of confusion and disappointment, said to the master, "But, Master, I don't understand. Every time I tell you that I will work harder, you tell me that it will take longer to reach the goal. I don't understand. How can this be?" The master replied, "My son, when you have one eye on the goal, you have only one eye on the path."

Having only one eye on the goal will burden you with frustration; you will be trying to reach the goal, and you are focused on the outcome. When you focus on the outcome, you focus on results, and when you focus on results, you can't concentrate in a relaxed way on the steps of the process.

So, if you weigh yourself down with the overwhelming burden of "getting a job" while you're trying to get interviews—or even go on an interview—you will inevitably perform poorly. But if you focus simply on getting an interview while you are trying to do just that, you are more likely to be more successful. If you focus on interviewing well while you are being interviewed, the job offer will take care of itself.

> **Key Point:** You can't control getting a job as much as you can control the process of getting a job.

The essence of this book is to make you aware of the process that it takes to find a job. If you manage the *process*, the *result* (landing a great job) will take care of itself. I cannot emphasize this enough. That's why great sports coaches like John Wooden, Bill Walsh, and Joe Paterno always encouraged their players to focus on the process. The score will take care of itself.

If you manage the process of finding a job and you do it in all the correct ways, then finding an excellent opportunity will just be a matter of course. It is that simple—not easy, but simple.

Passion, Intensity, and Enthusiasm

"To be a great champion you must believe that you are the best. If you're not, pretend that you are."
—Muhammad Ali, Heavyweight Champion boxer

Most individuals lose out in the job-seeking game because they don't develop a passionate intensity and enthusiastic approach to the process of looking for a job. Passion, intensity, and enthusiasm for the process of finding a job are conditioned emotions.

When most people look for a job, they are scared to death. They don't like looking for a job because that entails running the risk of rejection. No one likes to be rejected.

Interviewing from a defensive, scared, emotional position will never get you a job. At the start you may have to fake it until you make it through the ordeal. But you must learn to act like you enjoy this process. You could take six months to muddle through trying to find a job—during which time you become depressed, dejected, sad, and pissed off—only to realize that you need a psychologically motivated and enthusiastic way of finding that job. Or, you can rid yourself of all those garbage emotions now—even if it's a matter of pretending you like what you have to do and then doing it to the best of your ability.

What *matters* is your ability to organize and institute an effective job search that is going to get you employed in a new job as quickly as possible. The people you might think are being fake or false by acting passionate, enthusiastic, and loving every moment of it are the ones who get the jobs. They are not necessarily the most qualified candidates, but they are the ones selling themselves the best. Being passionate, intense, enthusiastic, and committed even when you do not feel that way takes a lot of practice. So, start acting enthusiastic about finding a job!

Being passionate and intense about finding a new job does not mean, however, that you jump up and down with excitement, become overly animated, or turn frantic. That kind of "passion" and intensity is short-lived; beyond the first one or two interviews, you can't sustain it. Instead, being passionate and intense about finding a job means that you don't postpone the start of your job search—in any way. You approach your job search as if it is a job itself. You look at it as a life-or-death matter. This is a 24-hours-a-day, 7 days-a-week, 365-days-a-year committed endeavor. You need to eat it, sleep it, drink it, and live it—until you find a job.

Finding a job takes a phenomenal amount of *practice*. And practice is one of the things that passionate, enthusiastic people do. In the beginning, most everyone is scared of looking for a job, even if they have looked for one before. But the smart people practice their scripts for getting an interview, they practice their scripts for initial interviews, they practice their scripts for follow-up interviews, and they practice their scripts for final interviews. They practice answering interview questions—over and over—until they get them right.

Looking for a job does not come naturally. One of the ways to overcome the fear, however, is to practice everything you will do during your job search—to the point where you execute it all flawlessly. I can't tell you the number of candidates I've interviewed over the years who think they are going to perform well in an interview without any practice beforehand. Reality: The candidates who practice the techniques I recommend always outperform even the most qualified candidates who do not practice.

Ways to Develop a Positive Attitude

> *"Attitude is more important than the past, than education, than money, than circumstances, than what people do or say. It is more important than appearance, giftedness, or skill. We cannot change our past. We cannot change the fact that people act in a certain way. We cannot change the inevitable. The only thing we can do is play on the one string we have, and that is our attitude."*
>
> —CHARLES SWINDOLL, MINISTER/AUTHOR

If you were to ask me the one, most important thing that marks the difference between people who change jobs successfully and those who don't, it would be *attitude*.

You have a choice in your attitude. You can adopt a positive mental attitude regarding your job search or a depressive, negative one. You can learn to appreciate the situation or you can curse every moment of the experience. Either you can develop a positive attitude about having to find a new job or you can settle for the normal, almost natural negative curse of it.

> **Key Point:** You will find a better job more quickly and have less anxiety about the process the sooner you get a positive attitude.

I recommend that you work on your attitude. You absolutely need to develop a super-positive mental attitude. The first step to developing this positive attitude is not only to accept the present circumstance but also to appreciate and actually be grateful for your present circumstance—exactly as it is. This first step means that you must embrace and begin to cherish the current circumstance because you know that you are going to grow from it. The sooner you start appreciating the positive aspects of looking for a new job, the better off you are going to be.

It is not as though you won't have some negative feelings or negative thoughts! When you are turned down for an interview, rejected on a job offer, or get told you're going to get an offer and you don't, you will feel negative, dejected, or depressed. What a well-developed, positive mental attitude will do is help you to *rebound* more quickly. You'll respond with an acknowledgment of your feelings, and you will move on to the next situation. A positive attitude does not mean that you must deny negative or sad feelings. Instead, you put those feelings into perspective and get over them quickly enough to be able to respond in a positive way to the next situation.

To maintain a positive attitude, you take massive action. You hang around supportive people. You read motivational books and listen to motivational tapes. You find an "attitude coach"—a friend or family member who will monitor your moods and keep them in check. You will see the "positive" angle in everything that happens.

The Need to Set Goals/Intentions

> *"Give me a stock clerk with a goal and I'll give you a man who will make history. Give me a man with no goals, and I'll give you a stock clerk."*
> —J. C. PENNEY, DEPARTMENT STORE FOUNDER

Success in any endeavor is pure chance if you don't have goals. You need to be thinking about changing jobs or getting a new job *all the time*. In fact, it may almost wind up being an obsession. The adage "Where the mind goes, energy flows" applies in the job-seeking effort. Just about every waking moment should have you mentally focused on getting a new job. It has to be a passionate, personal mission that doesn't end until you are successful.

Over the years, in researching and working with goals for others and myself, I have concluded that there should be an *intention* side of goals. So I have combined these concepts as one. Intentions have a softer side to them than strictly being goals. The challenge with goals is that by definition they need to be finite—that is, time sensitive. But that can be relatively harsh. People often become disappointed when they don't reach a goal. Intentions, on the other hand, are more subtle. They are spiritually deeper and more permanent.

There is going to be a tendency to bypass this section. Don't do that! In getting feedback from thousands of people who read the first *The Job Search Solution* and took the on-line course (www.thejobsearchsolution.com), I found that this was one of the most important, foundational things they did to lead to a successful job search.

Many people have a tendency to say, "Oh, yeah, I know all about setting goals. I get the message, but I need to move on to the more productive stuff." I assure you that the people who follow all of the things I teach—down to every detail—find that looking for a job is easier. Please don't overlook any aspect of the process I am teaching you. If you cut corners, everything will be more difficult.

Goals/intentions need to be SMART—an acronym used by Kenneth Blanchard in his book *Leadership and the One Minute Manager*. This means they must be:

- *Specific and Simple.* Stated in the present tense, with sensory-based language—auditory, visual, kinesthetic, even olfactory.

- *Manageable, Measurable, and Motivational.* I can, I do, and I feel.

- *Attainable and Achievable.* What I can control.

- *Relevant and Risk-Oriented.* Challenge/skill balanced. Meaningful, a stretch, hard but doable.

- *Trackable and Timed.* A process that can be measured, with dates set for accomplishment.

  More specifically:

- *Specific and Simple.* Goals/intentions should not be broad generalities. A statement such as "to get a better job and be happy" is not a specific goal/intention. Goals/intentions need to be stated in the present tense. You need to state them as though they were already accomplished. Also, it is best to state them in sensory—that is, seeing, feeling, hearing, and even smelling and tasting—language. An example of a specific and simple goal/intention in a job search situation is: "I see myself getting five face-to-face interviews a week. I can hear the sound of a hiring manager making an appointment to interview me. I feel the rush of success and anticipation for the opportunity to sell myself."

- *Manageable, Measurable, and Motivational.* Having manageable, measurable, and motivational goals/intentions leads to reasonable outcomes. Manageable goals are ones that you can personally manage. Having a goal/intention to grow wings and fly is not manageable. Having a goal/intention to become a better person is not measurable. A motivational goal/intention must be the kind of goal that you personally can get excited about, that moves you to action, and that truly inspires you. Many people make the mistake of developing a goal that really belongs to someone else. The goal of finding a new job has to be your goal/intention. It must motivate you.

- *Attainable and Achievable.* You need to develop goals/intentions that, even though they might be a stretch, can be attained, are achievable, and are within the realm of possibility relative to what you are capable of. You can control the activities necessary to get a new job; you may not be able to control getting a job offer.

- *Relevant and Risk-Oriented.* Your goal/intention must be meaningful and there needs to be a possibility that the goal/intention will not be attained. The goal that inherently does not have some risk to it is not a goal. Many people, for the sake of having a goal/intention, often write something that is easily within the realm of what they already do, and the chance of their not succeeding is very, very slim. The challenge of a goal must be balanced. For a goal to be valid, it must imply that there is reasonable risk and that there is challenge. In addition, the goal/intention must presuppose that the person has the ability, even if it is pressing the person to his or her limits to attain the goal.

- *Trackable and Timed.* Your goals/intentions need to be trackable and timed. Trackable necessitates numbers being associated with it. You must be able to measure goals by hard numbers. A goal for interviews would stipulate a certain number of interviews during a week. A timed goal/intention is a necessity. This may seem rather elementary, but many people design goals/intentions that don't have time limits. They let themselves off the hook at the beginning. The trackable, timed aspect of goals/intentions must be proportionate and relative to the size of the goal/intention.

An example of a SMART goal/intention is: "It is December 21, 20__. I am going to experience my first Christmas with my new company and my new job. I feel so grateful for my new opportunity. Most people are happy about Christmas—well, I am doubly happy. I feel so fulfilled with my new job. I see the new paycheck that is $ ___ a month. My spouse sees the paycheck, too, and is joyous. I am challenged every day. I am growing on a daily basis. I hear my family experiencing the shared happiness of my new job. I love my new job!"

This previous goal/intention encompasses all of the SMART attributes, but especially note that it is specific and stated in sensory-based language. It is also simple, measurable, certainly motivational, achievable, relevant, challenge/skill balanced, and timed.

Make Goals/Intentions Part of the Process

There are *process* goals/intentions and *outcome* goals/intentions. Outcome goals/intentions involve outperforming other people or focusing on a specific set of outcomes; process goals/intentions focus on the specific challenges of a situation.

In my experience, when it comes to looking for a job, process goals are much more important and reasonable than outcome goals. The reason is simple. With regard to being offered a job, the outcome is nowhere near as controllable for an individual as are the events in the process of finding a job. For example, setting a goal/intention of making a certain number of calls to employers to set interviews, or attaining a qualified number of interviews every week, is a lot more specific, manageable, measurable, attainable, trackable, and timed than the general goal of accepting a job offer. The timing in accepting a job offer, even though you are actively looking for one, is often too unpredictable to be an effective goal/intention. So, the idea is to set goals around the process of finding a job and let the result take care of itself.

Make Your Goals/Intentions Public

Research reveals that *public* goals/intentions are more effective than *private* goals/intentions. This simply means that a person needs to write out his or her goals/intentions and put them in a place where other people are aware of them. Psychologically you are more apt to achieve your goals/intentions if you know that other people are watching.

Make Goals/Intentions Positive, Not Negative

Research also reveals that goals/intentions need to be stated with a positive connotation. The mind and the emotions really don't know the difference between a positive statement and a negative statement. Many studies have been done to prove this fact, but goals/intentions stated in an "I don't want to . . ." manner simply reinforce whatever the person doesn't want to do. (Don't think of pink elephants! Think of pink elephants! Get it?)

Sample Goals/Intentions

Goals/intentions regarding a job search might appear something like this:

1. "Today is the first day of my job search. I see myself waking up excited about the opportunity of finding a new job. As I smell the fresh coffee that I pour, I feel confident knowing that I'm going to manage the process of finding a new job. As I sit, relaxing and drinking my coffee, I begin to think of how I am going to execute the plan that I made the evening before. I know that this is a little scary and I feel the trepidation of not knowing what is going to happen. I begin my plan for the day. This is an exciting day."

2. "After I've prepared myself for the day, I see my family smiling and giving me the encouragement to manage the process of finding a new job. By noon of every day, I will have accomplished at least thirty phone calls to prospective employers to try to arrange interviews. I hear myself speaking to prospective employers and I hear them granting me an interview time. I feel the rush of success in knowing that now that I have interviews, I am going to successfully sell myself."

3. "I see myself getting ten face-to-face interviews a week. That is an average of two interviews a day. I hear myself practicing the interviewing techniques that I am going to use in each individual interview. I feel well prepared for every interview I will have. I am confident. I feel great. I know that with this preparation, I will perform extremely well in each one of these interviews."

Since you should recite these aloud every day, they will also function as *affirmations*. Affirmations are assertions of belief. They are positive statements that reinforce an activity or a state of being. In this case, you are affirming with every sense you have the successful finding of a new job. The more you positively reinforce the emotional and spiritual parts of your psyche, the more likely the physical side will follow. Suffice it to say, affirmations, like goals/intentions, work if they are reasonable. They must be recited repeatedly to create the effect necessary.

4 : Getting Face-to-Face Interviews

HERE IS HOW ONE READER reacted to my chapter on getting interviews that appeared in the first edition of *The Job Search Solution:* "Thank you, Tony. I spent three months wasting my time trying to find easy ways to get interviews. Until I read this chapter, I didn't realize how simple it is. It wasn't easy to practice what you've taught me . . . but it sure works." That thank-you was from Todd S. in St. Louis, Missouri.

Unfortunately, most popular job search books and advisers focus on answering interview questions correctly. Knowing how to answer questions is good. But that isn't anywhere near as hard as getting a face-to-face interview. Most authors and career coaches don't know how hard this is to do because they aren't in the trenches, trying to find people jobs.

The most important thing you can do to get a job is *to interview.* Nothing else matters unless you can get a face-to-face interview with the hiring manager—a hiring manager with authority and pain (an urgent need to hire someone). But that's not easy. As I said in that first edition, "Those who say some people are just lucky because they are in the right place at the right time don't realize that the lucky ones show up at a lot of places a lot of times. It isn't a matter of luck; it's a matter of hard work."

When it comes down to the job offer, the real control is in the hands of the employer. No matter how well you might interview, in spite of what you might think, you can't really control *getting* a job offer. But you can influence a hiring manager to offer you the job by interviewing well and proving to the employer that, based on the interviews, you are the best person for that job.

> **Key Point:** While you cannot control job offers, you can control interviews—the number of them and how they are conducted.

Next to the interview itself, the hardest work you're going to have in the job search process is getting an interview. People are not comfortable with the idea of "selling" themselves—of offering themselves as the person to be hired. It can be a daunting, burdensome, and excruciating task.

No one likes being rejected. And there are few more clear-cut rejections than being denied an interview and being rejected for a job. Yet the risk of being rejected goes with the very process of getting interviews and being interviewed. The sooner you face that reality, and prepare for this kind of rejection, the sooner you'll to be able to find a job. Pristine résumés, brilliant research, great contacts, even superior previous job performance do not help you find a job to anywhere near the extent that getting numerous interviews and performing well in each interview does.

Exploring All Sources for Interviews

*"If you want to increase your success rate, double your failure rate.
You're thinking failure is the enemy of success. It isn't at all."*
    —TOM WATSON, PRESIDENT AND FOUNDER OF IBM

The initial interviews, if they're successful, will lead to subsequent second, third, or fourth interviews that will eventually land you a job. The most effective vehicle is going to be you, picking up the phone and calling anyone and everyone you can, whether you know them or not, to find people who might grant you time for an interview.

Studies have shown that most job seekers consider several different ways of getting interviews, especially in the beginning of the job search. And after a month or so, they abandon many of those ways and stick with one or two methods. This is a mistake. The key here is to use every one of the methods until you find a job. You need to be relentless about this.

It has been estimated that 60 percent of the people who find jobs have located them through networking. I guess that depends on how you define the word *networking*. With the advent of online networks like LinkedIn and social networks like Facebook and Twitter, the definition of that term has expanded. If you define networking as calling people whom you know, this estimate of 60 percent is probably an exaggeration. If you consider it calling anybody who might know someone who might know someone who might know you, then this statistic may not be too far off. I personally think that you should get an interview with anybody who will listen! Call and try to meet with as many people as you possibly can.

Previous Employers, Peers, and Subordinates

People you have worked with who have gone to other companies are great sources of opportunity leads. This group of people should be the very first you approach when you need to find a new job. Sit down and brainstorm the names of all the people you have worked with, or for, or have worked for you, in every company that has ever employed you.

LinkedIn has made this even easier. There are "groups" of ex-[name of companies] you can search. Don't hesitate to call previous employers, even if the individuals you worked for or with are gone. Just because you did not like working at a place five or ten years ago doesn't mean the same group of people, ownership, or culture is still there. Over a period of fifteen years or so, I placed the same packaging engineer with the same company three times. The company had changed hands four times during that span.

In case you haven't kept up with all the people you used to work with, LinkedIn is a great tool to find them. There are also a number of Web sites devoted to linking up alumni from different firms.

Caution: I do not recommend going back to work for an organization you have left unless the culture has completely changed. All the reasons you left the organization are usually still present. Even if you were laid off or downsized, the truth is that the organization thought more highly of its own self-survival than it did of you. Corporations don't change culture all that much. The principle should be to never go back to work for an organization that either you left or one that left you—unless there is a complete change in management, ownership, or culture.

Family Members

The larger your extended family, the better off you are. During the first few days of looking for a job, you should call every member of your family—brothers, sisters, parents, uncles, aunts, first cousins, second cousins, third cousins, any cousin, in-laws, and their cousins—to let them know you're actively looking for a job and you would like to talk to anybody whom they might suggest.

Some people are embarrassed about calling family members and letting them know that they are either out of work and looking for a new job or looking for a job change. Get over it! Would you rather be embarrassed by not being able to pay the mortgage or by letting your family know that you need a job? Call them, tell them that you're actively looking for a job, and ask them if they know of anybody who might be interested in your type of background. Offer to send one of your résumés. Keep a record of everyone you call and the response. Tell them that you would like their help, and that you would like to call them back in a week or so.

Friends

Talk to your friends just as you would talk to your relatives. Call them all and let them know that you're looking for a job; ask them if they would know of anybody who might need someone with your background. Offer to send a copy of your résumé. Make a note about when you called and ask if you can follow up in a week or so to see if they might have thought of anybody. Even ask your friends for their friends who might be of help in your job search, and ask them if you can use the friend's name when calling. With the advent of social networks, this ought to be easier to do. If you are a member of Gen X, Gen Y, or Gen Z, you get this.

Acquaintances

Acquaintances are different from friends. They are people you know, but not that well. They're people you occasionally, or even rarely, run into or contact from time to time. A study back in the 1970s found that people looking for jobs were more likely to find opportunities through acquaintances than through friends. The study concluded that often people make friends with people they work with or who occupy the same world. So when a large organization has a layoff, it's likely that a person's friends will be laid off, too. But acquaintances may operate within a completely different work world.

People in your church, athletic club, neighborhood, social club, golf or tennis club, or volunteer organizations, and parents of children who are friends with your children are all people you should make aware that you're looking for a new job. Even acquaintances of your spouse are people who might be able to help you.

Again, this concept is part of your life through social networks for Gen X, Gen Y, and Gen Z. Take advantage of it. (I will discuss social networks in Chapter 8.)

Competitors

Most of us know who our business competitors are. After talking to previous employers, it is a logical idea to call and solicit all of your company's competitors for a job. Capitalize on your familiarity with them. Candidates often tell me that they know a lot about their competitors, but they just would not want to work for one of them. This usually stems from an organization's painting its competitors as people with horns and tails. The truth is that most of us don't really know much about our competitors except in relation to the competitive situations with them. We don't intrinsically understand them. No matter what the party line has been about your competitors, you need a job and it is in your best interests to call them and see if they have an opportunity for you.

Caution: If you are in most forms of sales, and/or some tactical development types of positions, you may have signed a noncompete agreement with your current employer that, at least theoretically, prohibits you from working for one of your competitors. If you signed a noncompete agreement when you went to work at your current organization, pull it out, read it, and be aware of what you can and cannot do and the risk you might run.

If you can't find the noncompete agreement you signed, you had better get a copy of it somehow. You should have kept a copy of it when you were hired in your last or present job. If you are currently employed and you ask for all of your records in your personnel file, you are going to raise some eyebrows, though. Your supervisors are going to want to know why, all of a sudden, you're asking for your personnel records. This may be uncomfortable, but you need to find a copy of your noncompete. Some states are more liberal about noncompete agreements than others. You need to have a copy of yours if you are going to even consider working for a competitor. Noncompete agreements can cause you a lot of difficulty if you go to work for a competitor. Be prepared.

Suppliers and Distributors

Write down the names of all the people to whom you currently supply goods and services, as well as all the people who might distribute your goods or services to end users. The knowledge you have is probably applicable to the people who supply you goods and services and to the people to whom you distribute your goods and services. A software developer, for instance, develops software that may be sold through distributors. If you worked for the software vendor and you know how the software works, you are of value to the distributor. If your company manufactures parts that are sold to and by another manufacturer, you may have a great deal of knowledge that is of value to that other company.

Customers

In some situations, customers might be great people to approach for a new job. If you have sold to them or had reason to have contact with them and have built a good relationship with them, customers may have a great opportunity for you.

Caution: If you are presently employed, be *really careful* in soliciting your competitors, suppliers, distributors, or customers about a new job. No matter how trustworthy you think they are, you cannot afford to lose your job. No matter what you think, the probability of your actions getting back to your current employer is very high. I cannot tell you the number of times that I've encountered candidates who have lost their jobs because they told a competitor, supplier, distributor, or customer that they were thinking about changing jobs, and they got fired when it got back to their employers. You have to be very careful.

If you are employed and want to reach out to these people, call them—very confidentially. Speak to only the hiring authority, and if you agree to meet with the person, do it at a neutral site. I would not send a résumé unless I were very sure the company was interested in speaking with me. Again, be very careful—you can't afford to lose your job.

Trade and Professional Associations

Some professions and trades have more active associations than others. Some businesses are heavily involved in professional and trade organizations and some are not. *The Encyclopedia of Associations* lists 23,000 national and international groups for just about every occupation you can imagine. So if you haven't been active in an association, you can at least find the ones you ought to become involved with or at least become a member of. The most important aspect of being an active member in an association is that you receive a membership directory, which can be used for contacting potential employers. Some associations publish job opportunities for their members.

Trade shows for trade and professional associations not only give you great personal exposure, but you can often find out which companies are expanding and which are contracting. Often, trade shows have placement committees that organize publications of job opportunities. If you are out of work, these trade shows are a great place to interview many organizations in a short period of time. If you are presently employed, it may not be advisable to be that obvious, but as you introduce yourself, collect business cards and information about other people; this information can be helpful for contacting them later on a more confidential basis.

Alumni Associations, Fraternity and Sorority Members

Don't hesitate to take advantage of any contacts in these kinds of organizations that you might have. These organizations are an excellent source of many potential employers outside your normal sphere of influence. Alumni directories will give you the list of names and addresses and business affiliations of all members. Call fellow alumni and speak to them about their careers, companies, and industries. They may have job openings in their organization or know of openings somewhere else.

College and University Placement Offices

If you are out of undergraduate school more than a year or two, it's not likely that the undergraduate placement office at your college or university could help you that much. But you never know. Often, organizations that are expanding will list their current openings with the college or university placement office. You may be overqualified or too experienced for the positions that they might list, but knowing which organizations are expanding, no matter how much or little, provides great prospects for you to call.

It also doesn't hurt to list your name and experience with graduate school placement offices or at least call them and find out the listings that they may have. I have known of organizations that listed short-term project assignments in the graduate school offices of some MBA programs. It is amazing how often these short-term projects become long-term permanent positions. Take advantage of every resource that might be available to you. You're limited only by your own imagination.

Job Search and Career-Change Outreach Programs

The only difficulty I have with these kinds of organizations is that they can often be sophisticated pity parties. Sitting around with a group of people who are all bitching and moaning about the difficult employment market isn't going to find you a job. Make your own judgment! Go to these kinds of organizations and meetings if they indeed help you with your attitude. It's even possible that one of the other people in such a program will come across a job in your field that they are not qualified for and pass the information along to you. Just don't expect much in the way of actual job search results.

As I mentioned in the last chapter, over the past few years a number of churches throughout the country have developed some rather sophisticated job search support programs. They are usually free of charge or charge a nominal amount of money, but the good ones are well worth it. The CareerSolutions ministry, begun in Dallas, Texas, is such a program. It offers a twelve-week program to help people find a job or change careers. I'm quite sure there are similar programs in almost every major city in the United States.

Job Fairs

Job fairs were more popular when the employment market was much easier than it is now. These fairs are designed to have several employers come together and interview many people in one day. In recent years, job fairs have attracted thousands of people who are exposed to very few hiring organizations. If you are presently employed, do not go to a job fair. I have known of a few employed candidates who, since they were looking for a job, attended a job fair—only to discover their own organization was there. They were promptly terminated.

Religious, Community, and Social Organizations

It is important to tell people you know in these organizations that you are looking for a job. Common values are one major criterion that most people use in hiring others. This factor may not be obvious or even conscious to most people, but as I've mentioned before, we all have a tendency to hire people we like. And we have a tendency to like people whose values and beliefs are very much like our own.

Bankers, Loan Officers, Venture-Capital Firms, Lawyers, CPAs

These groups of people can be surprising sources of many opportunities that might lead to the job you need. Bank and loan officers, especially in small communities, know a lot of the businesses that are expanding or looking for people simply because they lend money to these organizations and often know who is on the rise. Small businesses, which make up 97 percent of the employers in this country, often establish great relationships with bankers, so the bankers can help them expand when they need to. These relationships are usually personal between the banker and the owner or owners of the companies. So it certainly doesn't hurt to ask the bankers and loan officers you know if they are aware of any organizations that might be expanding.

Venture-capital firms are organizations that provide money, typically for start-up companies. These companies have a tendency to fund many homogeneous types of organizations. It is not uncommon for the companies to impose one of their own members on a company that they have funded to see to it that their investment is protected. Whether they are just providing money or also have someone on the inside, these firms can be excellent sources of information on available jobs.

Attorneys who specialize in medium to small businesses, labor law, or certain other kinds of legal areas often know organizations that are expanding because they represent them or give them advice. I personally know an attorney who specializes in legal advice to high-tech firms. He knows just about every high-tech company in the region. He may not necessarily know of their expansion plans, but he certainly knows who they are. He helps the smaller ones incorporate and helps the larger ones with their legal issues. It is not uncommon for a company's external legal counsel to its growth plans.

Following the Script

This part of the instructions needs to be followed to the letter. Most people will read this, get the meaning of it, and then go off and do it their way. And that is where the mistakes will begin. Here, and in other places, I'm going to give you a carefully researched script that is likely to work. If you follow the instructions and do it exactly the way I teach you, the system will work. If you don't follow the script and end up ad-libbing, you won't be as successful. These scripts will work 90 percent of the time. So, please, for your own sake and for the sake of those who love and support you, follow the instructions exactly as I give them.

I provide for you a single script that can be used in different scenarios. Unless you have been using this kind of script on a daily basis, you need to practice before you use it. At first, the script isn't going to sound natural to you. To many people, some parts are going to appear very pushy and aggressive. No matter how difficult it might be for you to be this aggressive, the sooner you do it, the sooner you will be successful in your job search.

Eventually, the pain of either not having a job or of needing to change jobs gets so great that most people will opt to be painfully pushy in getting themselves interviews. All of the scripts I recommend take lots of practice. Most of them will be ones that you are going to deliver over the telephone. So, it is simple enough to practice them with someone who is supporting you in your effort. They are simple but very specific. Practice the scripts to the point where they sound natural to you.

Note: Throughout this book, I teach you to sell yourself. I teach you to sell yourself very, very hard. The kind of aggressiveness and assertiveness that I recommend is necessary in these days of a changing economy. To the vast majority of people, this kind of aggressive selling of oneself does not come naturally. It may be uncomfortable at first, but needing to find a job or change jobs is uncomfortable, too. It all depends on what you find to be more uncomfortable.

Since first writing about this in 2006, I have had literally thousands of people email me and tell me how successful these scripts were. They may be uncomfortable at first, but they are easy to get used to following and, above all, they work. Please use the script *exactly* the way I recommend. Some of these people who wrote about how effective the scripts were also mentioned that they didn't use them correctly at first. Most of the time, they just were afraid to be as downright *forceful* as I recommend. They would say namby-pamby, weak stuff like, "Do you think you might know somebody who might wanna hire someone like me . . . maybe?" instead of being businesslike and forceful. *Follow the script . . . damn it!*

Contacting People You Know

It is important that you record the telephone numbers and dates that you call people. *You may be calling the person back again in thirty, sixty, or ninety days.* Many people will not respond to you positively for a month or two. *You want to remind them that you need a job!*

Previous Employers, Peers, Subordinates, and Acquaintances

Name: _____

Company: _____

Date: _____

"Hello,_____, this is [your name] and I am presently looking for a new job. We know each other from [contact]. I called to ask you if you might know of any job opportunities available either with the firm you work for or any others that you might know about. For the past [period of time] I have been working at [name of company or what you have been doing]. I am presently looking for a job as_____ . Can you think of anyone who might need what I can offer?"

(continued)

[very long pause!]

If no, then say:

"I really appreciate your time. I'd like to send you my résumé, and if you can think of anyone who might be interested, please pass it along to them. By the way, I am not sure how long my search will take; I'd like to call you back in a month or so to see if you might have thought of anyone who might be interested. Would that be all right?"

Results: _____

_____

Family

Name: _____

Phone: _____

Date: _____

"Hello. This is [your cousin, brother-in-law, etc.] and I am presently looking for a new job. I called to ask you if you might know of any job opportunities that might be available. For the past [period of time] I have been working at [name of company or what you have been doing]. I am presently looking for a job doing _____ . Can you think of anyone that might need what I can offer?"

[long pause]

If no, then say:

"I really appreciate your time. I'd like to send you my résumé and if you can think of anyone who might be interested, please pass it along to them. By the way, I am not sure how long my search will take; I'd like to call you back in a month or so to see if you might have thought of anyone that might be interested. Would that be all right?"

Results: _____

_____

I present a different script for competitors, suppliers, distributors, and so forth later on in this chapter, when I discuss cold-calling in general.

Finding Businesses That Can Help You Get Interviews

There are many types of businesses that can help you get interviews in your job search.

Recruiters of All Types

The definition of "recruiter" has broadened over the last number of years. The term can include retained search organizations as well as employment agents and "placers." When I entered this profession, it was estimated that recruiter-type firms are responsible for 5 percent of the workforce hired. Today, it's more like 20 to 25 percent.

Yellow page listings and Internet searches will tell you how to find the most successful recruiters in your area. If the individual assigned to help you has any decent experience in the business, he or she will be able to give you a realistic idea of the opportunities that might be available. When the employment market is tight and there are many, many candidates to choose from, a hiring company expects to get exactly the experience it desires because it's paying a fee and the kind of experience wanted is readily available.

Talk to as many types of recruiters as you think can get you qualified interviews. I would not recommend limiting yourself to one or two, at least in the beginning. You will quickly find out who is going to be productive for you and who isn't. You need interviews! It is in their best interest to get you good interviews because that is how they're paid. If you aren't successful, neither are they.

The *Fordyce Letter*, the country's foremost authority on the placement and recruitment profession, maintains a database of some 33,000 firms in the United States that are, in one form or another, involved in the business of direct personnel placement. (This would include even the "casual" placers of people, temporary staffing firms, and companies that, as a part of their business, do some sort of placement.) For the past ten years or so, according to Kennedy Information, Inc., which publishes *The Directory of Executive Recruiters*, there have been approximately 5,500 permanent recruiting firms of all types in the United States. Some 35 to 45 percent of them went out of business over the past two years, only to be replaced by others. About twenty new recruiting firms open in the United States every week. It is estimated that one-third of these firms work on a retainer basis and the rest on some form of contingency. The average recruiting firm, according to the *Fordyce Letter*, has 3.1 "consultants" in it who successfully average recruiting and placing 1.5 people a month. The average tenure of these firms is seven years and the average "consultant" has been in the business for three years.

Traditionally, recruiters have fallen into two broad camps. The retained recruiter, who is just that—"retained" to find an employee—was one group, and the other was the "contingency group," whose members received their compensation only if they were responsible for causing a candidate to be hired. As I explain a bit later, this simple division is no longer applicable. Today, there is a broad range of contingency firms that you need to be aware of so that you can decide if they can actually help you find a job.

Regardless of the recruiter's arrangement, what you should expect and how you should deal with a recruiter totally depends on your understanding of the kind of recruiter you're dealing with. When you know the type, and his or her relationship to the employer, you will know how to manage your own expectations.

In general, here is what recruiters can do for you:

- They have access to and knowledge of opportunities with companies before they are "broadcast" to the world.

- For the most part (we see the exceptions below), they have a much more in-depth knowledge of an opportunity than an individual could gain on his or her own.

- They will "coach" you and sell you and your attributes, as well as sell around your shortcomings, better than you can for yourself.

- Because a recruiter knows how you compare with your competition for the positions, he or she can provide for you the advantage. Recruiters know their market.

- They will help you "manage" the process of interviewing and negotiating. Because a recruiter deals with this process daily, the individual knows how to do it better than you, even if you change jobs often.

- They are going to help you maximize your compensation possibilities. Most of the time the recruiter is compensated based on the salary package the candidate receives. It is in the recruiter's best interests to help you reach your compensation potential.

- They can provide you with more job interview opportunities, quicker, than you can stir up for yourself. Most people don't deal with job opportunities, career moves, and the like on a daily basis. A recruiter does.

- The help of a recruiter implies confidentiality. Most top professionals do not want their job search to be "floating around" the Internet or anywhere else, for that matter.

- A recruiter often has an intimate but objective view of the hiring company, the hiring authorities, and the "politics" of the specific hiring process.

- They are comfortable with all of the steps in the process of getting hired.

- They know what to do when things "go wrong" in the hiring process.

Here are some things that recruiters *cannot* do for you:

- They cannot get you a job. A recruiter can coach, teach, advise, strategize, and help. But you still have to be the primary force in getting the job.

- Top recruiters might give some career advice, but they're not counselors or career advisers. They are information brokers and hiring process managers. Unless the information or process is of current and immediate importance to the company or hiring authority they represent, they don't have the time to "counsel."

- They're not miracle workers. They can't get you the "job of your dreams." They can't get you an interviewing opportunity that you are not qualified for. They can't help you change careers when the economy won't bear it. They can't help you negotiate unreasonable compensation plans, and so on.

- They cannot do a lot of hand-holding or respond immediately every time you call or blindly email a résumé.

- They don't analyze every résumé that is sent to them. Unless they are a "boutique" search firm, they receive hundreds of résumés. Each one will get 10 to 15 seconds of attention, and unless what is on it is so obviously stellar and needed by their hiring companies, it will be stored in a database.

- They don't have time to give you advice about the job market or if it's time to "stick your toe in the water" to see if your skills or experience might be more valuable to someone else.

- Unless they are involved in the process of securing you a new opportunity, they're going to be fairly short on advice about "what you should do" regarding changing jobs down the line.

- For the most part, they're not going to give you advice about a job or career change that they are not involved in unless they have a longstanding relationship with you.

The biggest challenge we recruiters all have regarding candidates is the candidate's misperception of the marketplace and how his or her skills, abilities, and experience stack up against what is available to our clients. Our best candidates come from referrals or networking, or actually calling a currently employed person and presenting a possible better opportunity (recruiting). Some of us will respond to a résumé for a specific opportunity that we might advertise or will answer your phone call. Some of us will find your résumé on the Internet and call you.

Most candidates, even qualified candidates, have no idea how many excellent people there are available for most opportunities. Candidates, as I mentioned earlier, have a tendency to see the world through their own eyes and through their perceived ability to do a job. A good recruiter, even with a narrow search assignment, can usually begin with at least 100 to 200 "qualified" candidates or résumés. Even the top search firms, according to Kennedy Information, Inc., start out with 100 to 300 candidates in their database for each search they do. They then qualify, phone-screen, and narrow down those to 20 to 50 candidates, give in-depth interviews to 10 candidates, and present a final panel of 3 to 6 candidates.

Candidates are often surprised and enlightened when they understand the number of quality candidates available for most positions. Most candidates do not see themselves in the light of how they compare with other viable candidates. Most candidates evaluate themselves based on their own perceptions, and unfortunately they don't have the perspective of comparing themselves to 100, or even 50, other people at their same level of professionalism.

If you have absorbed most of the information in this book so far, it won't come as a surprise to you that the biggest challenge recruiters have with the hiring organizations is that they are dealing with human beings, who are flawed as we all are. Just because the organizations might need to hire a professional on any level, that doesn't mean that they're going to do it all the time. They will change their minds about the kind of person they need, or corporate politics, unrealistic expectations, mergers and acquisitions, buyouts, unexpected changes in the business climate, stock prices, product failures, and so on will govern their decisions at any given time.

Types of Recruiters

A recruiter might be able to help you, but you need to manage your expectations of what any recruiter can do for you and you need to help him or her help you. And what recruiters can do for you depends on the nature of the recruiters and their relationship with the hiring authorities or companies they are working for or representing.

In brief, there are many types of recruiters, with varying relationships with hiring authorities or hiring companies. The major types today are:

Retained/Executive Search Consultants

Traditionally, executive search firms—or search consultants—were never oriented toward a candidate. Their client is the organization that pays their retainer. They do not operate as an agent for the candidate. They are an extension of the client and they usually specialize in specific industries or professions. Whereas a recruiting firm that might work in a certain geographic area may work, from time to time, on a retainer basis, executive search firms usually operate on a worldwide basis. They usually have offices all over the world and they deal with only upper-level management positions. Over the past few years, boutique organizations have cropped up. They may have only one or two offices in a major city but they still specialize in a narrow category of executives.

A true executive search firm will claim that it is not interested in seeing or collecting résumés from individuals. The firm's stock-and-trade is to reach out and actually recruit certain types of talented people on certain levels who are not actively looking for a change in jobs. Traditionally, they have exclusive arrangements with their clients, and their clients, having paid part of a fee as a retainer, agree to the exclusivity. Along with exclusivity, there is usually an agreement not to solicit executives from the client for a period of time.

If you are aware of executive search firms specific to your industry or profession, don't hesitate to contact them and see if they might help you. Just don't expect the same kinds of results that you might get from a traditional employment/placement/recruiting firm that is more candidate-oriented.

Contingency/Search Consultants

These kinds of firms, of which mine is one, are paid contingent upon finding a candidate who is successfully hired. We work some retained searches, but most of our fees are earned on a contingency basis. Thus, we usually know our vertical markets very well. Whereas the retained search firm is not candidate-oriented, we can be. We will work for a group of candidates and for a group of client companies at the same time.

The ability of these types of firms to help you will vary greatly. It will depend on the firm's longevity and expertise in a particular market. Our firm, for instance, has been in business since 1952, and our average recruiter has been in the profession fifteen years. Other such firms could have opened their doors last week. Of course, you don't care how long they have been around as long as you can get good interviews. Again, speak to any of these organizations that might help you get an interview. Don't expect miracles.

Employment Agents

These organizations are strictly candidate-oriented. They find a candidate and call any organization that they think might be able to use the candidate. Many of us in the contingency/search business started out this way. Most of the people in this side of the profession don't have to have much knowledge of the businesses they call to solicit "job orders." There can be a broad range of expertise with these kinds of firms and the people in them. Again, if they can get you a decent interview, ask for their help. They are going to try to "screen you in" to the company as best they can and help you sell yourself.

Placers

These are usually people who search the country for one particular kind of candidate for one particular type of client that they deal with on a nationwide basis. I know of one "placer" who scours the country for payroll-processing salespeople and places them with his nationwide telecommunications client. That's all he does. If one of these firms finds your unique background will fit the client's needs, listen to what the placer has to say. But don't expect any other types of interviews.

Contract Recruiters, Internal and External

These are recruiters who work on a specific contract basis for particular clients. There are all kinds of arrangements that these recruiters have with their clients, of course. Some work on strictly an hourly basis and are evaluated by the number of people they recruit. Some work on an hourly basis plus a specific amount of money per person hired. Some work exclusively for one company at a time. Some work for two or three companies at a time. The arrangements can be endless.

The fact that this recruiter is a contract employee will be transparent to you. The individual will come across as an internal, permanent employee of the company being represented. It may not make any difference to you as long as the recruiter can get you an interview. Most of the time, though, since the recruiter works for one—or at most two or three—clients, the person is "searching" for very specific kinds of experience. And since the recruiter is contracted for a specific period of time or a specific number of hires, you may never hear from the individual again.

Internal Recruiters

These are people who are actually permanent employees of an organization. They are usually an extension of the HR department and may or may not devote all of their time to recruiting. Some know what they are doing and some don't. They spend most of their time trying to find the "most perfect" candidate. They are only going to help you if you are as close to a perfect candidate as they can find. Other than that, they're mostly going to try to screen you out.

HR Staff Recruiters and Screeners

These people may call themselves recruiters because they are trying to find candidates for their company. They are mostly part of the HR department, however. The "screeners" will not even tell you that they are trying to screen you out, but they are. If they help you get an interview, great—but don't expect it.

Research Consultants

These are people who simply do research for the companies they work for. They find candidates any way they can, and they pass these résumés along to their clients. Don't get excited if you get a call from one of the players simply passing your information along to someone else, usually an internal recruiter.

Consulting Firms for Long-Term Projects

These are consulting firms that actually offer a unique "solution" to their clients. Their solution usually entails assembling a group of people who will work on a particular project for an extended period of time, then "deliver" the solution. If you've worked with these kinds of services, you know how they work.

Management Consulting Firms

These are niche types of consulting firms that, as a part of their service, will do some recruiting. They usually have some unique expertise, and recruiting is simply a part of their overall service offering. If you are in the kind of business or profession that uses these firms, you know who they are.

Temporary, Staffing, and Consulting Firms

These used to be called temporary agencies. Traditionally, they were oriented toward secretaries and other office workers. Along with those for the secretarial and administrative staffing, the general labor staffing firms have been around for years. But today, these organizations staff all kinds of professional positions on a temporary basis. There are even staffing firms that place doctors, CEOs, CFOs, accountants, lawyers, technical writers, nurses and other healthcare professionals, HR professionals, drafters, designers, and engineers.

When you work for a staffing firm, you are actually an employee of that firm and you are contracted out to another business. Liability for payroll, taxes, workers compensation insurance, benefits, and so forth are all the responsibility of the staffing firm. The advantage to the client company is that it doesn't have to be bothered with any of these things and is free to terminate the relationship with the individual at any moment, with no serious business or economic consequences.

Since the mid-1980s, information technology (IT) consulting firms have grown to take on a significant amount of temporary information technology placement. These firms hire out their technical expertise, from very narrow and specific types of software development to general software applications. Most of these firms do not see themselves as staffing companies. They see themselves, and present themselves, more as consultants. They often work on specific projects for their clients; frequently these projects can last for many years. The client pays a high premium for this expertise, and as with general staffing, does not have the burden of long-term employees. The client can pay for the service on a time and materials basis, a project basis, or a flat hourly basis.

Many of these firms were spun off from the large consulting firms that developed IT expertise. In the tech wreck of 2000 and 2001, many of these firms had significant setbacks. They expanded again in the early 2000s, and although they had their setbacks in this last recession, they are still part of the business fabric today.

Advantages of Temporary Work

Working for most temporary staffing firms has many advantages. Depending on the kind of job you might get through staffing firms, you can often gain flexibility of hours; faster, almost immediate employment; a great entree into a company to experience what working there might be like; and a relatively fast paycheck. One major benefit of working for a staffing firm and being assigned to another organization is that, 15 to 20 percent of the time, the position can become permanent. This happens most often on the secretarial, clerical, and administrative level, but it is common in the higher level consulting types of positions, too.

If you have worked for any kind of accounting or IT consulting firm as a consultant, you know the advantages and disadvantages of doing so. In a tight market, it's hard to go from working as a consultant to having a permanent position. Companies are always concerned that since you have made more money as a consultant, if they hire you on a permanent basis you'll soon go back to consulting for a slight increase in money.

Disadvantages of Temporary Work

The drawbacks to temporary work are obvious. A temporary position—even on a very high level of a president or CEO—is still perceived as and is just that: *temporary*. The attitude toward a person working on this basis is often less than professional. The care and respect that is normally given to a person perceived as a permanent or regular employee is not given. The premium or markup that the client pays is higher than for hiring a permanent employee. That premium is paid for the right to terminate the job for the temporary person at any time.

The major concern from your point of view, however, is that keeping a temporary position can easily become more important than interviewing for a permanent position. It is not uncommon for an individual to have to work interviews around the temporary position. Since a temporary assignment is temporary, the individual knows that it can end at the whim of the client. Therefore, the candidate is often reluctant to schedule interviews for permanent positions during normal business hours while working at the temporary assignment. The immediate short-term benefits become more important than the long-term.

So, when accepting a temporary assignment, the thing to do is to be sure the client knows that you are actively seeking a permanent job and let him or her know that your schedule will have to allow the opportunity to interview for permanent positions.

Executive Marketing and Career Management Firms

The existence of these firms ebbs and flows with the economy. Their purpose is to counsel people in their executive career. They supposedly give advice on how to market one's self and provide career management counseling. Because of the many scams associated with this kind of consulting, several states have instituted licensing procedures for these firms. These organizations often purport to know a hidden job market and have secret connections to job opportunities, often untrue. These firms charge a fee for their "service." I have spoken to individuals who have paid up to $12,000 or $15,000 for this kind of expertise.

Caution: These firms do not find people jobs. They supposedly provide career counseling. I can only speak from personal experience, but in the years since 1973 during which I have been finding people jobs, I have never met anyone who used a career consulting service and felt he or she got what was paid for. There is no such thing as a hidden job market. Also, paying a fee for advice from someone who is not involved in actually finding jobs for people is a questionable investment.

I don't recommend paying a fee for any kind of service like this. Most of them are scams. They will tell you that they have this magical, mystical secret knowledge about how to find a job, have contacts with "hidden jobs," offer a magical format for your résumé, and then try to charge you a lot of money. Caveat emptor!

Résumé Services

There are fewer of these organizations since the advent of online résumé-writing advice sites. An experienced résumé-writing service may not hurt, but unless the organization is involved in helping people find jobs, its opinions about your résumé may be incorrect. In Chapter 5 I discuss a simple form of résumé writing that is the most effective you can use. The problem with writing a résumé is that you may think it looks good, but that does not mean it will be an effective résumé. There is a big difference between what works and what doesn't.

This is especially true since your résumé is going to be initially read online. In my book *Unbeatable Résumés* (AMACOM, 2011), I discuss the "new world" of résumé writing and résumé construction. I also offer the basic facts about how to write a résumé for today's technology in a later chapter of this book. Most of the books written by résumé writers and most of the advice given by the people who charge you to write a résumé *do not* take into account how your résumé will be reviewed. They are résumé writers—they don't find people jobs.

Distribution and Other Types of Services

These are organizations that, for a fee—usually a small fee—will "distribute" your résumé to 400 or 500 different job boards. I've never known anybody who got a job this way. I guess it depends on how you'd like to spend $10.

There are also other types of employment-oriented firms that provide employment services to employers, but they normally cannot help a candidate actually get an interview. For example, professional employment organizations (PEOs), which used to be called "employee leasing firms," undertake responsibility for an employer's workforce, payroll, benefits, administration, legal obligations, and sometimes other HR functions. They do not, however, recruit, screen, test, or interview prospective employees.

Similarly, outsourcing services provide personnel who can handle functions ranging from the mailroom to a telephone call center—all the way to totally revamping a company's information technology system. Over the past few years, *outsourcing* has connoted "offshore." This often means that the function is sent to a foreign country or the work is done by non-American citizens who are employees of the company itself or employees of the firm that is hired to perform a specific function. The most notable kind of outsourcing has been associated with large call centers and low-level IT functions, application development, coding, and so on. The majority of true outsourcing services for U.S. companies are done on the site of the company that did the contracting.

Outplacement services usually provide a facility for use by its terminated employees. This is where the former employees can base a search for new employment. The service may include office space, telephones, fax and Internet access, a message center, and so forth. The former employer usually pays the fee for this service.

Getting Interviews with People You Don't Know

We now come to a portion of the process that can make one of the biggest differences in how fast you find a new job. The procedure is simple: You get on the telephone and present yourself to a prospective employer and ask for an interview. It's called a cold call. It is simple and direct. The results you get will be immediate. The cold call will either result in an interview or it won't.

The process of making cold calls is very simple, but the manner in which you do it is sophisticated and takes a lot of courage and practice. The reason it takes courage is that you are running the risk of being rejected and refused in as short a time as ten seconds. On top of that, you are going to have to make 100 of these calls before you get an interview. So, you have to expect one heck of a lot of rejection and refusal before you get positive reinforcement.

I'm sure that I received more than 3,100 emails after publishing the first edition of *The Job Search Solution*, most from people thanking me for this script. A few people, one in particular, who wrote a review of the book for Amazon.com, criticized the script as being too canned and implied that it was insulting to a hiring authority. People are certainly entitled to their opinions, but I must tell you *this script works!* It doesn't matter what you might think of it. You need interviews and this script will help you get them. But if you don't feel comfortable using it, don't.

I prefer to call these *warm calls* because neither you nor the prospective employer is cold. Keep in mind that when you make this call, you are trying to get an interview regardless of whether there is a position open or not. You are selling an *interview*, not necessarily the idea of getting a job. It is extremely important that you recognize this difference. The purpose of this call, this warm call, is to get in front of that prospective employer so that you can sell yourself and your skills. You are purposely going to ask for a meeting with the prospective employer without asking him or her if there indeed is a need. You are selling a date, not marriage. Don't confuse getting hired with an initial interview. All you're trying to do is sell an audience with that person.

The reason you are just trying to sell the initial audience, or interview, is that, very often, hiring managers will interview potential employees whether they have an opening or not. As you will see, the script does not ask if there are any openings; it asks for an appointment, an interview, and it only presupposes a current or upcoming actual position opening.

Warm-calling is the most productive activity to get an interview you can perform. It is also the most difficult and creates the greatest amount of immediate rejection and refusal possible. I can't tell you how essential this practice will be in limiting your job search time. Most people *don't like it*, and they *postpone it*, doing everything they can to avoid it because *it is hard*! But, if you learn to do it well, your job search is going to be a lot easier.

After preparing for your job search—that is, setting goals, writing out a daily plan, writing a good résumé, and picking up the phone and calling a prospective employer to ask for a face-to-face interview—this is *the most important step* in the job search process. I have received literally thousands of emails over the years expressing gratitude for information on how to do this. If you do this correctly and often—daily—you'll have more interviews than you thought possible.

Some critics of the first edition of *The Job Search Solution* and the online program www.thejobsearchsolution.com have made fun of this script, calling it stupid and insulting to prospective employers. But they apparently weren't the people who really needed to find a job. The people who needed to find a job and used it found it to be very productive.

> "I didn't like this script at all when I first read it. It was way too pushy for me. But after three months of unemployment and not getting interviews any other way, I practiced with my husband until I could overcome my fear. In my first week of using it like you suggested, I got two interviews. Within two weeks, I found a job."
> —Marianne L., Norcross, Georgia

Whom to Warm-Call

If you don't know the name of a hiring manager at a firm when you call an organization, simply ask for the name of the manager of the department that you would normally report to. If you are an accountant, ask for the name of the controller. If you are a controller, ask for the name of the vice president of finance or the CFO or, when it comes down to it, anyone who is in charge of the finances for the company. If you are a salesperson, ask for the sales manager, the regional sales manager, the vice president of sales, and so forth. If you are an administrative support person, ask for the administrative support manager. In short, when you call, ask for the manager of the kind of department that your skills and ability would best fit. It is that simple.

In larger organizations, the people answering the phone are instructed to *not* give out that kind of information. They may tell you that they are "not allowed to give out that information," or they will tell you that they don't know, or that they don't have the titles of the people in the company. So, you can do two or three easy things. First, you can go online to the company's Web site and find the names of the people who are in charge. Second, you can ask for the customer service department or the person in charge of customer service. That individual will be quite helpful. Third, you can ask for the accounts payable department. These people are so used to getting beat up every day by vendors who are asking for money that, when they speak to someone nice who is just asking for a name, they are usually so grateful that they will tell you anything, especially something so simple as who the managers are.

Now, if you get "lost" in a voice-mail system that only allows you to spell the names of people you know, you are going to get very frustrated. If you know the name of the person you're trying to reach, of course, spell that name. Some companies' voice-mail systems purposely *don't* include the names of some of the managers. (I know it's stupid. and it makes absolutely no sense, but I don't write the rules.)

If you run into this problem, your goal is to speak to just about anybody. So hit any "common name" first letter like "S," and speak to whoever answers. Ask for the accounting department, sales department, customer service department, and so on. If you don't know the name of the manager of the department, and you get a voice mail from one of the administrative people, you have no choice but to leave a message and ask the person to call you back. I would not recommend saying on the message why you are calling; when the person calls back, be as nice and cordial as you can. You want to speak to the department manager. Most of the time, since administrative types want to help, they will give you the name of the manager. Try to speak to the manager then.

If you have skills that can transfer from one industry or profession to another, you can warm-call just about anybody. Any kind of administrative experience, accounting experience, bookkeeping experience, sales experience, and so forth can carry over to a lot of different businesses. So, you can warm-call from just about any reference book that might provide names of companies and their telephone numbers. Don't overlook the white pages of businesses or the online telephone book itself.

The Warm-Call Script

"Hello. Who is your [controller, vice president of sales, IT director, CEO, etc.]? Fine, let me speak with_____."

[pause]

"Hello,_____, my name is and I am with [feature] and have a great track record of [advantage and benefit]. I would like to meet with you to discuss my potential with your firm. Would tomorrow morning at 9 a.m. be good for you or would tomorrow afternoon at 3 p.m. be better?"

If you get a response like, "I really don't have any openings," then your response will be:

"I understand, and the kind of people whom I want to work for probably do not presently have an opening. I would just like to take fifteen or twenty minutes of your time because I am a top-notch performer. I am the kind of person whom you would want to know to either replace your "weakest link" or to know of my availability when the next opening does occur. Now, would tomorrow morning be good for you or is tomorrow afternoon better?"

You will either get the appointment or hear a more insistent response of, "I really don't have any openings. There is no reason for us to meet." Your response, then, is:

"I understand that you don't have any immediate openings, but I have a great track record of_____ . Mr. [or Ms.____], I am the kind of professional who is better than 90 percent of the employees that you might have now. It is in your and your company's best interest that you at least talk to me and be aware of my availability. If not for now, then maybe in the future. My experience has taught me that, often, great talent comes along when you don't need it. But, it is always a good idea to be aware of talent on a face-to-face basis. I will take only a few moments of your time and it may wind up being beneficial for all of us. Would tomorrow morning or tomorrow afternoon be better?"

If the response is, "Well, can you email me a résumé?" Then your response is:

"I can, but my résumé is only one-dimensional and it is of value for both of us to associate a face and a personality with a résumé. I'd like to bring it by, hand-deliver it to you, and spend maybe fifteen minutes of your time so that you know what my accomplishments are and how they can benefit you and your company. Is tomorrow morning good or would tomorrow afternoon be better?"

If the response is an emphatic, "Just email me the résumé!" (which is just a nice way of saying no), then your response is:

"I will, right now. I will call you back tomorrow to be sure you have received it, and then we can set up a visit."

If you get a very emphatic no and it is clear that you're not going to get any kind of face-to-face interview, you then need to pause for two or three seconds and say:

"Do you know of any other opportunities that might exist in your firm with another manager?"

If you get a person's name, ask:

"May I use your name as a reference?"

If you get the name of another manager, also ask for his or her phone number. If the answer is no, then ask, after a two- or three-second pause:

"Do you know of any other organization that you might have heard of through the grapevine that might need someone of my experience?"

If you get the name of an organization or a person's name, ask:

"May I use your name as a reference?"

Key Point: Warm-calling is a numbers game. The more calls you make, the more likely you are to get an interview.

Script for Following Up on a Referral

If you get a referral to a particular person or organization and the person who referred you said you could use his or her name (this is an indication of how strong the ties the people might have), here is the script:

"Hello, [Mr./Ms. _____], I was referred to you by _____. I am [name] with [type of experience] and a great track record of [accounting, sales, customer service, etc.]. I would like to meet with you to discuss my potential with your firm. Would tomorrow morning at 9 a.m. be good for you or would tomorrow afternoon at 3 p.m. be better?"

You will be amazed at the number of job opportunities you will uncover this way. Controllers know other controllers. Vice presidents of sales know other vice presidents of sales. Engineering managers know other engineering managers, and so on. It is not uncommon for one type of manager to know a number of other types of managers, both within and outside of his or her own company. These managers are often asked by their counterparts in other organizations if they know somebody to fill vacant positions. You may get a productive response once out of every forty times you try this approach. But don't be discouraged. *The one interview you get as a result of asking that question is worth the forty or fifty times of asking.*

Whether you get a referral or not, it is a very good idea to end the conversation with the following:

"Thank you for your time, I would at least like to email you my résumé in case something changes with you or someone you know."

Nine out of ten times, the person on the other end of the phone will be willing to receive the résumé. No matter what the person's response, whether it is positive or not, end the conversation by saying:

"I'd like to give you a call back in thirty days or so to see if there might be any openings there or if you might know of any with friends of yours."

Again, nine out of ten people will agree to your doing that. To a certain extent, that lets them off the hook for the moment; but they know, in the back of their minds, that they could easily have a position open up at any time.

If the hiring manager just plain dismisses you or insists that you deal with the HR department, you can say:

"My experience with company HR departments (as far as identifying top talent when there isn't an immediate need) just hasn't been good. I am sure they are wonderful people, but I need to be talking to decisive managers who can make immediate decisions. Is there any other decisive manager in your firm that has an opening?"

Analysis of the Script

This is very simple but very strong stuff. The idea is to sell a face-to-face interview, whether the hiring manager has a position opening or not. You are not asking if there is a job opening or asking to be hired; you're simply trying to get a face-to-face interview. The script is meant to be forceful and to the point.

- You do not ask the person answering the phone who might be doing the hiring. If you ask who does the hiring, nine out of ten times you'll be relegated to the HR department and that for the most part is a dead end.

- Once you get a hiring authority on the phone, you have to provide *features*, *advantages*, and *benefits* as to why you should be interviewed. This is very important! If you simply call and ask for an interview without giving specific features, advantages, and benefits to the prospective employer, you won't get to first base. This is, again, simple stuff if you are aware of what you are doing.

Your Features, Advantages, and Benefits

Here are some examples of how to present your personal features, advantages, and benefits to the person on the other end of the phone:

> "Hello, [Mr. or Ms.], my name is [name] and I am a [*features*] solid mechanical engineer. I am registered with fifteen years of very stable engineering experience. I have worked my way up in two organizations from the ground floor to a senior engineer position. The *advantage* that I bring is stability and performance. The *benefit to* you and your organization is that you would have a long-term employee with a great track record. I would like to meet with you to discuss my potential with your firm. Would tomorrow morning at 10:00 a.m. or tomorrow afternoon at 2:00 p.m. be best for you?"
>
> "Hello, [Mr. or Ms.], my name is [name] and I am an accomplished [*features*] IT professional. I have ten solid years of experience: five with a Fortune 500 firm and five with a small $100 million distribution firm. I have attained nine IT certifications [*advantage*], as well as saved each one of the firms I have worked for thousands of IT dollars. I would like to [*benefit*] continue this kind of a performance with an organization like yours. I would like to meet with you to discuss my potential with your firm. Would Tuesday morning at 9:00 a.m. or Wednesday afternoon at 3:00 p.m. work the best for you?"

The purpose of this script is to briefly and succinctly tell a hiring authority your personal features and advantages so that they can be perceived as benefits to the hiring authority's company. So, your job now is to come up with a *features, advantages,* and *benefits* statement for yourself. The question is, and always will be, on the part of that hiring authority: "Why should I hire you?" The whole interview process centers on this question.

Keep in mind that features, advantages, and benefits regarding you and your possible employment do not have to be mystical, miraculous, or mesmerizing. They can be simple and rather uncomplicated. In fact, simple and uncomplicated reasons for hiring somebody are the best.

A *feature* is an aspect of you or your career that makes you unique. It can be the number of years of experience. It can be grades in school. It can be things like hard work, determination, persistence, and dedication. A feature, in a job-seeking situation, is simply a unique aspect about you that is going to be translated into being a good employee.

An *advantage* is something that the feature does to set a person apart from the average. So, if a person graduated cum laude from college and worked his or her way through college with two jobs (features), that person demonstrated hard work and commitment way above that of the average person (advantage).

A *benefit* would be the gain that a company would realize from hiring a person who brings unique features and advantages. So, the features of graduating at the top of your class in addition to working two jobs demonstrate your advantage to perform on a higher level than average; therefore, you will perform in the same way for whomever you work for and the company will benefit from your work.

So now, write out your own:

Features: _____

Advantages: _____

Benefits: _____

Remembering that you are selling yourself and that you are briefly giving a prospective employer a reason to interview you, write a features, advantages, and benefits statement about yourself:

> "Hello, [Mr. or Ms._____], my name is [name]. I am a [profession]. I [*features*], which are [*advantages*] and, therefore [*benefits*] you and your firm."

Practice writing this statement, and in just a few minutes you can write three or four features, advantages, and benefits statements on yourself to fit just about any situation. *Remember: The purpose of this statement is to intrigue a hiring authority enough to want to interview you.* Do not try to sell the whole idea of hiring you in one phone call. The purpose is to get the interview by giving a hiring authority a brief statement about what you can do for him or her.

The closing question, "Could I see you tomorrow morning or would tomorrow afternoon be better?" is a minor choice resulting in a major decision, which most salespeople learn in their first training class. This concept is so simple it is almost too good, and yet a phenomenal number of people will avoid using it because it appears too obviously manipulative.

It definitely is simple, but it definitely works! At the end of your features, advantages, and benefits statement, ask the minor choice and major decision question. It works. Do not ask questions such as: "Would you be interested in talking with me?" or "Could I come by and see you?" or "Can we set a date for an interview?" None of these questions is nearly as effective as: "Could I see you tomorrow morning at ____ a.m. or would tomorrow afternoon at ____ p.m. be better?"

Please, please don't try to be coy or cutesy by making this more complicated than it needs to be. Simply make the features, advantages, and benefits statement and ask the alternative choice question. Then, *shut up!* Don't say another word until you have a response.

Now, most people who are not in sales, and even some who are, will have a difficult time using this statement and question, especially in the beginning of the job search. I have been using this format for finding other people jobs since 1973, and it has resulted in more than 80,000 interviews for my candidates. It works better than anything else you can imagine. You want to start getting results, or interviews, as fast you can. It works—don't fix it!

So, there you have it. A features, advantages, and benefits statement followed by an alternative choice question that will get you the results that you need. Now all you need to do is to *practice!* You have nothing to lose but your anonymity.

Should You Leave a Voice-Mail Message?

Somewhere along the line you're going to be faced with leaving a voice-mail message. Unfortunately, more and more businesspeople *never* answer their phone. Some managers in sales are rarely in their offices, and some managers in accounting and engineering departments aren't "people people" anyhow, so they let everything go to voice mail.

You diligently practice a warm-call presentation and then you get voice mail! So, you ask, "Should I leave a voice mail, or not?" It's about the only way you're going to be able to "communicate" to a prospective employer.

First off, I would call the same hiring manager at least two or three times, trying to make a presentation to him or her before I would leave a message on voice mail. If I concluded, after even the second time, that I'm not likely to catch this hiring authority answering the phone, I would leave a voice-mail message.

The script for the voice-mail message isn't much different from the script for speaking with a live person. The ending, however, is slightly different. It goes like this:

"Mr./Ms. [_____], my name is [name]. I am a [position]. I have [*features*] that are [*advantages*], which would be [*benefits*] to you and your firm. I would like a chance to meet with you. My phone number is [number]. Again, that is [your name] and my phone number is [number]."

Be sure to repeat your telephone number at the end of the message twice—say it once and repeat it very s-l-o-w-l-y so the person can write it down as you record it the second time. It might be even advisable to mention your phone number after you give your name in the very first part of your script, so you are offering your phone number three times.

When people have a ton of voice-mail messages on their system, they find it tedious to go back and listen to the whole message a second time just to get a phone number. By putting your phone number right after your name in the beginning of your message, you give them a chance to go back to the very beginning of your voice mail, get your phone number, and not have to listen through your whole talk just to get your telephone number. If you say it slowly in the beginning of the message and repeat it even more slowly at the end of the message, people are more likely to write down the number and return your call.

If you don't get a response the first time you leave a message on voice mail, don't hesitate to record a similar message four or five times for the same person. This sounds a bit excessive, but my experience has been that if there is even the slightest pain of needing someone now or in the near future, this kind of message will get the attention of a hiring authority.

You may ask, "Why would I leave that many voice mails for the same thing? If they have a need for what I do, they are going to call me back after the first one, right?" Wrong! The answer is, "No, they aren't!" Well, they might, but it is not very likely. Here's why: Looking for a job is *your* highest priority. But a hiring authority has many priorities and hiring someone may be a top priority one day but drop to priority number 22 the next day. If, at the moment the hiring authority gets your voice mail, filling that position is the number 1 priority, you'll get a callback. If it isn't you won't.

What's going through the hiring authority's mind when he or she listens to your voice mail? It likely is, *Damn, I really need to fill the job; now that Leroy's been fired, I have to hire someone else . . . get ready for this surge of business we're going to have . . . replace Rhonda because she's going on maternity leave . . . get rid of Ralph because he's late all the time . . . replace Susan because she is transferring to another department. But I'm late for that meeting. I'll give that guy or gal a call later.*" And later never comes. The third time you leave a message for the hiring authority, you make it really easy for him or her to pick up the phone and call you back.

There is a tendency for job-seekers to think that when companies need to hire someone, they do it in a thirty-day period or so. People think, *Well, they had an opening a few weeks ago . . . They must've filled it.* Based on what I've learned since 1973, I guarantee you that it takes more like 120 to 150 days to fill those positions, even when the hiring authority says it's high-priority. Candidates can be offered jobs, say they'll take them, then the day before they're supposed to show up, they decline. Or, candidates accept the job, show up, and a week later another opportunity they were considering comes along and is better, so they leave the first job. Maybe the company never finds anybody it likes when it starts interviewing and other things happen that become a higher priority.

Companies begin interviewing candidates and, after a while, decide that they want to change their criteria or they don't see anyone they like and then decide to start all over. The hiring process always takes longer than anyone thinks. Remember, you have everything to win and nothing to lose by leaving a voice mail.

After leaving eight to ten messages similar to this and not getting a response, you should stop calling, at least for now. If your experience has been with a similar kind of organization where your value might be greater than the average candidate looking for a job, call back a number of times down the road. But, for now, stop calling after eight or ten messages.

If you don't get the courtesy of a callback from a hiring authority, don't take it personally. You'll be surprised at the number of people who call you back simply because they admire your persistence. They'll tell you that they don't have an opening, but they appreciate your calling. This is a great opportunity for you to ask for a referral of someone they may know. And again, ask their permission to call back in a month or two.

The In-Person Cold-Call Visit

One great way—and one of the most effective ways—of getting an interview and the attention of a hiring authority (the person with pain) is to simply show up at his or her office and ask the administrative person if you can have a few moments of the hiring authority's time. Then you just wait in the office until he or she sees you.

Once you are meeting the person face-to-face, even if it is a brief moment in the lobby, you state the following as you hand the person your résumé:

> "Mr. or Ms. [Employer], I understand that you are looking for an excellent candidate to fill your position of [_____]. I am an excellent candidate and would like to spend a few moments with you to discuss my qualifications. Do you have a few moments?"

Do not expect that you are going to get an interview right then. That will happen only occasionally. If the hiring authority says that he or she does not have time right then, ask when there will be a better time: Be persistent about setting a specific time. When you have the boldness to do this kind of thing, you have everything to win and nothing to lose.

Keeping Track of the Process

This may not come as a surprise, but you absolutely *must* keep good records of all these calls. Your job search, whether you like it or not, may take six, eight, or nine months. I hope, for your sake, that it doesn't, but you need to be prepared for that possibility. If you follow my advice properly, you're going to talk to numerous people whom you have warm-called many times. Just because a company, or an individual within the company, says there is not an employment opportunity today, it does not mean that there will not be an opportunity in the future.

The probability of your discovering a vacancy when you initially warm-call like this is about one or two in 100. You will almost double those odds by calling back a second, third, or fourth time. So, it is important to recognize that warm-calling the individual or organization is not simply going to be a one-time thing. At the second or third call the person you're calling is more aware of who you are and what you're doing, and there may be more possible employment opportunities in the organization.

Simple manila folders can be used to keep records of each organization you approach or interview with. A daily planner can be used to make notes every day or into the future. Microsoft Outlook is a great way to keep track of these calls, too. The alarms keep you from forgetting to follow up, and, if your job search is prolonged, the software is more efficient than paper records.

When a person starts out looking to either find or change jobs, he or she usually has no idea how long it is going to take to be successful. There is a tendency to have a lot of activity in the beginning of the process; however, the process may carry on for much longer than a person would imagine. Good record keeping helps the momentum in the beginning to be sustained over however long it takes.

Take heart. There were also quite a number of people who have written me and told me that although this did not come naturally to them, they practiced and practiced and practiced until they learned it well enough to do it. Remember what Goethe wrote: "Everything is hard before it is easy."

Best and Worst Places and Times to Have an Interview

Anyplace other than a business office is not optimal to have an interview, including over the phone. Some of the worst places (beginning with the worst) include airports, train stations, and bus depots; any kind of vehicle; sporting events and company social gatherings such as holiday parties and picnics; your or the hiring authority's personal residence; anyplace outdoors; restaurants and coffee shops; and the manufacturing plant floor.

Some of the worst *times* for a face-to-face interview (beginning with the worst) are Sunday evening; anytime Monday morning, especially before working hours; when you are really sick (other than that, *go* to the interview—you may not be able to reschedule); Saturday; the first morning the hiring/interviewing authority is back from vacation or a long business trip; the day before a holiday; after 6:30 p.m.—especially on a Friday; while you or the hiring authority are on vacation; on your way back from anything personal like shopping or dropping the kids off at school; or on a religious holiday during the week that you or the hiring/interviewing authority may celebrate.

5 The Unvarnished Truth About Résumés and Cover Letters

I PERSONALLY RECEIVE 200 to 300 résumés a week. I use 200 résumés a week to find people jobs. Being on the front line, in the trenches, I know what works and what doesn't regarding résumés. This isn't theory; this is *reality*. This is the *truth*.

In this chapter I present the ten biggest mistakes you can make when preparing your résumé. I crush the myths about résumés, and tell you what hiring authorities really want to see on your résumé. There's expert guidance on *what* you should be including, on *how* you should be presenting that information, and *why* it's the best way to get you an interview. I expand on the basics to offer some tips for developing an even better résumé than you thought possible. Finally, I tackle the topic of the cover letter (or email) and explain why it's just not that important. Here is the information you need to produce a résumé that gets desired results: a face-to-face interview.

> "I spent $550 on a résumé service. What they sold me looked great to me. But I got zero interviews using it. I read your *Unbeatable Résumés*. Wrote it myself using your advice, and got three interviews in the first week." —Connie L., Chicago, Illinois

Top Ten Mistakes of Résumé Writing

Here are the top ten BIG mistakes people make when preparing their résumés:

1. *People overestimate the value of a résumé.* I discuss in depth later the reasons people overestimate the impact of a résumé. But suffice it to say that the value of your résumé's getting you a job, let alone an interview, *isn't what you think!*

2. *People overestimate the attention that will be paid to their résumé.* The average résumé gets *scanned* in 10 seconds. Most people think that someone is going to peruse, di-

gest, dissect, and read their résumé over and over. The truth is that interviewing or hiring authorities glance at résumés. They look for companies they recognize, longevity of jobs held, and maybe a few other things. That's it! They then determine to read it in depth at a later date. If your résumé doesn't grab their attention in 10 seconds, it is filed in the circular file.

3. *People underestimate the number of résumés interviewing or hiring authorities receive.* It is not uncommon for an interviewing or hiring authority to receive 200 to 300 résumés for every opening. With the advent of the "send" button, these people get overloaded with résumés even when they aren't looking to hire.

4. *People overestimate the qualifications of the people who will screen, read, and or "pass" their résumé along.* If you think the "right" people are reading your résumé, guess again!

5. *People include the wrong information in their résumé.* Even the most experienced professionals put the wrong content in their résumé. They write résumés that *they* understand instead of résumés that will be understood by the people that matter—the ones who can get you an interview. If a high school senior, who doesn't know you, can't read your résumé and understand exactly what you have done, who you have done it for, and how successful you were, you have the wrong content in your résumé! For instance, people list the names of companies they have worked for, never explaining what the firms do. They assume that since they know who the companies are and what they do, everyone else does, too. Oh, boy!

6. *People use distracting résumé formats.* This appears elementary, but most résumés don't get read because of their distracting formats. These formats, even those recommended by supposedly professional résumé writers—who never found anyone a job—don't work!

7. *People overestimate the value of the cover letter.* Cover letters are as overrated as résumés. Most cover letters destroy any chances that even a good résumé will get read. I like to call this "cover letter cover-up!"

8. *People assume one size fits all!* This is the mistake of sending the same résumé to all of the people or job opportunities you are perusing. You should know how to "dumb down" your résumé and how to *customize* it for success in different environments and for different opportunities.

9. *People flub the basics.* They make mistakes on such things as length, objective, summaries, dates, titles, and other basics. It is amazing how the execution of these sim-

ple matters can defy common sense. The sheer length of most résumés, for instance, ensures that they will *never* get read. On the vast majority of résumés, including an "Objectives" statement will *eliminate* most candidates right off the bat. And a "Summaries" paragraph can kill your chances of being interviewed.

10. *People have the wrong résumé "strategy."* Ask the average job seeker what kind of strategy he or she has for ensuring that the résumé will get attention *and* lead to an interview, and you'll get a blank stare! In other words, other than the "send" button, the average job-seeker has no strategy. Big mistake. There are strategic activities candidates should do *before* they send the résumé, as well as *after* they send it.

Things have really changed regarding résumés since the first edition of *The Job Search Solution*, but the mistakes people make haven't changed. So please, listen up!

The Truth About Résumés

Most hiring authorities and people who review your résumé really don't know what to look for in a résumé. Your résumé needs to be addressed to hiring authorities who have pain—the actual current need to hire someone. You are trying to get your résumé read by hiring authorities who are accountants, controllers, sales managers, engineering managers, plant managers, officer administrators, and so forth.

As a professional recruiter, I've learned a lot about résumés since I began in 1973:

- Sixty percent of résumés received for a particular job opening are *never reviewed* by the hiring authority.

- Seventy percent of all résumés received for a particular opening are reviewed by a *third party*—that is, a Human Resources individual, internal recruiter, or some administrative person, who may or may not be qualified to interview, let alone recognize what a prospective employee's résumé ought to look like.

- Sixty percent of third parties reviewing a set of résumés have *no direct experience* with the job they are recruiting for.

- Forty percent of résumés that are "opened" to be read are deleted because the reader can't understand what the candidate has done, who they've worked for, and so on.

- The average résumé gets "scanned" for 10 seconds before/if it is read.

- There are at least 100 résumés received for every job posted to the public.

The Kind of Résumés That 3,000 Hiring Authorities Want to See

For my book *Unbeatable Résumés*, I surveyed more than 6,000 hiring and interviewing authorities; 3,129 people answered the survey. They were hiring authorities who ranged from first-line hiring managers to CEOs, and firms employing from six people to more than 1,000 employees. For our purposes here, this is a summary of what they like to see and what they don't like to see:

What They *Like* in a Résumé

- Reverse chronological order

- Names of companies that the person has worked for and a clear indication of what the companies do

- Clear, concise articulation of skills and experience

- Direct evidence of success

- Written by the candidate (not professionally written)

- Easy-to-read format

- Pertinent information that relates to the job being filled

- Clearly stated experience that relates to the opening

- Stability

- No more than two pages

What They *Don't Like* in a Résumé

- Functional résumés

- Objectives and Summaries at the beginning of a résumé

- Longer than a page and a half, or at most two pages

- Long, unclear descriptions of the present or previous jobs

- Grammar, spelling, or punctuation mistakes

- No factual achievements

- Mention of anything before college

- Written by a résumé service

- Written by copying the published job description

- Fluff, generic competencies like "dynamic leader," "excellent communications skills," and "effective listener," "integrity," "honesty," etc.

We found that the average number of résumés reviewed for each position is sixty. About 86 percent of those surveyed didn't think a cover letter was very important. Thirty-nine percent said their HR departments screened the résumés before they got them. And 56 percent said that they spent less than a minute on each résumé they reviewed. (They embellished. They want to *appear* more interested than they are. The truth is that they spend about 10 seconds on each résumé.)

Based on the survey results, your résumé needs to be written in reverse chronological order and clearly describe the functions of the companies you work for, as well as your duties and responsibilities at each of those companies. It must highlight your accomplishments in terms everyone can understand and relate your own experience to the job you are applying for. The résumé should communicate longevity at each job, with specific dates. It must be no more than two pages, and it should rarely include an objective statement or a career summary—and then only if it relates to the job you are applying for. Your résumé should feature accomplishments that make you stand out from the crowd because it is one of 60 being reviewed.

The Medium Affects the Message

Probably 99 percent of the résumés you submit will be sent via the Internet, so you need to know how images and information are read differently on-screen from how they are viewed when they are physically held. For example, keep in mind that:

- People spend 39 percent less time looking at images and information online than they do when it is printed.

- The average person looks first at the center of an online document and then moves around the screen to view other details. One study found that people have a tendency to scan the screen in search of content and that our eyes follow an F-shaped pattern, beginning at the top, then going down the left side of the page to the middle, quickly scanning across text in search of the central nugget of information.

- People have a tendency to read "down" a screen rather than across, looking for information.

- People's reading online tends to be shallow, with more scanning and skimming. As one researcher put it, "The screen-based reading behavior is characterized by more time spent on browsing and scanning, key word spotting, one-time reading, nonlinear reading and reading more selectively, while less time is spent on in-depth reading and concentrated reading."

- People are interrupted more when reading online and tend to "bounce" from one document or image to another.

- Most people print out a résumé only if it looks good to them, and then they read it in more depth in printed form. But the first yes or no decision is made by viewing it online.

- Mark Zuckerberg, founder of Facebook, has said that communication on the Web needs to be seamless, informal, immediate, personal, simple, minimal, and short. And with your résumé, it *especially* needs to be seamless, immediate, personal, simple, minimal, and short.

- Dr. Gary Small of UCLA has discovered that people suffer from "Continuous Partial Attention" when working online. And they'll do the same with your résumé.

Since your résumé is likely going to be read first online, it needs to be clear and direct. And with research showing that the middle of the screen is the online reader's focal point, position your most compelling information in the center of the "page." Then, after you write your résumé, ask friends or relatives to read it online, and then check to make sure that it has communicated to them what you want it to communicate.

A Simple Message

I recommend that you keep the message of your résumé on a level that a high-school senior could understand. If your résumé is more sophisticated or esoteric, it is going to miss the mark. This does not suggest that you cannot explain complicated experiences in your résumé. But it is the difference, for example, between explaining the splitting of atoms to a high-school student and explaining it to a nuclear physicist.

Most people write résumés that *they* understand. They describe events and experiences in ways that make sense to them, so what their résumé says is usually clear to them. Let me stress again that the hiring people at 97 percent of the companies in the United States probably do not even know what they are looking for in a résumé. If they come across something they don't understand, the easiest thing for them to do is just discard the résumé.

Alternative Versions

I would advise having several different résumés that you can use in different situations and for different opportunities. This is simple to do on a computer, which allows you to add or delete information in your résumé within just a few minutes, then save each version you create.

In fact, I recommend that you try to customize your résumé every time you send it. This is especially true when you might be sending a résumé in response to a particular need that a company might have. For instance, if you're an accountant and you are applying for a finance or accounting position with a business where cost control might be an important aspect of the company's accounting function, you might emphasize cost control in your résumé. If you're an administrative support person and you are applying to an organization that has to meet tight schedules and deadlines, you can emphasize in some of the job descriptions your ability to deal with the pressures of deadlines.

Optimum Timing

I encourage you to send a résumé to a hiring authority *only after you have spoken to him or her on the telephone*. If indeed you accomplish this and you then email or send a résumé, you will have found out specific information, or hot buttons, that will be of interest to the hiring authority. You will then highlight those parts of your résumé that reflect those interests. You might need to put a different spin on your résumé before pursuing each specific opportunity.

The point is to think creatively and be prepared to target certain positions with the exact experience that might be requested.

The Résumé Pitfalls and Perils

There's a lot of advice out there about writing your résumé, and not all of it is good advice. Here are some common problems with today's résumés.

Overrating the Value of a Résumé

The first big issue regarding résumés is that people have a tendency to think that there is some kind of magical tool that is going to get them a great job. A résumé never got anybody a job—and it never will. The idea that there is some secret science to it is simply untrue.

Another reason that people tend to overrate résumés is that people can control what they write in one. It is one of those activities that can be confused with productivity. I encounter people all the time who devote three or four days to writing a résumé. It may take five or six hours if a person starts from scratch, but beyond that, it is a waste of time. Because it is one of the things in a job search that an individual can control, people have a tendency to think that if they devote enough time to it they will get a better job.

If you are changing jobs or looking full-time for a new one, of course you need a well-written résumé. I show you how to do that in this chapter. However, even a well-written résumé is just a résumé. Getting interviews and managing the process of interviews are one hundred times more important than having a good résumé. Most people looking for a job would be better off devoting half the time they normally spend in writing a résumé and using that time cold-calling to get themselves into an interview.

> **Key Point:** The purpose of a résumé is to get you into the initial interview and to give the interviewing and hiring authorities an aid to help them decide in the interviewing process if you are a person they should hire.

Let me stress once again that the average résumé is read for ten seconds. When you couple that with the fact that hiring authorities are literally receiving a hundred or more résumés for each opening they have, you might begin to appreciate what happens when they look at a résumé. Think about it—*ten seconds*! If your résumé cannot interest somebody in calling you in for an interview in ten seconds, all of your artful, miraculous, cosmic, inventive, or unique formatting or wording isn't going to matter.

So, what do most hiring authorities scan for initially in the ten seconds they look at a résumé? They want to know for whom you have worked, how long you were there, what position or positions you held, and your accomplishments and successes. Those four things are what everybody looks for. If the initial scan is palatable, the résumé gets read further—maybe even read two or three times. The initial scan deals with who, how long, and what.

Being Galactic/All Things for All Companies

There is a tendency for people to try to sell themselves in the same way that they would sell any other kind of consumer product. These people present themselves in what I call an all-galactic fashion. It means that people are trying to present themselves as though they are and can be the biggest bang for the buck. But, most of the time, candidates *overstate* how wonderful they are and actually ace themselves out of many good, solid opportunities.

If you are a vice president of finance for a multimillion-dollar Fortune 500 telecommunications firm and you are laid off, it doesn't matter how "all-world" you are. There are damn few positions out there for which you will be hired. It doesn't matter how wonderful your experience is, how much responsibility you had, how many millions of dollars you have managed, or how many hundreds of people you have supervised. You cannot do anything about the availability or, should I say, lack of availability of those kinds of jobs.

The Career Summaries and Objectives Turn-Off

I'm not a big fan of the Summary and Objectives sections that appear at the beginning of most résumés. Obviously, the employers we surveyed feel the same way. Though many résumé writers will tell you they're a wonderful idea, that's because you're paying them and they're stroking your ego and making you look bigger than life. Unfortunately, these sections will backfire more often than they'll help in getting you an interview. Here are two reasons for this:

1. *Hiring authorities don't care about your objectives.* They care about *their own* objectives. They only care about what you want if it also gives them what they want. So, in looking to show how you will fill their needs, don't bother telling them what your needs are.

2. *A hiring or interviewing authority is generally looking for specific skills to fill a specific position.* The vast majority of Objectives and Summary statements are so broad that they don't mean anything.

While there are some exceptions to this proscription, it's risky to use an Objectives or Summary statement when you can't be sure that it won't annoy the person reading your résumé. Consider this: One of the résumés that came across my desk recently featured this Objective and Career Summary statement (yes, both):

> [Candidate's name] provides profitable return while working in a highly effective environment of success and reward. He is a proven leader with 24 years of experience providing creative information-based solutions in executive management, global sales leadership, strategic planning, new business unit development, technical management, and operations management. He has demonstrated the ability and the resolve to develop and implement strategic business initiatives, initiate innovative solutions to complex problems, and manage high-performance teams that have significantly contributed to bottom-line results.

This candidate was seeking a sales job. His statements are not objectives at all, but more like a career summary. Overall, the statement doesn't say anything specific. What does "global sales leadership" mean? What are "strategic business initiatives?" Many hiring authorities don't think of their organizations as having a "highly effective environment of success and reward." Most are not looking for a "proven leader" but simply a good "follower" who goes out and does the job on a daily basis. See my point?

Now, how about this Objectives statement that I recently received:

> Seeking a position with an emerging company that possesses best-of-breed product or service that is looking to rapidly expand into new markets.

Surely, 99 percent of companies in the United States do not consider themselves "emerging companies." Most of them will not consider themselves to have a "best-of-breed product or service." And most might well be afraid of a candidate who wants to join only a company "looking to rapidly expand."

I'm sure these Objectives and Summary statements were important to the people who wrote them. But they mean absolutely nothing (or, nothing good) to a hiring or interviewing authority. It's all fluff. In fact, that fluff may well keep the candidate from getting an interview. There are, however, occasions when a Career Summary may work—when it's a *specific description* of what you have accomplished that would be meaningful to the prospective employer. One example of this type is:

Offering successful consumer product marketing and product management. Responsible for a successful, first-year, $15 million healthcare product initiative into the Mideast.

Obviously, this kind of Summary statement would be of value only to an organization looking for this type of experience. So, unless your Career Summary or Objectives statement can be that specific, it's best not to write one.

Key Words and Phrases

The use of key words is a relatively recent résumé phenomenon. With the advent of talent-management software used by companies to scan résumés and supposedly catalog them, many so-called authorities recommend a Keywords section. However, the vast majority of companies in the United States do not use applicant-tracking software that scans résumés for these key words. In fact, less than 1 percent of companies actually have this technology, and most of them don't use it. So the importance of including a special section devoted to key words is overrated.

In technical professions such as information technology, healthcare, and engineering, however, using key words may be of value. These key words need to be highly specific, though. I'm sure you're already aware of key words in your profession and in your industry. Of course, résumés have always included mention of certifications, such as MBA, Ph.D., CNO, and RN.

These new technologies suggest that résumés will be searched for "concepts" instead of key words. For instance, "intelligent search technology" is supposed to overcome the idiosyncratic aspects of résumés and provide more accuracy in locating individuals with applicable talents. Most of the large job boards like Monster and CareerBuilder are promising this kind of technology for recruiters and subscribers. If it is advantageous to include key words for your profession, such as in information technology or accounting, then do it. I personally don't think you need a section devoted exclusively to key words. These key words will be recognized in the body of your résumé.

Fuzzy key words and phrases should be avoided, in any case. These include *customer oriented, excellent communication skills, leadership, integrity,* and *character*. These fuzzy words and phrases lack meaning and do absolutely nothing to help you get an interview.

The organizations that do pick up on key words are more likely to look for words that refer to titles. Most likely they will retrieve these words from the body of the résumé, rather than from a Keywords section. So, words like *customer service, account management, controller, accountant, manager,* and *vice-president* may help you there. However, know that one company's "customer service manager" is another company's "client services leader." That variation in terms and titles is the primary challenge in using key words and phrases.

I recently received a résumé that used the words *honesty, sincerity, character, integrity,* and *determined*. Oh, brother! Show me a company that doesn't want these characteristics in its employees. It is senseless to include these words.

A recent book on résumés devotes four pages to a list of key words for inclusion in résumés. The suggested key words include *complex tasks, visionary, servant leadership, creative, professional,* and a whole page of "action verbs." Cut it out! What hiring authority is going to respond to this kind of stuff? Visionary? What's that? (The book also suggests designer résumés using clip art and colored boxes.) Oh, no! Please don't go there!

Nix Your Photo

Get the photos off of your résumé, if you've put them in there. You are looking for a job, not a date. You may think you look wonderful in the photo, but others may not agree! Remember: You are trying to get an interview, and anything that risks getting you eliminated doesn't help your cause. It's too easy for people to draw conclusions from your photo that might eliminate you. For their purposes, you could be too old, young, blond, bald, attractive, or otherwise. No reason to run that risk!

Writing the Most Effective Résumé

The clear message of an effective résumé needs to be: You need to interview (and subsequently hire) ME because this is what I have done in the past FOR OTHERS and therefore THIS IS WHAT I CAN DO FOR YOU! Prospective employers don't care about what you think of the résumé and your track record. They care about what you can do for them.

The most effective résumé for finding a job is a simple straightforward reverse chronological history of your employment.

Length

A résumé should never be more than two pages. A résumé that is more than two pages is simply not going to get read in any kind of detail. One-and-a-half pages are ideal, but if your experience is more than fifteen years, you might end up with a full two pages. The survey we did supports this reality. (Academic, scientific, and healthcare résumés may be exceptions to this rule.)

Name, Address, Email Address, Telephone Numbers

Your name, address, email address, and telephone numbers are the basic things that should appear on the top of a résumé in black, bold printing. Simple printing! No fancy script. Nothing cute. Just plain, black, simple, bold type.

Content

Let's review what hiring authorities look for in the few seconds they have to scan your résumé:

- The companies you've worked for and what they do

- How long you were there

- The position(s) you held

- Your accomplishments and successes

The initial scan produces the answers to the *who, what, how long,* and *how well* questions. These are the four things that every hiring authority looks for. If the initial scan is palatable, the résumé gets read further, maybe even two or three times. Your best bet, then, is not to distract that hiring authority with a Career Summary or Objectives statement that he or she may well regard as meaningless.

Reverse Chronological Order

Don't let anyone try to convince you to use any kind of format other than a chronological one. And always use a *reverse* chronological format. That is, you list your present or your most recent job first, and then work backwards. You state the name of the company you work or have worked for and the dates of your employment—month and year. Then you describe, in detail, what your job function was and how well you performed—again, in terms a high school senior could understand. You don't even have to use full sentences (e.g., you can begin statements with verbs). And each statement should not begin with "I." Just make sure that what you write is short, to the point, and easily understood.

A paragraph format works well. Bulleted lists also work well, as long as they highlight the important points. Bullet points without a descriptive paragraph don't seem to be as effective, though. And too many bullet points can become tedious and make your résumé too long.

Technology has altered the way we read, and so bullet points are common and expected. Quite a few studies have documented how the Internet has changed us from a culture of written media to one of visual media. So bullet points—even bulleted sentences, paragraphs, or short paragraphs— are visual aids for getting the reader's attention.

The bullet points have to communicate *specific, meaningful performance* qualities or else they won't work. After the first few bullet points are read, the rest will be ignored unless there's substantive information given. So, use bullet points to convey information that is:

- Specific

- Meaningful

- Performance based

This seems like a simple concept, but *it isn't that easy to do.* Many people include fluffy, meaningless material in the body of their résumés. To weed out the fluff, you will have to think, write, and rewrite—many times. Keep what you write simple, but specific and powerful. Remember, you're trying to get the reader to interview you, based on what you say you've done and how successful you say you've been.

Caution: Don't use a functional/accomplishments format. Functional/accomplishment résumés are, unfortunately, rather popular. Instead of a reverse chronological listing of prior employment, these list all of the functions a person has fulfilled, and often their accomplishments, in the body of the résumé, without relating them to particular jobs. In fact, most often the functions and accomplishments section takes up the vast majority of space on the résumé. Then, at the very bottom of the document, the companies a person has worked for are listed.

Using a functional format immediately communicates that you are trying to cover up something—too many jobs, gaps in your work history, or something else that a chronological format would expose. As a result, a functional/accomplishment format communicates distrust and deception. And with hiring authorities receiving scores of résumés, they quickly look for reasons to weed some out. Most of the time they just reject functional/accomplishment résumés without further review.

Another problem with this format is that, while it communicates what you did and how well you did it, it doesn't do so within the context of *when*, *where*, and *with whom*. Whoever reads the résumé can't associate the accomplishments with particular jobs or companies, and so the information is viewed as useless.

Some résumé services advise people to use a functional résumé if they are re-entering the workforce, leaving the military, pursuing a different job function, or are seeking their first job. In these instances, it is possible that a functional résumé *may* get read. But they will be more likely to get attention when our economy is booming and when there are only a few candidates for the jobs available. For now, when there are too many résumés for each job opportunity, stick to the reverse chronological format.

Your Dates of Employment

Starting with your most recent position, write the times of your employment clearly, including both month and year. Do this for every job that you've had for at least the past fifteen years. Dates, companies, and functions dating back more than fifteen years can be consolidated.

If you've been out of work for more than three or four months, or have been between jobs more than twice, record just the years and omit the months. Be aware that hiring authorities may draw unflattering conclusions about your using just the years and you run the risk of being passed over, but putting down the specifics is more likely to call attention to the gap and get you eliminated from consideration.

If you have changed jobs within the same firm, don't list each job separately, as though you had changed companies. Often, résumé readers simply look at the dates of employment; if they see a one-year stint followed by another year's stint, followed by yet another one-year stint, they may consider you as having had too many jobs. So, if you've had a number of promotions or different jobs with the same company, put the comprehensive dates next to the company name. Then, you can list the dates next to each position within the company, detailing the titles or duties.

Your Employers and What They Do

Write the complete names of the companies you have worked for. If a company's name would not be easily recognized, also state what it does. If you work for a company whose business is not extremely well known, many résumé readers will dismiss your résumé simply because they aren't familiar with the company!

The point is that you need to be certain the person reading the résumé understands who you have worked for and what that business entails. Even if you worked for a large, well-recognized organization, it doesn't hurt to name and briefly describe the division as well. For example, stating that you worked for IBM is meaningless unless you name the division or group, as well as what you've done.

Titles and Positions

You list your job title after the name of the company. If it is not clear from the title exactly what you did, or if the title is in any way confusing, change it to something more consistent with the industry or to a title people might recognize more readily. If you have an oddball title but, for whatever reason, you feel you must use it, put it in parentheses, next to the traditional title. For example, your title of Client Advocate might actually be the same as Customer Service Representative or Account Executive elsewhere. You be the judge, but remember that you want to convey the function of your job at that company.

Titles can be confusing. There are lots of VPs, for example, who are really just sales reps. They are told to use the VP title to help get them in the door of a potential customer. The same goes for Regional Manager, Director, and similar titles. A hiring authority looking for a Salesperson will often immediately dismiss the résumé, thinking *I'm not looking for a VP or Director; I'm looking for a Salesperson!* So, tailor your title, if necessary, to fit the category of work that the hiring authority will recognize.

Descriptions of Prior Experience

After you've listed the date and title for each job you've had, describe in three or four sentences exactly what you did there. Use language a high school senior would understand, keeping it simple and clear. You may want to devote more space in the résumé to your recent jobs, especially ones that are more applicable to the position you are applying for. However, if you've been in your current position for only one year and have spent fifteen years in your previous position, hiring authorities will likely be more interested in the previous fifteen years than in your past year. The longer you have worked in an organization and the more recent your experience, the more detail you need to provide.

Educational Background

Some people leave information on their education for the end of the résumé, while others put it at the beginning. Baccalaureate degrees, especially if you graduated with high honors from a prestigious school, may be worth putting at the beginning. In the business environment, advanced degrees from prestigious schools should probably be noted as well. If you're listing your degrees on the résumé, always include the dates you received them.

If you have a graduate degree, such as a Ph.D., consider preparing one résumé that includes this information and one that omits it. In the business environment, a Ph.D., among other advanced degrees, may communicate that you are overqualified. The academic, scientific, and healthcare environments are different, of course. An undergraduate degree with an MBA is reasonable to report; however, more advanced degrees scare some business employers, who may think, *Why would someone with a Ph.D. want to work here?*

Here is an example of an education statement, placed in the beginning of the résumé because of the prestigious school and the candidate's outstanding athletic success:

EDUCATION

U.S. Military Academy, West Point, NY (B.S. Engineering Management 1989)

- 4-year Army Football Varsity Letterman and Senior Captain at Strong Safety
- Awarded Colonel Gillespie Memorial Award for "Leadership, performance, contribution & dedication to the Army Football Program"
- Selected as Graduate Assistant Army Football Coach for first active-duty assignment
- Sun Bowl vs. Alabama, Peach Bowl vs. Illinois, Emerald Isle Classic vs. Boston College

---

Personal Information

I never recommend including personal data, and the reason is simple. While what you include in a résumé may work in your favor, it may also work against you. For example, being married with three kids may sound to you like you're a stable, solid citizen, but to a hiring authority looking for someone to travel 60 to 70 percent of the time, that personal information may keep you from being interviewed. Similarly, mentioning that your hobby is golf might communicate to prospective employers that you're going to try to spend two days during the work week playing golf. In short, there's just no good reason to include personal information that may keep you from getting the interview or the job.

Also, forget the ancient history. If you are more than thirty years old, no one cares about your having been an Eagle Scout or having held the high school state record in the high jump.

Reasons for Leaving Previous Jobs

Never include mention of why you left an organization. That information suggests too many reasons you shouldn't be hired this time. In an interview, when a prospective employer asks for the reason you have left the prior organization, for some reason your *verbal* explanation satisfies the question, whereas a *written* explanation never seems to work in your favor.

A few years ago, I had a candidate who, after each job listed on his résumé, included an explanation of why he had left the job. After four of such explanations, he wrote "Laid off due to downsizing." Now, what do you think a prospective employer will think of that? *When I have to eliminate someone, I will eliminate this guy!* With all those résumés out there, hiring authorities are looking for reasons *not* to interview you as much as they're looking for reasons they *should*. So, it is in your best interest not to explain in your résumé why you have left any organization. Wait for the interview to answer that question.

Money Matters

Don't *ever, ever* include your past, present, or desired earnings on your résumé. This will automatically eliminate you from too many opportunities.

Confidentiality

Any time you email a résumé to a prospective employer, you run the risk of your job search being discovered by your present employer. This matter has become more complicated, now that résumés are posted on literally thousands of Internet sites or job boards. No matter how confidential you try to be, if you're looking for a job while you are presently employed, you may be discovered.

If you are worried, and rightfully so, about confidentiality, then you need to send your résumé to specific hiring authorities only after you've spoken with them on the telephone. Unless you are soon to be out of work or don't care if your present employer finds out you're looking for a new job, be careful about where you send your résumé. Keep in mind that including the word *confidential* on your résumé does *not* help keep it confidential.

Often, candidates state "Employer *confidential* 2010–Present" instead of including the name of the company. Don't do this, either. Potential employers want to know who you have worked for. They have too many other résumés to choose among, and with this missing information, yours won't get read.

References and Endorsements

For openings in most traditional business environments, there's no need to include references. With some academic curriculum vitas or political, scientific, and research-oriented résumés, however, it may be appropriate to provide a list of references. It also may be appropriate to just state, "References upon request." Depending on the situation, you may want to give different references for different positions.

There are exceptions to this guideline, of course. If your references are high-profile people, it could be of value to include those names on your résumé, provided you have checked with the individuals first. Since most of us don't have those kinds of references, it is usually better to leave off any names.

The same advice is true for quotes from people who "endorse" you personally. Unless these quotes are from the president of the United States or someone else who is readily recognizable, it's a waste of space.

Tips for Better Résumés

Here are some tips for better résumé content and format.

Stories Sell and Numbers Tell

Numbers, statistics, percentages, and the like on a résumé get attention, especially if you put them in bold type. Use truthful statistics on your résumé, and don't go overboard. Statements like "150% of sales quota," "Increased profit by 28%," "Came under budget by 30%," etc., get the attention of the reader and communicate performance.

As for including stories of your accomplishments, consider brief statements that could prompt questions in the interview that would enable you to tell success stories. People love stories; they humanize the numbers behind your accomplishments and inspire admiration. Stories are particularly effective when they distract from or counter any biases that the hiring authority might have toward certain applicants.

How do you plant in your résumé the seed of story? A number of years ago, we had a candidate who held an engineering degree from Texas A&M. He was born and raised on a chicken farm, which he noted on his résumé. Subsequently, in interviews, he told stories about his childhood on the chicken farm—how hard the work was, what he learned, and so on. The company that hired him admitted that what made him different from other candidates was that his stories gave them confidence that he would be a hard worker.

Target Your Résumés

Earlier in the chapter I suggested having different résumés for different situations and different employment opportunities. This is a matter of developing targeted résumés, something that is simple to do nowadays with computer word-processing software. Make sure to save each version you create.

A targeted résumé is simply one that is customized to stress the relevancy of its content to the specific job you are applying for. If you find a particularly narrow job posting that your experience fits very well, add to your résumé the terminology used in the posting. For instance, if a posting reads something like, "Manage a staff of six senior accountants and four junior accountants," and your résumé reflects that you have managed an accounting department, you may want to alter your résumé to reflect the number of accountants, both junior and senior, that you managed. Try to be as specific as you can.

Similarly, if you're an engineer with both design and quality control in your background, and you're applying for an engineering position with a major emphasis on quality control, you can emphasize the quality-control experience in the résumé you send. Likewise, if you're a bookkeeper who has worked for a comptroller where you used Great Plains software, you may not want to put that information on your master résumé. Rather, paste it into the résumé when applying for positions where knowledge of Great Plains will set you apart from other candidates.

Customize your targeted résumé with anything you might know to be of value to a particular employer. For example, if you are an HR professional and you read about a company that is fending off union organization, you could emphasize that you have helped your previous employer defeat attempts at union organization. In short, the more precisely you customize, the better off you are.

Get the Particulars

For information about jobs, don't simply rely on the ads posted on the Internet. Those ads are usually quite generic, and most of the time they are not written by the person actually feeling the pain (the one needing the person to be hired). Use any specific insights you might have regarding a particular position or any information you might have gleaned from someone else. Especially, if you speak to the hiring authority before you forward your résumé, you may collect excellent information to customize your résumé.

You might even try investigating the opportunity with someone in the organization other than the hiring authority. For instance, a company looking for someone to manage a group of purchasing agents or a purchasing department has subordinates for the job in question whom you may want to talk to. Subordinates can give you lots of information about what is needed. The more specifics you get, the better targeted your résumé will be.

Caution! Sometimes people put different spins on their basic résumé. In fact, they sometimes go overboard with so many different résumés they forget which ones they use for which situation.

Simple Format, Clean White Pages

Avoid the fancy-schmancy layout, font, and other special effects. Once in a while, I get a résumé written on colored paper, paper with a cutesy background, maybe with yellow balloons; others are printed in italics, with some nontraditional script, or with flowers in the margins. Please don't do this! Unless you are in an artistic field, where appearance is paramount, an unusual presentation will amuse the recipient but eliminate your résumé automatically.

Stick to the traditional font of Times New Roman (or maybe Arial), 9- to 12-point size, black type against a white background. You might want to vary the type size for your name, the companies you have worked for, and perhaps your titles. But try to be consistent. Too many variations in type size make the résumé look cluttered. Also, allow a reasonable amount of white space on each page. Some résumés are so "crowded" that they would never get read. Your résumé needs to be pleasing to the eye, whether printed out or on a computer screen.

Especially, go easy on the boldface type, italics, and underlining. Tables, text boxes, icons, and graphs on your résumé might impress you, but often they get messed up or eliminated when you email your résumé. So keep the graphics to a minimum, if you use them at all. When a résumé can't easily be read online, it will likely be passed over in favor of the 100 other résumés that are easier to view online.

Do not place your résumé in a table format or use a template, especially if you are planning to give it to a placement service. A recruiter or placement service will always submit résumés with the firm's logo at the top and a disclaimer on the bottom. When résumés come with a table/template format, they become distorted or lose their formatting if placed within the placement service's own template. Similarly, when you e-mail a résumé formatted in a table or template, your lines will show if the recipient's computer has the "show gridlines" button turned on. Just prepare your résumé in a simple Word format that can easily be viewed on most computers.

Truth, Not Lies and Misrepresentations

An unacceptable form of "spinning" the facts on a résumé is to take credit for successes that weren't all yours. I have had candidates claim on their résumés that they were individually responsible for megadollar sales deals. Often, though, a reference is checked and it turns out that the candidate inherited the sale or was part of a team that made the sale. The candidate *embellished* by taking credit for something that wasn't all his own doing.

Think that you wouldn't embellish—or even lie—on your résumé? A large number of studies show that people do embellish or even outright lie at least once every time they rewrite their résumés. There are a phenomenal number of studies that prove that the majority of people will lie or embellish about most anything if they believe they won't be caught. (Too much to go into here, but a very interesting and provocative topic. Kinda sad.) Lies on a résumé run the gamut from statements of expanded duties and responsibilities, to factual matters of job titles, degrees, or length of time in a position. The most common lie is made to cover up a job or jobs that, for whatever reason, a person doesn't want to include on the résumé. Candidates simply extend the dates of employment for other jobs and hope the difference will never be discovered. Admittedly, these fabrications are the most difficult to detect or discover.

Another common lie is to expand on successes. As I mentioned previously, this involves taking credit for more than is reality—for example, claiming an innovation that was the product of a team.

One of the most common lies is declaring to have a baccalaureate degree when that's not the case. I've never quite understood why people will lie about having a degree. It's so easy to verify this information. There are even clearinghouses that perform this task for hiring organizations.

If you lie on your résumé and it is discovered beforehand, it is unlikely that you will be hired. If you lie and it is discovered *after* you are hired, you will likely be fired. Many companies verify a candidate's dates of employment, especially the most recent employment, *after* the individual is hired. So if you put on your résumé "2007 to Present," and you left that job six months prior to being interviewed, you'd best correct the dates before you accept the job. If you don't and it is discovered, you may well be fired.

In spite of our preaching about truth, at least twice a month we have candidates lose out on an opportunity because they lied on their résumés. Five or six times a year, we have candidates get fired *after* they were hired because a lie on their résumé was discovered. Dan Ariely, in his book *Predictably Irrational* (Harper Perennial, 2010), reports on numerous studies as to why and how people lie. One of the major reasons people lie or embellish is that they don't believe they will get discovered. A résumé is a perfect opportunity for people to bend the truth. The best way to be sure that you don't lie or embellish on your résumé is to: (1) remember the commandment, "Thou Shalt Not Lie," and (2) think about how stupid and at a loss you'll feel when you are discovered. *Don't lie!*

A Standard Résumé Example

This is a standard reverse chronological résumé. Read it, study it, see how it compares with your current résumé, and adapt it to your situation, if necessary.

YOUR NAME

your address   phone number   email address

Experience

April 2011–Present NAME OF COMPANY [Short explanation of what the company does or explanation of the division of a large company, so that anyone can clearly understand its function]

TITLE: [Make sure the title is commonly understood; if not, explain it in common terms.] *A specific, understandable explanation of your duties and responsibilities, as well as specific accomplishments that are highlighted. Write all the way from one margin to another so that you can get as much information on one page as possible. Write no more than a three- or four-sentence paragraph that a high-school senior could understand. Remember, the résumé is to communicate why you should be interviewed.*

January 2006–April 2011 NAME OF COMPANY [Same as previous example]

TITLE: [Same as previous example; if your title is odd, you may want to change it to make it resonate better; just be sure to explain to an interviewing or hiring authority what you have done during the interview.] *Again, explanations of duties need to be clear to anyone who may read them. Remember that numbers and statistics get recognized and paid attention to. So if you can quantify what your successes have been with numbers or statistics, do so. Percentages of sales quotas, cost savings, size of a department, even amounts of budgetary responsibility are noticed. Highlight or bold any outstanding numbers that will set you apart from other candidates.*

August 2000–January 2006 NAME OF COMPANY [Same as previous example]

TITLE: [Same as previous example] *The further back you go in your job history, the less you have to explain about what you did and how you did it. Highlight the outstanding performance, but one or two lines of information will suffice. A hiring organization is most interested in what you have done in the past few years.*

How to Handle Previous Experience

If your experience goes back more than fifteen years, you could summarize all of it in two or three sentences. You may want to highlight the names of the companies and the success you had with them, if it is appropriate to do so. For example, if you began your career with a prestigious organization that is noted for its training programs, such as IBM, Xerox, Procter & Gamble, or Perot Systems, you may want to feature that fact in this part of the résumé. Some people simply leave off their résumé anything before fifteen years of recent experience. Remember, the résumé is supposed to help sell you into an interview, not get you a job. Don't feel like you have to communicate your whole life story. On the other hand, don't leave out important facts that might help you get an interview.

How to Handle Education

List your college or university attended and type of degree, beginning with the graduate degree first and year of graduation. If no degree was conferred, simply put the years of attendance. Any honors such as high grade point or scholarships should be noted. Any formal school less than college does not need to be reported. Any continuing education (such as certifications, sales courses, or negotiation courses) could be mentioned here (stay away from any personal growth programs that might be religious or political—mention nothing controversial).

Cover Letters and Emails

Cover letters and introductory emails are as overrated as résumés. A well-written cover letter needs to be short and to the point. If a résumé is read or scanned for only ten to fifteen seconds, a cover letter probably gets five to ten seconds, at best.

My experience is that cover letters just don't get read unless they are brief and full of impact. Our survey with hiring authorities supports this. They simply aren't read like the writers think they are.

The purpose of a cover letter and introductory email is to briefly introduce the highest points as to why you should be interviewed, as well as to accentuate the facts in your résumé that might be most important to the prospective employer to whom you are sending it. If you have not spoken to the hiring authority, then you might highlight in boldface or bullet two or three things that you believe would be most important to know about you—what you would want to know if you were in the hiring authority's shoes.

A good cover letter or email should read something like this:

Mr. or Ms.[ ]:
You should read my résumé and interview me because:

- I have ten solid years of experience in your business.

- I have been a top performer.

- I give you dependability, leadership, passion, and commitment.

Read my résumé and interview me this week.

Sincerely,
[Name]

If you are emailing or sending a cover letter to someone you have previously spoken to—which is what I recommend—then your cover letter or email should mention your brief conversation and highlight the discussion points that you might have had with this person. A previous conversation before the receipt of your cover letter or résumé makes all the difference in the world as to whether your cover letter or a résumé is read. In this situation, your letter would read:

Subject: Our Conversation

Mr. or Ms. [ ]:
Our discussion today was brief but informative.

You stated that:

You wanted someone who had at least ten years of experience in your business—**I have twelve!**

You wanted someone who was a top performer—**I have been one for twelve years!**

You wanted someone with leadership skills, dependability, passion, and commitment—**I have all of these!**

(continued)

> My attached résumé highlights my experience, performance, leadership, dependability, passion, and commitment. I will call you tomorrow about arranging a personal interview.
>
> Sincerely,
> [Name]

Following up this type of cover letter or email and résumé with a phone call is more likely to secure the interview.

When the Résumé and Cover Letter/Email Work Best

This fact is so simple and yet rarely advised: A résumé and a cover letter/email are most effective when they are supported by *a previous telephone conversation* with the hiring authority. Your résumé is 85 percent more likely to be read if you have had a previous phone conversation with the prospective hiring authority. It is just like the warm call we discussed. A résumé associated with at least a voice has a better chance of being read.

Getting your résumé read is governed by the same threshold as getting an interview—the pain threshold. The greater the hiring authority's pain of needing a new employee, the more likely your phone call and résumé will get the appropriate attention.

The most effective way of using a résumé and a cover letter is as follows:

- Warm-call the prospective hiring manager and uncover pain or interest.

- Email your résumé and cover letter, highlighting the hot buttons you heard in the conversation; be sure to use the exact words or phrases the hiring authority used.

- Follow up with a phone call confirming the hiring authority received the résumé and ask for a face-to-face interview.

Don't be surprised if you have to call several times. Most people have a tendency not to want to call at all, let alone call as many times as might be necessary. Well, being a pest is a lot better than being out of work and needing a job.

It is possible to secure an interview by sending a cover letter/email and résumé without the telephone calls. In a very narrow profession, where there are few people with the experience that you have at the kind of organizations that you are targeting, firms receive so few résumés that each one probably gets read; in these rare cases, the standard process doesn't apply.

Picking out a group of companies to simply email your résumé to, when you have no appreciable experience that would be of great value to them, is probably nothing but a waste of time. However, picking up the telephone and selectively calling potential organizations and speaking directly to potential hiring authorities, and then emailing them a résumé, will have a much greater statistical probability of getting you an interview. *So, get on the phone and discover a potential employer's pain!*

In the case where you know that a company has an opening for someone with your kind of experience, follow a similar process. Don't just send a résumé to the email address for the response—probably five thousand other people are doing exactly that. Pick up the phone and call the person who would be the logical hiring authority. Even if you have to leave several voice-mail messages for that person, this tactic is going to produce better results than simply emailing your résumé to the address posted on the advertisement.

And whether or not you think it sounds too "pushy," one of the best ways to distribute your résumé is to go to an employer's office and physically deliver it as you request a face-to-face interview.

6 : The Myths and the Realities of Today's Job Market

HERE'S WHAT I'VE BEEN HEARING at least once every workday since 1973:

> "I had no idea looking for a job would be so hard, or it would take so long . . . I just had no idea!" —Jonathan S., Davenport, Iowa

The vast majority of people—in spite of knowing that unemployment is high, that people they know or have worked with have been laid off, or that their neighbors have been looking for work for a very long time—always think that it's different when it comes to them, personally. They just never imagine that looking for a job is going to be as hard as it normally is. Even when they have a job but need to find another one, they are still amazed to find out just how difficult it is.

I've seen six economic recessions come and go since I got into this profession, and with every one of them, the recovery of the employment sector lagged far behind the official economic recovery. And in some places, for some professions, it never recovered.

None of us can keep these recessions and the cycles of bust and recovery from happening. I can, however, help you see some of the myths and realities of today's market so you are prepared.

Common Myths and Misperceptions

Yes, there are many myths about hiring that can lead job candidates off in the wrong direction. If you are prepared, though, your search will be easier. This chapter discusses the myths and realities of the hiring process.

Myth #1

Companies are always proactive in finding good-quality employees and will hire them even if they don't need them immediately.

Don't let anybody kid you; this is total B.S. The vast majority of companies in the United States hire people only when they need to—especially when they are coming out of a recession. For now and the foreseeable future, companies hire more out of "fear of loss" than with any "vision of gain." The blunt truth is that they're afraid—afraid of the economy, afraid of their own business acumen, and afraid of making a mistake in hiring. This means that you need to show prospective employers that you are not a great risk and they should not be fearful in hiring you.

If you're like most candidates, you can't imagine why any company *wouldn't* beg you to grace its halls by hiring you immediately. Why wouldn't any hiring authority in his or her right mind just jump at the chance of hiring you? After all, you are an exemplary employee with a fantastic record.

Well, it ain't necessarily so. In fact, it *isn't* so at all. For now and in the foreseeable future, organizations are going to hire only when they absolutely have to, and when they do, they are going to be very, very cautious. They are going to try to find the "perfect" candidate. Ah, but who's perfect, you ask? No one. But that doesn't mean they'll stop trying to find the perfect candidate. In spite of your glorious experience and great background, you're going to have a difficult time convincing them that you are that perfect one. That's because they will view you as a potential mistake, in spite of what you may think.

Myth #2

Hiring authorities and companies really know what they're doing when it comes to hiring.

A good part of this book addresses the fact that most hiring authorities, managers, and companies have no idea what they're doing when it comes to hiring people. They have only a vague idea of a process. Some do it better than others, and some are even surprisingly successful at it. But you should expect idiosyncrasies, inconsistencies, and relative chaos.

Myth #3

Companies approach hiring with common sense, logic, and good business acumen and consistency.

Consistency in hiring, even from day to day, is certainly a myth. Don't expect common sense, logic, or consistency. There is nothing you can do about this reality, so you need to accept it and deal with it. Common sense isn't very common.

Myth #4

The Human Resources department streamlines the hiring process.

Most people running Human Resources (known as HR, which really means "Hiring Roadblock") departments in U.S. businesses are not decision makers. They are record-keepers, and their presence blossomed in the late 1960s when the push for adherence to Equal Employment Opportunity (EEO) standards began. At that time, the function of the HR department was to keep track of interviewing and hiring, and to be able to answer any governmental investigations about the company's hiring practices. Over the years, though, the Human Resources departments gained tremendous responsibility, and since the departments were keeping records about hiring, the initial functions of recruiting and hiring fell within HR's purview when hiring authorities were just too busy or too inept to do it themselves.

Because the initial stages of interviewing and hiring represent an interruption in the flow of everyday business, it was easy to rationalize someone else's doing the activities. The problem with an HR department initiating the hiring process, though, is that its personnel don't normally know or understand the give-and-take of experience and background that a particular department might need. Most HR departments are not capable of assessing the total package of a less-than-perfect candidate. The bottom line is this: *You do not want to seek a job through the efforts of a Human Resources person.*

I am not saying that no one ever gets hired through the HR department. It happens occasionally. I have known many wonderful people who work in HR departments. However, they are not hiring authorities. (By the way, most hiring authorities in most medium to large companies don't like the HR department either. They are just as stuck with HR as you are.)

Myth #5

I can find a job on the Internet and through social and business media networks.

We've come a long way in the past few years when it comes to using the Internet to help people find jobs. We'll discuss this in detail in Chapter 8, but please don't put jall—or even the majority—of your eggs in this basket. The Internet and social media are simply one tool that can help you find a job.

Where the Internet can help you is by giving you a lot of information about companies that you might approach for work. The Internet can supply wonderful background about companies, their competitors, their industry, their growth or lack of it, and so forth. It can help you find the names and telephone numbers of hiring authorities in those organizations. Then, armed with that information, you can pick up the phone and call them. Use the script I've given you in chapter 4.

Now, if you are in a profession that is in high demand, like the medical profession, health care, or certain types of niche professions, just posting your résumé on any one of a number of professional job boards will get you lots of activity. But unless you are in one of those rare categories, the probability of your finding a job on the Internet isn't good.

Myth #6

They've advertised a job on their Web site, so there's an opening there that's perfect for me.

Based on my recent experience, at least 25 percent of the time companies advertise because they *think* they might have an opening at the time they post the ad—and then it never materializes. Something like 30 to 40 percent of the time, they already have in mind who they're going to hire and they are simply advertising to politically look like they have tried to find other candidates. I know companies that "post" jobs just to give the appearance, especially to their competitors, that they are growing. But they have no intention of hiring anyone at all. Many times, they either fill the position or stop looking and just don't bother to remove the posting from their Web site.

Myth #7

There is a time formula for finding a job depending on your job level and earnings.

For years there used to be all kinds of time formulas for predicting how long it would take a candidate to find a job, based on the amount of money he or she made.

Whoever came up with this idea wasn't living in the real world. How long it takes to find a job depends on what you do and the market for it. Duh! If you did software maintenance and made $90,000 in 2009, but your job got shipped off to India, you may still be looking for a job and delivering pizzas at night. There is absolutely no way that anybody can predict how long it's going to take you, or anyone else, to find a job.

Myth #8

You can still find your dream job.

There have been more than thirty books written in the last two years that address how to find your dream job. I cannot tell you the countless numbers of candidates I have interviewed over the years who have read those books about finding their dream jobs. These candidates honestly, seriously thought that just because they described their perfect job, it existed and—what's more—they were going to get it! For any job, your probability of getting it depends on your ability to perform as well as your ability to get it.

Just because someone dreams about being in a particular type of position doesn't mean it will automatically happen. Now, if people are in the economic position where they don't have to work to feed their family, pay a mortgage, or have a car loan, and they wish to pursue their dream of being an actor, stunt pilot, writer, musician, or whatever, that's okay, I guess.

For example, someone like pro basketball superstar LeBron James has his dream job. But just realize the amount of talent it takes to get that kind of job, as well as the opportunity to show that talent. Most people are unrealistic about the competition out there, let alone the skill and the experience it takes to get that "dream job."

Myth #9

I've paid my dues, so now someone will pay me what I'm really worth.

This idea ranks close to the top of egocentric self-centeredness. It usually comes from people who are told that they are underpaid and underappreciated by everyone except the people who really matter—their present employers. Employers are going to hire you based on what they need, not on what you need. It is obvious, in view of the most recent economic situation, that putting time in at a particular profession has nothing to do with what anyone deserves or what he or she is paid.

We live in a business world of, "What did you do for me today?" You are worth exactly what you were getting paid. If you don't think it's fair, you certainly have the right to take your skills elsewhere. But don't expect to get more money—or more of anything—just because you think you're worth it.

Myth #10

I have great transferable skills that an employer will love. They make me a great candidate.

This statement is usually followed by a list like: great communication skills, critical thinking, teamwork, integrity, creative, leadership, blah, blah, blah.

Cut it out! You might as well add "strong heartbeat." This kind of stuff tells an employer absolutely nothing about what you are going to do for him or her. Stop this! Transferable skills and traits without the context of performance mean nothing.

Myth #11

Since I'm looking for a job anyway, this is probably a good time to change careers.

In this scenario, a candidate has usually been in a particular type of business or a profession for a number of years. For some reason, he or she thinks that it is possible to change careers and that someone is going to pay him or her at the same level as that previous career or current employment.

The further away you get from what your documented skills or demonstrated knowledge is, the harder you will find it is to get hired. Unless you're willing to either start over at the bottom or take a drastic cut in pay—and even then it is difficult—changing careers is a near impossibility. Why do you suppose lots of career-changing folks start their own businesses? Because they have a hard time getting a job with someone else!

People who want to change careers say things like, "But I know I can do it." Okay, maybe you can, but it is going to be rare for a company to take a chance on you when they can hire a person with direct experience. And when unemployment is high and the market is flooded with all kinds of people having all kinds of experience, getting hired to do something you have no documented skills in is near impossible, let alone to make reasonable earnings at that new occupation.

Be prepared to start at the bottom, no matter what you decide to do. Even if you can get someone to hire you in a business you know absolutely nothing about, you're still going to have to prove yourself. The probability of your being hired in a business you know nothing about, by someone who doesn't know you, at a decent salary, isn't very likely.

If you're truly intent on changing careers, you're most likely going to have to make it a good business deal for a prospective employer—worth the risk involved in taking a chance on someone without proven experience. You'll have to say something like, "Look, I've been a successful accountant for the past fifteen years, but I want be a real estate appraiser. I'm working on certifications. I'm willing to go to work for half of what you would normally pay an appraiser. I am willing to start out at the bottom and work my way up. I am a good employee. I will make the risk worthwhile for you."

Myth #12

If I change jobs, I need to make more money.

Depending on the economy, and the market for your particular skills, this may or may not be a realistic statement. If you are out of work in a tough economy, finding any job at all, regardless of the pay, may be a necessity. But it is a bit misguided to insist that in changing jobs you will always get more money.

Myth #13

I've done my research; I know what kind of money I'm worth on the market.

This is usually preceded by, "I know I am underpaid." What is your house worth? Nothing—until the day you sell it. There is no objective "range" of money for anyone's skills. You won't know what kind of money you might be worth until you actually get job offers.

Myth #14 master Bull-A--! Most MBA are not smart!

An MBA or graduate degree makes me a better candidate.

It is a myth that an MBA, or any other kind of a graduate degree, in the business setting will automatically get you a better position or more money. This may be true in academic circles or pure scientific organizations, where a Ph.D. can get you a promotion. But in the majority of businesses in the United States, having an MBA or graduate degree doesn't get you a better job or more money.

I have never seen a candidate hired just because he or she had an MBA—or any other graduate degree. Now, I have seen situations where an MBA was preferred, and since the employer suggested the advanced degree as a criterion, the company limited itself to interviewing candidates with MBAs. However, the MBA was not the reason the successful candidate was hired.

Universities sell the idea that an MBA is going to make you a better businessperson. Universities love to offer MBA programs because these programs are cheaper to run than any other kind of graduate program. The ratio of student-to-professor is extremely high in contrast to graduate programs in scientific and technical fields, where the student-professor ratio is very low: more students per class, lower costs for the university. It's all of these MBA programs that help universities pay for all of the other graduate programs they offer.

The truth is that people who earn graduate degrees are also people who are diligent about many other things, including their jobs and their careers. These people would get ahead anyhow, with or without the graduate degree. People with MBAs do often make more money than employees who don't have that degree. But it's not *because* of the MBA. The high earners are people who want to do better, and since America seems to promote the idea that more education is better, these people get MBAs. They wind up being successful, with or without the MBA.

Myth #15

The most qualified candidate gets the job.

The candidates who get the jobs are the candidates who sell themselves best in the interviewing process. More often than not, the most qualified candidates are *not* hired unless they have sold themselves better to the hiring organization.

I cannot overemphasize that *qualifications* are the 20 percent threshold; that threshold needs to be crossed over to get the interviewing opportunity. But 80 percent of getting the job comes down to the people who are not only reasonably qualified but who also sell themselves the best in the interviewing process.

Myth #16

I know I'm good; just get me in front of them.

This is the egotistical approach to interviewing. These candidates usually assess their success and ability based on the job they are in currently or the one they had been in most recently. Unfortunately, this kind of attitude does not take into account the competition these candidates are going to encounter in the interviewing process. Candidates with this arrogance have no idea how difficult the interviewing process is going to be. They may well be in for a rude surprise.

Myth #17

Interviewing and hiring is a two-way street.

The idea that interviewing has any kind of give-and-take between candidate and hiring authority is simply not true. The interviewing process is a one-way street, at least for most of the process. And that one-way street belongs to the hiring authority.

The reason is simple. In most interviewing situations, the employer has several qualified candidates available to do the job. The objective, then, is for the candidate to sell himself or herself as hard as possible for the offer. The candidate can then qualify for the opportunity. Then, and only then, does the interview process become a two-way street.

Myth #18

Offshoring and outsourcing are killing jobs in America.

This is not a myth, but it is a misguided statement. Every fifteen years or so, we hear that America is going to be devastated as a result of companies outsourcing jobs so as to use cheap foreign labor. Other claims are about offshoring, which is when domestic companies establish divisions in other countries to take advantage of that same cheap labor.

While it is true that some people lose their jobs to cheaper foreign labor, the predicted impact has never been as devastating as feared. Today, especially in the technology sectors of business, the fear of U.S. jobs being lost to India, Russia, or Brazil runs rampant. However, outsourcing has always been with us. It is part of American free enterprise.

It is true that over the last ten years, U.S. multinational companies have cut their domestic workforces by 2.9 million while boosting hiring abroad by 2.4 million. But only 1 percent of the companies in the United States are multinational. These kinds of companies are recognized by the media so often that their activity is overemphasized.

America has been "offshoring" since World War II. A cheap labor market will always attract a lot of demand. But when the demand for that cheap labor market increases, wages go up here in America or anywhere else in the world. Eventually the cost advantage of that so-called cheap labor no longer exists, and then some of the jobs either come back to the United States or move to another part of the world. Then the cycle repeats itself.

One of the reasons that offshoring and outsourcing are currently such a large issue is that advanced technology has made the practice take place in more countries, faster than we have ever dreamed possible. Therefore, it affects more people than ever before.

America taught the world free enterprise, ingenuity, hard work, and innovation. Now these principles are being used to compete against the United States, yes. But we have a choice. We can curse the darkness that we perceive the world to be engulfed in or we can take those same principles of free enterprise, ingenuity, hard work, and innovation and use them to compete with the rest of the world. In order to compete, though, we have to be better and work harder.

Myth #19

If you're really good, people will want to hire you and you will always have a job.

Try selling this myth to most of the IT, telecommunications, electronics, and manufacturing people who have been either laid off or downsized in recent years. Some of these people have been looking for jobs for two or three years. They're really, really good people. There is just no market for their skills.

Myth #20

I want to find the last job or company for the rest of my career so I'll never have to change jobs again.

Unless you are sixty-two years old and plan to retire at sixty-five, this concept is really misguided and borders on insane. The average job is going to last from two to three years—either within the same company or at a new one. Now, you may beat the averages, and the opportunity that you find may last for the rest of your working career. But the probabilities of this scenario being accurate are not very great. So, you need to be prepared to change jobs every two to three years. You may not like it, but that is reality.

Myth #21

I know the market for my skills. I get calls to recruit me all the time.

This statement is usually followed by one that says that, since the candidate keeps up on his or her industry or profession by reading and keeping in contact with people in the same profession, he or she knows exactly what the market will bear in looking for a new opportunity.

Don't flatter yourself. There is a big difference between knowing a general, broad, overall market and actually finding a specific job opportunity that might be the real deal. Getting a call from a recruiter, or hearing someone talk, or reading an article about the market for your skills may not be close to reality.

Myth #22

Networking is the only way to find a job.

Concentrating on any single method of finding a job is misguided. Most people begin looking for a job in several ways. They start out by doing some networking, contacting recruiters, talking to previous employers and subordinates, and so forth. By the fourth week, however, most of these people focus on only one or two means to get interviews. *This is a big mistake.* The key is to work as many different angles as possible to get interviews.

Myth #23

Being employed while looking for a job gives a person leverage.

Trying to find a job while you have one does not give you any kind of advantage at all. Most hiring authorities who have "pain" and need to hire someone don't really care whether you are currently employed.

If you are currently employed and don't have to change jobs that badly, it may be less risky to negotiate and run the chance of being refused because of demands that you might make. It is comforting when you have a job—even one that you may not like—to know that you aren't desperate and don't have to take a job just because it's offered.

A hiring authority with pain needs that pain alleviated by the best-qualified candidate he or she can find. Unemployed candidates feel that they are at a distinct disadvantage in the hiring process because they do not currently have a job, but it is more of a psychological and emotional inferiority complex than a reality.

Myth #24

I'll "stick my toe in the water" and casually look for a job, just to see what's out there.

I have known candidates who have approached finding a job this way for years, and they've never found one. They are still at the same job they've had since they started looking for a new job. The truth: There can be nothing casual about looking for a job. You're competing with people who are not casual about looking for a job. You are going to lose out to anyone else who really wants to go work—and acts like it.

Myth #25

If I'm recruited, they have to sell me. After all, I'm not looking for a job.

It is true that if you are happily employed and an organization—either through a recruiter or on its own—approaches you about changing jobs and joining another company, you have somewhat of an advantage. Just be aware that once you get into the interviewing process, you have to sell yourself just as though you were going after the job on your own. A laid-back, "Give me a good reason why I should come to work here" approach will simply leave the door open for your competition.

Myth #26

When companies "stroke" you, they're signaling that you've got the job.

"You're by far the best candidate we've seen." "We'd love to hire you." "We'd love to have people like you in our organization." "You're exactly what we want." Sounds good, right?

These are some of the most misleading statements that you will encounter in the job-finding process. They can also be the most emotionally debilitating, especially when an offer does not formally materialize. Even the statement, "You've got the job," means nothing unless it is accompanied by an actual job offer. I have known hiring authorities who told three or four candidates simultaneously that they would like to hire them for the same position, and then never hired anyone.

Myth #27

Big companies have more security.

There is no more stability in large organizations than there is in small ones. The average job is going to last two to three years, whether you are with a big company or a small company. It really doesn't matter.

The only difference between a big company and a small company is that people seem to have more sympathy and understanding for someone who has lost a job at a big company. I've never figured this out. When a big company lets a person go, it is called a layoff. When a small company lets someone go, there is a tendency to think, "The SOBs fired me!" In either case, you're out of work, looking for a job.

Myth #28

It's not what you know, but who you know.

It is true that the more people you know, the more opportunities for interviews you may get. It is true that the more people like you, the more opportunities you might have for going to work. However, who you know can often backfire on a qualified candidate. I cannot tell you the number of qualified candidates I have seen who did *not* get hired because of familiarity.

This is a difficult concept to communicate, and even a little harder to accept. What it comes down to is that your friends, or people who you think are your friends, don't really want to hire people they know personally. When people get to know others, they also get to know their strengths *and* their weaknesses, the positives and negatives about their personalities. Often people whom you know fairly well really don't want you around in their organization because you know *their* positives and negatives, too.

The old adage "familiarity breeds contempt" comes to mind. Don't trust people you know to help you any more than the people you don't know.

Myth #29

I asked around and got great advice from _____ about the kind of job I should take.

You fill in the blank! I love it when candidates talk to others (two or three or five or fifteen or twenty people) who have changed jobs in the recent past and have given them advice.

Unless these people have skin in the game, take all of the so-called advice they give you with a big chunk of salt. Unless someone is willing to offer you a job, their opinions are often just that—opinions.

Myth #30

I changed jobs a few years ago, so I know what I'm doing.

Job markets change. You really don't know anything about the current market for you and your skills. Every time you go to look for a job, the market is different from how it was before—even as recently as a year ago. Assume nothing.

Myth #31

Finding a good job is more luck than anything else.

Luck is *preparation meeting opportunity*! The harder you work, the luckier you get.

If it's luck to sell yourself into lots of interviews, to know what to say when you get there, and to get a good job offer as a result, then I guess some people are just lucky. This is a numbers game. Babe Ruth hit a lot of home runs, but he also struck out a lot. Was he any luckier when he struck out than when he hit the ball? Hard work creates a lot of "luck."

Myth #32

I'm too shy to thrust myself at a prospective employer.

I really understand. Many people are just not good at pushing themselves onto other people. I read one book that said that the alternative to thrusting yourself at a prospective employer was to simply email your résumé. You may be more emotionally comfortable hitting that "send" button, but it isn't going to get you a job.

If you practice all the scripts I offer, you will become confident in your ability to secure and perform well on an interview. You can overcome your shyness with practice. I didn't say it would be easy, but it is necessary.

Myth #33

I don't want a job like the last one; I really got burned.

This concept is a symptom of people's running away from what last hurt them. There is a tendency to generalize about what doesn't work out—to turn those companies or people with whom you have had bad experiences into universals. Just because one business or one organization hurt you, it doesn't mean another one will. People are sensitive about their last bad experience. But it doesn't always follow that, just because you worked at one organization that was poorly run, everyone else in that profession or industry is of the same ilk.

7 : Mastering the Telephone Interview

MORE OFTEN THAN IN EARLIER YEARS, even our better clients, who trust our judgment in qualifying candidates for them, are asking our candidates to interview over the telephone. Even local organizations will often insist on talking to, screening, or interviewing candidates over the phone first, before they consider a face-to-face interview. What's this all about? And how does a job-seeker handle the matter?

What's Going On?

With so many candidates to choose from, companies find that the telephone interview is a great way *not* to have to interview a large number of people. It has become the de facto terminator of prospective candidates. Consider the following email train:

> FROM Tony Beshara [tony@babich.com]
> SENT Thursday, June 23, 20—4:21 p.m.
> TO Al Bingham
> SUBJECT Ron English telephone interview
>
> How did his interview with you go?
>
> RESPONSE (Client)
> He is not a cultural fit.
>
> RESPONSE (Tony)
> What do you mean?
>
> RESPONSE (Client)
> I asked him one question. He talked nonstop for 22 minutes.

The door is shut. There's a bad initial impression made, before there's been even the slightest consideration of qualifications. How does a candidate avoid this plight?

Unfortunately, 35 to 40 percent of the time, the telephone screener is not the hiring manager. This makes the situation even worse. The screener's objective is to pare down a large number of probable candidates to two or three possibilities. That is, the screener's job is to *eliminate* candidates. That means . . . *YOU.*

Now, those screeners will tell you that their mission is to discover the best candidates, but it becomes a game of musical chairs. There is a random stopping point for deciding who wins the face-to-face interview, and you may be the one who's left without the chair when the music stops.

Awkward and Uncomfortable Phone Situations

I recently placed a candidate with a company that, over the course of three months, screened him via the phone three different times for two different positions. He was eliminated each time by the HR screener. Finally, I got him the face-to-face interview with the hiring authority because he was such a good fit. Of course, we didn't tell the hiring authority that he had thrice been eliminated. The company hired him. In fact, the hiring authority wrote me a month after the candidate had started working there, telling me he was the best hire he had ever made!

With the initial telephone screening now so important, what's a job candidate to do? Especially those candidates who find telephone interviews uncomfortable?

> "Tony, they told me they were going to call me at 8:30 a.m. I waited, but had to take the kids to school. They called at 8:50 a.m., while I was driving back from the school. In fact, I was in a school zone when I answered the phone, got pulled over by a policeman for being on the phone in a school zone, and had to explain that to the person calling me. Needless to say, our conversation was short. I told her I'd call her back. How should I handle it?" —Ted, *The Job Search Solution* radio program caller

The skills you need for getting beyond the telephone screening are different from those you use in a personal, face-to-face interview. Here are a few tips we have found that can make a telephone interview successful.

To begin, if you get a call from a prospective employer in response to a résumé you sent, and you are not prepared or ready for the call, take down the person's number and say you will call back at a designated time. Don't feel that you need to talk to someone just because the person called you, especially if you don't know whom you're talking to and what company the individual represents. Most of the time, whoever calls is going to tell you that he or she would like to set up a telephone interview with you. But even if the person wants to interview you right then and there, set a specific later time and, preferably, *you* place the call. (There is a psychological advantage to initiating the call.)

Here are a dozen tips on what to do when it comes to telephone interviews.

Change the Message on Your Phone

Whether it's your cell phone or your landline, change the message so that people know exactly whom they are reaching. When you can't answer, the caller should hear a message like, "This is Tony Beshara. You've reached 214-823-9999. Please leave a message."

Many people, especially for their cell phones, let the automated message state their phone number. Okay, you say, "so what's wrong with that?" Well, here is what's wrong.

Hiring authorities may keep your résumé for two or three years—maybe even longer. If an opening comes up in the future, companies often search through the résumés on hand. If yours is one they like, they may want to call you. When they call the phone number on the résumé and hear the automated message, they are not sure that it is you and so they hang up. You may have just lost out on one of the best opportunities that ever came along, and you don't even know it. So, state your *name* and *phone number* clearly on your recorded message so that people know they have reached your voice mail.

And it should go without saying, make sure it is a professional message. Hearing something stupid like, "Wa-d up . . . this is T. Leave a message, bro," is not going to sit well with the hiring authority. I had one candidate sometime back who had a song as an intro to her message, with romantic music and a female voice softly singing, "Come away with me. . . ." The lady was almost my age, had over twenty-five years of professional experience, and had a master's degree. What's even more sad—or stupid, depending on how you look at it—was that she was insulted when I told her that she had to change her message.

Set an Appointment Time for the Call

If possible, set a phone date. It makes the call more important to all parties. Avoid a casual response like, "Call me any time." If you initiate the call and need to leave a message, let the person know you called and leave a message that you will call back after five minutes. Do not leave a number. Place the call again. Keep doing this until you reach the interviewer. (Leave a number only when you know, for certain, that you're going to be available and focused when they call back.)

Research the Company and the Position

There may not be much time to gather information, especially if the call has come out of the blue and you're calling back in fifteen minutes, but the more you know, the better off you are. This is another reason you should try to avoid starting the interview immediately upon receiving the call.

I have even had some candidates who make a quick pre-call to the interviewing/screening authority to find out who it is, how long he or she has been there, and so on. They ask questions like, "What is the purpose of the call? How many people will I be speaking to?"

Prepare for the Interview

Make sure that you have time to prepare for the telephone interview. Write out several open-ended questions that show you have done your research about the company. Asking even tough questions about the company's financial statements (if it is a public company) or the success of a product that the company has developed shows that you have taken an interest in being informed.

Know Who Your Interviewer Is

Establish beforehand exactly who you are interviewing with. Hiring authorities are much better to speak to than screeners. The hiring authority is going to be more flexible than a third-party screener. He or she also has a much better idea of how to evaluate your qualifications and experience in regard to the job at hand.

Know What the Hiring Criteria Are

Rehearse addressing those needs. If you are being screened by a third party who does not have a feel for the give-and-take in a position, the interview will be harder. This person does not have the personal pain of needing someone, so he or she will be more rigid about what is wanted.

For instance, a screener is going to evaluate you based on factual rather than qualitative issues. A screener in HR may not have one iota of an idea about what it takes for an accounting candidate to file an SEC report, but he or she will ask why you had three jobs in three years. So, if you try to sell the idea that quality writing of SEC reports outweighs the circumstances of three jobs in three years, you're gonna lose!

Remind Yourself: This Is Not a Real Interview

Remember, this is a *screening* call, and usually the objective for the screener is to screen out candidates. It is not a face-to-face interview, so it doesn't take into account your image, body language, or visual communications. It's strictly voice-to-voice. Overall, this can be even more difficult for you than a face-to-face interview because it's so much easier to *screen you out* over the phone.

Sell Yourself Hard

Since there is more of a tendency for the interviewer to screen out than to screen in, you must sell yourself a little harder. Remember, the objective of a telephone interview (from your point of view) is to get the face-to-face interview. Psychologically, from the caller's point of view, the purpose is to eliminate you.

Keep to the Point

Be concise. The more talking on the phone that you do, the more likely you will be screened out. And that is the last thing you want. Say what you have to, but stay focused on getting the personal interview.

Be Prepared

Have your résumé in front of you, along with any research you have done on the company. Have a legal pad of paper and pen handy so that you can take notes. Also, have a glass of water nearby in case you get dry. If the interviewer, hiring authority, or screener is calling you from another city, there may be a number of telephone interviews before you get a face-to-face interview.

If you are interviewed over the phone by another person in the same organization, you'll come across as more professional if you mention the name of the last person you spoke to on the phone. You will sound like you really know what you are talking about when you say things like: "Well, when I spoke to _____ last, he mentioned that _____." So, take really good notes. (I can't tell you the number of my own candidates, whom I have coached, who forget to do this. They get to a second or third telephone interview and literally forget what they told the first one or two people they interviewed with.)

Smile

It doesn't hurt to have a mirror in front of you. Be in a good mood, friendly, and in the selling mode. People can hear smiles over the phone! Be upbeat and energetic. Sound interested and engaged.

Anticipate the Length of Time

Be ready for a psychological time frame of about twenty minutes. That's if the call is being conducted by a screener. Most screeners aren't going to admit this, but the truth is that they don't know what else to ask after about 20 minutes. Even if interviewer/screener has a set of questions to ask (which most do not), after a while the conversation tends to ramble around. Just be prepared for this and start closing early for a face-to-face interview.

If you are even a reasonably seasoned professional and you feel like you are being asked stupid questions by a person who knows little about the specific opportunity, you may become frustrated, even mad. However, you cannot afford to come across as condescending or too good to be having this conversation with such an ignorant person. Be patient and bear with it. The conversation is the road to a face-to-face interview.

On the other hand, if the telephone interview is being conducted by a hiring authority with pain, you should be specific and elaborate on your possible contributions in terms the hiring authority would recognize. Be careful, though, because you can establish great rapport with someone over the phone and forget to push for a face-to-face interview.

If a phone interview with a hiring authority goes beyond 20 minutes, and there is obvious interest, it is likely that the conversation could go on longer. I've known phone interviews to go as long as two hours. Be prepared for this. You don't want to come across as poorly prepared by, say, after about 45 minutes of a productive conversation having to conclude with something stupid like, "Oh, my, I'm going to be late to another appointment. Can we pick this up at some other time?"

> **Key Point:** Relax and practice this kind of interview before you need to do it.

What Not to Do

Just as there are "do's," here are nine "don'ts."

Don't Take It for Granted

Don't take a telephone screening or interview for granted. It's just as serious as a face-to-face interview. In fact, it's going to be more difficult.

Don't Use a Cell Phone

Avoid using a cell phone for a telephone interview unless you absolutely have to. Some people now use a cell phone exclusively and have discarded their landlines. I recommend that you conduct any telephone interviews from a landline, if you can. Admittedly, cell phone technology is better than it used to be, but I still don't like cells for telephone interviews. It's not because I'm an old fuddy-duddy. It's because, psychologically, people have a tendency to be casual on cell phones; also, if the connection drops in the middle of an interview, it just plain isn't good.

I have had candidates try to carry on telephone interviews inside buildings where the reception was poor. I've had them carry on screening conversations while in their car and lose a connection (we'll get to that in a minute). Cell phone connections can easily drop in the middle of a conversation and in some places service is not available. We have known many instances where the telephone interviewer couldn't reconnect with a candidate after one or two tries, so he just moved on to the next candidate.

Don't Interview in a Noisy Place

Avoid carrying on a telephone interview in a busy place or where there's a noisy environment. If the interview must be conducted from home, make sure there are no kids, dogs, television, or radio in the background. (Don't laugh; people do that kind of thing all the time.) Likewise, don't make the call from the car or on a speakerphone. Speakerphones are especially annoying. No matter what you think, they communicate big ego—too big and important to pick up the phone.

If the interviewer or the screener begins to use a speakerphone, ask the person to pick up the phone by just stating that you cannot hear him or her very well. Speakerphones do not communicate a personal, one-on-one relationship. As a candidate, you especially do not want this kind of situation. So, it may come across as a bit pushy, but it is a good idea to ask callers to please pick up the phone so that you can understand them better.

Don't Lose Your Focus

Don't carry on a telephone interview when you cannot focus completely on the questions and the interview. This is critical. I can't tell you the number of candidates who get screened out because they had the phone interview in the wrong place. Don't do it on your cell phone, or while you are driving, or when you're with someone else, or while you're watching TV, or when you are in your office and have to whisper lest people overhear. If necessary, pull off the road and park. And, by the way, don't be reading your emails while you're carrying on a telephone interview, either.

Don't Discuss Money

Don't talk about or bring up money or salary in any kind of depth in a telephone interview. State what you have made before, if asked, and address the money matter when the opportunity arises later.

Don't Ask "What Can You Do for Me?" Questions

These kinds of questions are the major reason telephoned candidates do *not* go beyond the phone screening. When asked, "Do you have any questions?" keep your questions open-ended, such as "Why is this position open?" or "Mr./Ms. [Employer], why do you work for the company?" Any question that relates to what the company can do for *you* will most likely eliminate you as a candidate.

In fact, when the interviewer asks, "Do you have any questions?" you should take the opportunity to ask, "When can we get together face-to-face?"

Don't Talk Too Much

Answer the questions directly and conversationally, but don't ramble. It is easier to become confused in a telephone conversation than it is in a face-to-face one. So err on the quiet side. In fact, it is a good idea to end every statement with a question—even if the question is, "Did I make myself clear?"

Don't Avoid Obvious Sensitive Issues

Things like listing too many jobs on your résumé, being out of work for an extended period of time, or being fired are red flags. Whatever you do, don't trip over or avoid tough questions, though. Explain the situation directly and be to the point. Do not appear to avoid them or cover them up with the proverbial "it doesn't matter" excuse.

Don't Say You Know Something That You Do Not

There is nothing wrong with admitting, "I don't know" in response to a question that you shouldn't know the answer to anyway. Know the difference.

> **Key Point:** Prepare for the phone interview or telephone screening in the same manner as you would for a face-to-face interview. Take it seriously and sell yourself!

8 : Finding a Job on the Internet

DON'T HOLD YOUR BREATH. You can believe me now or believe me later, but you're not going to find a job on the Internet. The Internet might help you find a job, but it's not going to find you that job.

The Internet has revolutionized the way people go about looking for work. However, here's the truth: It is nowhere near the magic tool those in the Internet business would have you believe. When I first got into this profession, résumés were delivered by mail. Résumé delivery was then speeded up by faxes—do you remember those? (In 1983, I placed a salesperson with the Burroughs Corp., hired to sell fax machines for $100,000 each. Boy, has technology changed.) Today, resumes are sent over the Internet in rapid response to job openings listed online.

There are, however, a number of other ways you can use the Internet to job-hunt, including social networking. At the end of this chapter, I describe the results of a survey we conducted regarding candidates' use of Facebook, Twitter, MySpace, and LinkedIn. It was revealing of the great impact the Internet has had on the job search process.

But, before we begin to discuss the potential, here's a general caution.

Beware Internet Scams and Solicitations

If you post your résumé on the Internet, you really need to be extremely careful about giving out information to anyone who contacts you as a result. Identity theft and fraud account for almost a billion dollars a year, and much of it comes as a result of a job-seeker's posting his or her résumé on a job board. These scammers pose as potential employers and dupe candidates into revealing personal information.

These schemes can be very sophisticated, and they may not always involve outright theft of your money. It recently happened in our organization. Some scam artist ran an ad on Craigslist for a proofreader/transcriptionist. The individual used an email address similar to that for our company, Babich & Associates. A woman responded to the ad and corresponded three or four times with an individual who made an agreement with her to work on a contractual basis. He vaguely referred to our firm. She was to work out of her home, editing and rewriting technical information. She received the material by email, edited and rewrote it, and returned it by email. She agreed to $10 an hour as compensation, and she was told she would be paid every two weeks. After two weeks' worth of work—90 hours, to be exact—the payday rolled around and she received nothing.

When she called the listed phone number, no one answered. She emailed the address she had been sending the work and received no response. Once she realized she had been cheated, she called our organization. It soon became clear that the whole thing was a scam. This kind of thing is hard to imagine until you experience it.

In fact, the news is full of stories of people who unknowingly either email or in other ways give out private information like Social Security numbers, credit card numbers, and so on. For job candidates who have posted their résumés on job boards, the scam involves being contacted by "potential" employers that claim they have to do a background check before the interview. They ask for all kinds of private information and often get it.

You can assume that your personal information, whether on your résumé, on a personal Web site, or on a social network site like LinkedIn, Facebook, MySpace, or Twitter, will float around in cyberspace, readily available for just about anyone to use or see. So, you might want to consider using a different email address while looking for a job; you can easily cancel the address if this kind of stuff gets out of hand. (I get five to ten emails a day sent from people I know whose email addresses have been "hijacked," offering me every imaginable drug known to man. I'm not as bothered by it as most people are, but my friends are embarrassed. They end up having to change email addresses.)

However, it is simple to avoid most of these problems. Just don't give any personal information to anyone until you have interviewed with someone face-to-face and you know you are dealing with a legitimate business. Even when the person sounds legitimate, verify the facts. A number of years ago, a prospective employer called our organization. He told us he was an executive with a company that was going to establish an office in the Dallas–Fort Worth area. He told us he was flying into town and wanted to meet a number of potential office managers at the hotel where he was staying.

It was our long-time experience as recruiters that signaled this as fishy. We called the corporate office of this supposed new client to find out that an executive's briefcase had been stolen. Someone was using his identity and credit cards, pretending to be him. So, even if the person sounds good, don't provide personal information until you are certain you're giving it to a legitimate person with a legitimate business.

If you are requested to do something that appears odd, be suspicious. A legitimate organization interested in you as an employee is going to follow traditional steps. If you don't get a face-to-face interview after a few conversations, be leery. Check on the legitimacy of the opportunity and the company.

It is easy to say, "Come on, can't people figure out when they might be duped?" But when a person is desperate for a job, suffering emotional "disease," and receives come-ons like these, he might think, *Maybe this is okay . . . I need help.*

Expect also to get legitimate franchise and business investment opportunities, insurance solicitations, credit card offerings, and the like as a result of your résumé's being posted on the Internet. I guess that's part of free enterprise. This can be irritating, too, and it has led many job-seekers to avoid posting their résumés or to respond only to specific opportunities and specific people. But if you're careful, and can put up with a few unwanted solicitations, posting your résumé on the Internet should not be a problem.

The Internet for Company and People Research

By the time you read this, there will be new innovations involving the Internet that will be helpful in your job search. However, understand that the Internet is only one tool to be used in your job search. For instance, the Internet cannot conduct your interviews for you, though if it is used right, it may help you get those interviews. Likewise, the Internet isn't going to "sell" you any better than you can sell yourself. As before, getting the interview is the most important thing you can do in the job search—provided you sell yourself well.

Know Before You Go

The most effective use of the Internet for a job-seeker is to research companies and locate individuals who might interview you. For example, you can use a search engine like Google to find out about any hiring authority you are going to speak with. You can visit the Web sites of organizations to obtain information that even the people you interview with may not know about their companies. The more extensive research you do about individuals and organizations you are going to speak with, the more likely you will interview well.

There are hundreds of ways you can use the Internet to promote your résumé as well. However, the return on investment relative to the time you spend is low. Skillfully using the Internet to research companies, the people who work in them, the hiring managers you will speak with, their competitors, and anything else you can find of interest still yields the best return on time invested.

Everyone, objectively, knows to research the organizations and people they may interview with, but some people stop with the basic information even when there's that little something extra out there that can be helpful in the interview. For example, we have placed a number of people with a CEO who has written a couple of books about his favorite hobby. If you Google his name, you will find out about his avocation. Nothing impresses this guy more than a candidate who asks about the books he has written.

So use the Internet to research *everything* you can about the organizations and about the people who might interview you. You never know what information you uncover may prove useful.

Expand Your Searches

You'll be amazed at the number of local companies and job opportunities you will uncover using this simple Internet search tool. A Google search, or entering the key words that relate to your situation, will produce company names. When you find an organization that may need the skills you have to offer, pick up the phone and call it.

By the way, if your Google search uncovers the news that a particular organization is expanding in one area, don't assume it may not be expanding in other areas as well; the company may need the kind of expertise you offer. If a company is hiring three or four inside salespeople, for instance, it may very well be in need of an accountant, bookkeeper, or administrative person also. "Bodies in motion tend to stay in motion"—and that goes for companies that are expanding as well.

Job Boards

There are basically four types of job boards on the Internet: national job boards, like Monster.com, HotJobs.com, and CareerBuilder; regional job boards, which focus on your state or metropolitan area; profession-specific boards, which cover one profession or industry; and company job boards, which are specific to an individual company. There are also some job boards that link many job boards; you can save some time by posting your résumé on one of those.

There are thousands of job boards. (I read one report that said there were 55,000 of them.) In fact, there are now Internet services that post your résumé for you on multiple sites. You post your résumé once, and for a fee the service distributes it to hundreds of job boards. There are even Web sites that send your résumé to over 8,000 recruiters—for a fee.

Many job boards are going to ask you to reformat your résumé to conform to their format. You may not have much choice in this if you decide to post your résumé on those particular job boards. Different job boards keep your résumé active for different periods of time, so you should check with each one so you know how long your résumé will be posted. How often you update your résumé is up to you, but don't confuse this activity with productivity.

Most job boards provide keyword searches for their users. That is, if you are a specific type of engineer, or specific type of accountant, most job boards will produce your résumé for those users who use those key words. General résumé submittal forms may work for you; however, by using them you may limit yourself to your ideal job or ideal company. The same holds true for indicating any preference for company size. Try to be as open as possible to various situations so that your résumé appears in a company's search for suitable applicants.

Post your heart out, but don't expect a big return on your investment. Studies have shown that only 2 to 5 percent of candidates receive a worthwhile response from an Internet posting. I've seen this figure go as high as 10 percent, but that depends on how one defines a "worthwhile response." If a company calls you because it found your résumé posted, and the caller asks about your skills or availability, is that a positive response? If you get a call from a recruiter who finds your résumé on a job board, but you never hear from that recruiter again, is that a positive response?

The results from Internet job board postings are often overrated. Every year, the employment consulting firm CareerXRoads conducts a survey of human resource managers at large companies. The 2011 survey showed that just 13 percent of recent external hires were found from job boards, while 27 percent were found through referrals—that is, people who work at the company. In fact, the percentage of external hires from job boards has averaged between 12 and 13 percent since 2005.

This won't come as a surprise to most perennial job-seekers, but when the market is flush with candidates, as it has been for the past few years, employers or recruiters with job opportunities call even less. Your attitude may be, "Well, I only need one good opportunity." You're right! The hard part is finding that good opportunity.

Weddle's is a leading publisher of print guides to the 100,000+ job boards now operating on the Internet. It has conducted a poll since 2004 regarding the best online employment job boards; here are Weddle's top finishers for 2011:

Weddle's 2011 User's Choice Awards: The Elite of the Online Employment Industry

- Absolutely Health Care
- AHACareerCenter.org
- AllRetailJobs.com
- Climber.com
- CoolWorks.com
- EHSCareers.com
- FlexJobs.com
- HEALTHeCAREERS
- HospitalDreamJobs.com
- Job.com
- JobFox.com
- Monster.com
- SimplyHired.com
- SnagAJob.com
- VetJobs.com

- AfterCollege.com
- AllHealthcareJobs.com
- CareerBuilder.com
- CollegeRecruiter.com
- Dice.com
- ExecuNet
- Hcareers.com Network
- HigherEdJobs.com
- Indeed.com
- JobCircle.com
- Jobing
- National Healthcare Career Network
- 6FigureJobs.com
- TopUSAJobs.com
- WSJ.com/Careers

Responding to Web Site Job Postings

Applying directly to a company that has posted a job opening can be one of the most frustrating experiences you will have. There's a tendency to think that if a company posts a job opportunity, it has a real opening. Well, at the time someone posts the opportunity, maybe it does—but maybe it doesn't.

Don't Hold Your Breath

Don't assume that there is really an opening; 25 to 30 percent of the time, companies post these openings just to be able to say they did it. They're going to promote from within, and they knew this to begin with, or the nephew of the VP of sales was already told he would be hired. Why do companies do this? They need to justify their internal or "brother-in-law" hire by saying, "Well, we searched all over the place for qualified candidates and couldn't come up with anybody better than the person we hired!"

At least 20 percent of the time these companies never hire anybody at all, even when they start out needing an employee and post the job opening. I know this because, as a recruiter since 1973, I have experienced this over and over. Our clients give us a search assignment, expend effort in interviewing candidates, and then claim they're not going to hire anyone. Happens all the time. Job opportunities are posted on company career sites for all kinds of business and political or legal reasons.

There's no question that it is frustrating to be looking for a job, see a job posting you know you are well qualified for, apply for it, and never hear a word. You probably will apply three or four times and never hear a word. You will get frustrated and angry, as well as downright disheartened, about the whole experience. The problem is, you have no idea if the job is really open, why it was posted in the first place, and of quality of the 473 other candidates who have applied for it. So, do respond to postings on company Web sites, but don't hold your breath waiting for a response.

Call the Company

The specific questions that companies ask on a Web site posting may very well eliminate you right away. Most of the time, you are forced to enter on the Web site the money you have earned before. You know that the likelihood of being eliminated is great if you put down the wrong figure, and the money you earned in the past really has nothing to do with the money you would consider today, especially if you've been out of work for any length of time. Unfortunately, if you leave this entry blank, your application often will be automatically eliminated.

Most people who advise on job hunting and résumé preparation will tell you not to call the company or the appropriate individual. Don't buy this advice. You need a job. The ad will say, "Do not call." Well, I can't tell you how many times I have earned thousands of dollars in fees when I was told not to call and I called anyway.

So, you say, "Well, what if I make them mad?" First, hiring authorities who really need to hire someone—that is, those who have a great deal of "pain"—don't really care how they find the best candidate. The HR (i.e., Hiring Roadblock) people are trying to protect their jobs and keep a hiring authority from having to answer the phone, so they dictate the "Do not call" order.

You say, "Well, I really don't know whom to call." Cut it out! If you're a salesperson, you call a sales manager. If you're an accountant, you call the comptroller. If you are a comptroller, you call the CFO. If you're an administrative assistant, you call the office manager. You know whom to call—don't use that wimpy excuse! Pick up the phone and find the hiring authority with "pain" and call that person. Tell him or her you would make an excellent employee, and you need to interview as soon as possible.

Your odds of getting an interview this way are much greater than if you take the passive route. You can either believe me now or believe me later, but you will eventually come to this conclusion. Yes, you may make five or ten calls to a hiring authority and never get a call back. Okay, that's life. I didn't say it was going to be easy. But I absolutely guarantee you'll get more interviews doing this than if you apply online and wait for someone to call you.

Break Through the HR Barrier

You might be pleasantly surprised to find out how frustrated hiring authorities are with the ridiculous "recruiting" process their company has likely burdened them with. Yes, you read that right. Most hiring authorities don't like the recruiting process that the HR (Hiring Roadblock) department imposes on them. How do I know? I talk to tons of these folks every year. They want to find quality candidates, quickly. Most company recruiting processes don't work very well because hiring people isn't the primary job of the HR folks. They are primarily record keepers; they perform an administrative function.

I have, as you see, been referring to HR departments as "Hiring Roadblock" departments. I know that is a strong accusation, and there are some HR folks who are really good at what they do. But most of their processes and procedures center on what is good for them, rather than what is good for you as a candidate or the direct hiring authority who has the "pain." Most hiring authorities would rather manage the interviewing and hiring process themselves. They are as stuck with the HR department as you are. And most of them will admit that, off the record.

I know this because I have spoken to thousands of direct hiring authorities since 1973. Just realize that if you get relegated to the HR department, your odds of getting an interview, let alone a job, are drastically reduced. That's just the way it is!

The average company in America has sixteen employees! Fortunately, most companies don't have an HR department. Even the ones that do don't recruit very well. So, pick up the phone and call someone at the company who can get you an interview. Be relentless! You're the one who's looking for a job!

For example, suppose you go to the company Web site for a business in your local area and see who their employees are. Maybe you know some of them; if you do, call them! (LinkedIn is great for this, as you will see later.) Ask them about the job and the hiring authority, and find out how they might help you get an interview. Don't be bashful.

And if you don't know anyone directly, you may know someone who knows someone who works there, especially if you are in the same or a related business. This is a great way to use your second and third levels of contacts through LinkedIn or another social/business network. Call the person and ask for an introduction to the hiring authority.

Again, don't be shy. Don't worry about irritating anyone. If you are professional and pack a powerful message—that is, why you would be a good employee—the person won't be irritated. And, in the back of his or her mind may be the recognition that the roles could be reversed somewhere down the line and he or she may be calling you in the future.

Develop Your Own Brand

You can go well beyond the process of posting your résumé on job boards, following up with people you know, and calling people you don't know to try to get interviews. Now, you can build your own professional "brand." This ability is an outgrowth of the powerful Internet, coupled with the reality that, on average, people change jobs every two-and-a-half to three years. In other words, you need to be prepared to look for a job at any time. Developing and sustaining a personal identity, a brand, will make that easier.

Alison Doyle's *Internet Your Way to a New Job*, third edition (Happy About, 2011), provides a good foundation for establishing your personal brand. The concept is that you, as an individual, *create* a professional presence on the Internet, *market* yourself, *connect* with others who can help you find a job, and *help* prospective employers find you. The goal is to create an online presence that sells you as a candidate, much like a consumer product or service is marketed. People, especially prospective employers, are able to locate you through online media and, therefore, know what you can do for them.

This concept is fascinating and represents a new approach to the job search, but unless you have the time (are looking for a job full time and can also devote time to developing the brand), its effectiveness is questionable. If you have the time, it certainly can't hurt.

Caution: If you are looking for a job while you still have one, think twice about having a large online presence. I recently had a candidate who, while still at his job, began to look for a new one. He updated his LinkedIn contacts to include me. Alas, his boss was also one of his contacts, and when he saw that I was newly added, he asked my candidate if he was looking for a job. Of course, my candidate denied he was looking for a job, but their relationship was strained. So, if you are presently employed, be careful what you post or what contacts you add!

Here are some ways you can develop your online brand. By the time you read this, of course, there may be dozens of other possibilities.

PowerPoint Résumés

I have personally received a number of these. They involve ten or twelve PowerPoint slides with creative images, pictures, and graphics about the candidate, which take the place of a traditional résumé. The concept is simple and can be done very creatively. The major problem is that when 123 other candidates are also submitting traditional résumés, the hiring manager, although amused, may not really know what to do with all this.

Reviewing the PowerPoint presentation may be interesting, but if the reader, as most do, decides to print out some of the résumés of people to pursue, he or she is going to think twice about printing out a lengthy PowerPoint presentation. And it is unlikely the printed version is anywhere near as effective as the online presentation.

A PowerPoint presentation is most effective as a follow-up communication with prospective employers and hiring authorities—*after* an initial interview. My candidates have had excellent responses to their candidacy when they developed creative PowerPoint presentations based on information they gleaned during the initial or follow-up interviews. For example, a hiring authority is often impressed with a well-done PowerPoint presentation on "Why You Should Hire [Your Name]." A creative slide

PowerPoint summary of your features, advantages, and benefits (*value proposition*) is a killer follow-up to any interviewing situation.

Video Résumés

Traditional résumés can carry add-ons such as videos and links to projects or Web sites, or be totally video as posted on YouTube. Again, these can be creative and somewhat entertaining. Some Web sites provide a service that helps you create these kinds of visual résumés. They can be printed and easily updated, as well as connected to LinkedIn, Facebook, Twitter, and Plaxo—in fact, to any of the social media you might think of.

If you are going to develop a video résumé, consider the following tips:

- Keep it short—under three minutes, and sixty seconds is even better

- It should be professional looking and demonstrate your skills, features, advantages, and benefits

- Be sure you are photogenic

Again, if you are presently employed, posting a video résumé may not be a good idea, even though many of these sites will tell you they are secure. Video-sharing sites are often available to the public (Yahoo Video, Metasafe, Buzzquest, etc.). Another disadvantage of video résumés is that employers are busy. If they take only 10 seconds to read a traditional résumé, who is going to take 60 to 180 seconds to review a video résumé?

People under age 24 might be comfortable with hazy, fuzzy pictures and clips from an iPhone. These are social! Video résumés are supposed to be *professional*. Google "video résumés" and look at a bunch of them. Most are awful. These people could practice for years and never look or sound any better. Would you be encouraged to interview any of them?

I consulted my long-time friend, and America's first career columnist, Joyce Laine Kennedy. She has been writing for four decades about careers, has a syndicated column (*Careers Now*), and has published seven books about careers, changing jobs, résumés, and interviewing. Her take on this new buzz is about the same as mine. The only people who may get ahead are the ones who are charging a job candidate for making the video résumé.

Consider how you really look on a video; it may not be complimentary. In fact, most people are not that photogenic. Unless you really look good, reconsider. Until it becomes more "traditional and practical," most employers may not give video the time of day. In fact, I don't know of any companies that use them. Even if they present a candidate well, the major problem with video résumés is the same problem educational TV had in the '60s and online video training now has: There is *no* personal interaction between people and *no* feedback exchange between candidate and employer. Things may change, but as of this writing, the time, money, and effort to produce a video résumé may not be worth it.

Facebook and MySpace Profiles

Keeping your Facebook profile up to date, especially for professional reasons, will help you build your brand. Keep in mind, however, that whatever you write on Facebook, or any other type of Web site, is going to be there forever, even though you may think you are editing it as you go along.

As of this writing, I'm not convinced you need a Facebook presence to launch a quality job search. We have had candidates whose profiles on Facebook were a little racy. In doing their due diligence, employers often review a person's Facebook profile. Even though the profile is intended to be "social," it does say something about you.

When a job market is really, really tight, potential employers are looking for just as many reasons *not* to hire you as they are reasons to hire you. Don't give them the ammunition to eliminate you. So, if you insist on having a Facebook presence, make sure it is professional. Don't give me that nonsense about, "That is my personal life and has nothing to do with my professional life." In case you haven't caught on, how you present yourself personally is just as important to a prospective employer as how you present yourself professionally. So, don't put anything on there you wouldn't be proud to show your mom, your present or future spouse, or your present or future children.

The developers of Facebook and MySpace claim that these sites are excellent tools to help you find a job. Read the survey results later in the chapter and draw your own conclusion.

Twitter Accounts

You already know about Twitter. By the time you read this, there may be other rivals. There are now ways of tweeting your résumé, as well as keeping in contact with recruiters and hiring authorities. Again, read the survey results later in this chapter and draw your own conclusions.

Personal Web Sites

If you are presently employed, you certainly can't develop a Web site announcing that you are looking for a job. However, if you are looking for a job full time, you may have the time to develop your own personal Web site. This is another way of building your brand. You can create a pretty compelling profile of yourself. Be sure, though, that everything is businesslike and professional, including your picture (make sure it is professional—you are not trying to get a date). It goes without saying that you need to be careful with what you put on your Web site.

Don't put all of your faith in your Web site to get you a job. I've had candidates who have developed their own Web sites and assumed that interested companies and hiring authorities would automatically visit it. Think about it: When a hiring authority is receiving 140 or 150 traditional résumés, he or she may not take the time to visit your personal Web site, no matter how good you think it is.

Blogs

A blog, or Web log, is another popular way to build your brand and share your credentials with the world. Like your personal Web site, it can take a lot of time to prepare. Maintaining it is fairly easy, once you get the hang of it.

You can connect your blog to your Web site, LinkedIn, and Twitter, as well as include its address on your traditional résumé. If you are going to write a blog, though, you better have something to say that's worth reading, and it had better be information the reader can't get any other way (taken from another source). If you don't have expertise on what you are writing about, and a prospective employer reads it, you won't look very professional. Having a blog just to say you have one isn't going to help you get a job.

The Value of Social Media for Getting a Job

The Internet has expanded the opportunities to locate job openings and publicize your availability for work. Only time will tell how effective these various options are. I'm not convinced that either a personal Web site or a blog will necessarily help you get a better job.

I recently had a candidate who had a personal Web site and a blog, which he directed readers to by noting the addresses at the bottom of his résumé. A company I referred him to was interested in hiring him, so one of the administrative personnel visited his Web site. His Web site communicated that he was a very devout Christian. In fact, on his blog, he continually wrote about how no one would be saved without having Jesus Christ in his or her heart.

The owner of the company was sympathetic to the candidate's belief, but after the information about the candidate's Web site was passed around to a number of people in the company, several employees warned that they did not want a "bible beater" in the company who was going to try to convert them. The employer decided not to hire the candidate, simply because he didn't want to create any more hassles than he already had to deal with.

The lesson is clear. If you are looking for a job, you cannot afford to have anything floating around in cyberspace that might get in your way. For those of us who are Christian, this is a sad commentary. I read the guy's Web site, and I admit that it was rather judgmental; it made clear the writer was convinced Jesus Christ is the only way to salvation. However, that doesn't mean the candidate would try to convert everyone to his persuasion. The owner could have checked the guy's references and bluntly asked previous employers if the guy was on a mission to convert folks and if he made people uncomfortable at work. But the employer just didn't want to go to that trouble and, more important, did not want to run the risk of making his present employees uncomfortable. So stay away from controversial stuff.

Our Survey on Facebook, MySpace, and Twitter

Because there is so much hype about these social media, I decided to do a quick survey of job candidates and determine their success in using these three tools to get a job.

We asked over 9,000 local candidates who registered with our firm over the last few years; 3,600 of them responded to our survey. The group represented just about all generational levels, from recent graduates to boomers. They ranged widely in profession, from sales and accounting to information technology, healthcare, and administrative support. Earnings varied from $25,000 to $250,000 a year. Also, 60 percent of them were currently employed and 40 percent were looking for a job full time. Some have been looking to change jobs for as long as two years, while others have just started looking. Without being too scientific, they represented a valid cross section of solid employment candidates.

Now, don't shoot the messenger, but only *five* of the 3,600 people surveyed said he or she had found a job through any of these social media—and it was through Facebook. *Three* of them reported that they secured interviews as a direct result of being on Facebook. That was it! Many others stated that they had contacted people via Facebook about a job *after* they knew their names. Three other people said they found contract/freelance jobs by using Twitter and Facebook.

These results are a bit surprising, since the Internet resources proclaim how lots of people get jobs as a result of using the media. The vast majority of respondents stated that these social media helped them get jobs by being able to make new contacts through existing contacts. But as far as actually getting a job directly from one of these contacts, or being contacted by someone offering a job, none of these media seemed to work for anyone except the three previously mentioned. So, you may feel you have to use these tools, but don't get too hopeful you are going to land a job by using them.

What one of the respondents said sums up our conclusions as well. When asked the question, "Has Facebook, Twitter, or MySpace helped you get an interview or a job?" he answered, "No. Facebook, Twitter, or MySpace have not yielded me any interviews nor my friends. After seven months of looking for a job, my thought is they simply create false, busy activity—not meaningful connections."

It seems to be a matter of hype rather than reality. Here are some other responses:

- I keep my social life *social* and my professional life *professional*—I don't have the time for this kind of stuff."

- "I use Facebook and MySpace and Twitter extensively . . . but I haven't found a job through any of these—I guess they are just social."

As of this writing there are a number of major corporations that are developing within their HR departments the expertise to focus on recruiting certain types of candidates through the social media. I have spoken to three that have told me the approach is working well. Time will tell how popular and successful these efforts will be.

LinkedIn: A True Resource

Unlike Facebook, MySpace, and Twitter, the network LinkedIn actually *does* seem to help people in their job searches. It is very easy to create a profile on LinkedIn and begin linking to many new contacts. You can update your profile regularly and get recommendations from colleagues, previous bosses, and clients. You can find out where people with your kind of background are working, determine where people came from, see if a company is hiring, and most important, find out who the hiring manager (the one with "pain") might be.

We surveyed more than 3,600 people in our company's database over the last five years—both candidates and hiring authorities. A full 500 of these people were also surveyed about Facebook and Twitter. We asked these two questions:

1. Has LinkedIn made your job search easier? How?

2. Is LinkedIn simply another tool to get interviews or does it really enhance your job search and make it more effective?

Over 60 percent of respondents said that LinkedIn definitely helped them in their job search and made it easier. Fifteen percent of the respondents were employers who said LinkedIn helped them in the hiring process. Only 10 percent of the respondents said they actually found a specific job as a result of being contacted directly by either an employer or a recruiter from their LinkedIn profile.

However, having said that, it appears that LinkedIn is extremely useful in helping people get jobs or employers find good candidates. Being "discovered" for a specific job opportunity by a specific person may be rare, but LinkedIn enhances your job search in a number of ways.

Activity Confused with Productivity

In the final analysis, creating an online presence and branding yourself might be good tools, but they are just that—tools. I had a candidate a few months ago who kept trying to send people to his LinkedIn profile, his Web site, and his blog. He spent all kinds of time and effort doing this, but he wasn't getting many interviews. He asked me what might be the problem. It turns out that he simply wasn't *asking for interviews*. He was assuming his online presence would sell him into the interviews and then get him a job. This wasn't going to happen.

Looking for a job is an emotionally difficult thing to do. After the death of a spouse, a child, or a parent, or divorce, it is the most emotional thing we go through. People don't like being rejected. They often spend all kinds of time writing a résumé, building an online brand, and doing any other job search activity that appears to be of value as a way of avoiding rejection. They confuse activity with productivity.

One respondent said that he thought all of this Internet activity would eventually lead to "Internet overload." He might be right. Can you imagine getting 125 or 130 Tweets a day while monitoring LinkedIn, managing a Web site, writing a blog, getting interviews, and still being able to do your job? Could you do that even if you're looking for a job full time? This would be unmanageable for most of us.

None of these activities matter unless you get interviews and perform well during the interview. Any technique that lands you an interview and helps you perform well is of value. Anything that doesn't get you an interview and help you perform well is a waste of your time.

The Connected Generation

Having said all this, change may be right around the corner. If you exclude LinkedIn from social media (and some don't), it appears that the hype is greater than the reality of finding a job directly through social media. Taking into account that today's 16- to 24-year-olds are online on average of *six time*s longer per week than boomers and *twice* as long per week as GenXers, social media may still have a great deal of promise in helping a person find a job. Only time will tell how it will be used effectively.

One final note: The Internet and other electronic resources available to us today certainly have sharpened our focus on what's happening and have honed our research skills, but at a price. For a thoughtful view of the long-term effects of our reliance on the Internet, check out *The Shallows: What the Internet Is Doing to Our Brains*, by Nicholas Carr.

9 : Making the Initial Interview Successful 95 Percent of the Time

THE JOB INTERVIEW IS A STAGED, contrived event. It is not an event that has anything to do with a person's ability to do a job. Although purportedly the job interview is a mutual evaluation of your past record and talents and a prediction of how you're going to perform in the future, as well as your personal evaluation of the organization, it is rarely any of these things.

Each party in this process is putting his or her best foot forward, and rightfully so. Candidates are responsible for selling themselves to the employer, trying to convince the employer that they are the best person for the job. The company (or the individuals representing it) is trying to find the best person to do the job and, at the same time, both selling the company and screening out the candidates it does not think will be capable of doing the job or fitting in.

This chapter reviews the top ten mistakes most job candidates make in the initial interview, then presents two basic versions of a four-phase interview process, including some tips and the scripts you can follow to avoid these mistakes. Important: The ideas here work. Here's what one reader said as a result of incorporating them into his job search process.

> "I've been out of work for four months. I had quite a few interviews and nothing seemed to work. I wasn't getting hired. Then I got your book. The chapter on interviewing made all the difference in the world. I was doing it all wrong. In three weeks I got three interviews. I nailed them all by following your steps and scripts. I got two offers. I start work on Monday. Thank you so much." —John A., Colorado Springs, Colorado

The Interview: An Overview

The essential four-part question to be answered by a hiring company in the interviewing process is, "Can this person do the job? Do we like him or her? Is he or she a minimal risk? Can we work the money out?" That's it! For the employer, it is no more complicated than those questions. The answers to this four-pronged question are the whole reason that individuals go through the interviewing process in the company.

As a job candidate, it is your job to communicate the following: that you can do the job, that you are liked, that you offset any risks that you pose to the company, and that you are reasonable about the money. That's it! For you as a candidate, it is no more complicated than answering those questions. That is the essence of the interviewing process. It is very simple—just not very easy.

The best experience that money can buy, the most significant accomplishments that an individual can attain, and all the knowledge attained from the best MBA schools in the world will never be investigated or revealed (or, more important, hired) unless you can sell yourself in the interviewing process.

So what this means is that, in spite of the fact that interviewing is a staged, contrived event, it is absolutely necessary that it be done, and preferably done well. The better your ability to interview is, the better your opportunity to get a good job.

> **Key Point:** You are going to get a job based on your ability to interview well, rather than on your ability to perform in a job. When you fully comprehend this idea your interviewing process will be easier.

The Top Ten Mistakes Candidates Make in an Initial Interview

> "This is the fifth book I've read in my job search and no one has explained the technique of interviewing this well." —Charlotte M., San Diego, California

It's easy to get off track in the initial interview. Have you made any of these mistakes?

1. *They forget that this is a selling situation—and don't ask for the job.* A candidate's objective in an initial interview is to sell what he or she can do for the prospective

employer. Some candidates, though, feel they are unique and would be so valuable over and above every other candidate that it is obvious they should be hired. Therefore, the candidates have absolutely nothing to decide about until there's a job offer. Truth: Success in the initial interview is the first step to that job offer. So candidates have to constantly be asking, "What do I need to do to get the job?"

2. *They think that interviewing is a "two-way street."* Most candidates think that the interview should be a give and take on the part of the candidate and the interviewing or hiring authority. Truth: an initial interview is a "one-way street." Hiring or interviewing authorities are going to have available a plethora of initial interviews for every job they have to fill. The candidate has to prove himself or herself superior to all of the other candidates before there's an "equal" exchange with a potential employer.

3. *They focus on what they want in a job.* Most candidates are intent on what they want in a job rather than what they can do for a prospective employer. They don't recognize that if they give the hiring authority good enough reasons for why they ought to be hired, a hiring authority can give them plenty of good reasons why they ought to go to work there.

4. *They don't know what they're really selling to an employer.* Most candidates, even if they know they need to sell themselves, don't know what they should be selling. Their attitude is, "Hey, I'm a good person, you'd be lucky to have me. When can I go to work?" They forget to sell specific *features, advantages, and benefits* that they can provide the employer.

5. *They cannot articulate or "bridge" for the employer their specific abilities.* Most candidates "know" they're good, and even if they're aware of their specific features, advantages, and benefits, they can't articulate them specifically. In other words, they need to say, "This is what I've done for others, so, therefore, I will be successful for you." This takes practice and doesn't come naturally.

6. *They have poor communication skills.* It is hard to believe that candidates don't practice looking people in the eye and communicating clearly and concisely what they can do for a company that nobody else can. If you mumble, slouch, don't look people in the eye and can't speak clearly, you won't get hired. It's not that hard to practice even if it doesn't come naturally.

7. *They dress improperly or poorly and/or their body language is unprofessional in the interview.* There are still people who dress casually for an interview, slouch or lay back in their chairs, have poor eye contact, and do unprofessional things in an interview.

A candidate should, at least in an initial interview, dress like a banker and be well groomed. Candidates need to practice sitting up in the chair leaning forward, looking the interviewing or hiring authority in the eye, and being relaxed yet serious.

8. *They don't research the company or the position they are interviewing for.* I'm always amazed at the number of well-educated, professional candidates who don't do research on the company or the job they're interviewing for. Cursory research won't do. The people who are getting the jobs usually know more about the company and the person they are interviewing with.

9. *They are unable to articulate what they would like in a new job or company.* I'm not talking about salary, title, and so on. I'm talking about people who don't know what their professional goals are, don't have a clue as to where they would like to be in the future, and haven't an idea what they're striving for personally and professionally. Too often they come across as, "Well . . . I just need a job."

10. *They badmouth their present employer.* Most candidates don't recognize that employers identify with employers. Whatever you say about your present employer or past employers, you will say about them. Your present and past employers have to appear positive.

Here are some other sins: discussing personal problems in the interview, being late for the interview, not apologizing for being late to the interview, not "closing" the interview properly, not asking what the next steps are going to be, and not asking about the competitive candidates. Are you guilty of any of these?

Sell Yourself Through to the Next Interview

"Find a system and stick to it."

—General Douglas MacArthur

I'm going to offer you a format and script that I have developed. It is the most successful technique that can be used to make your initial interviews successful 95 percent of the time. This is a bold statement, but it is true. If done correctly, you will be successful in at least the initial interview, if not beyond. Remember, you are trying to sell yourself through to the next interview. That is all you're trying to do: to get from one interview to the next interview to the next interview—so that you can be in the final group of people who are interviewing for the job.

There are two versions of this format. The first edition of *The Job Search Solution* recommended the first technique over the second one. After tons of feedback from readers who have used both of them, though, I've come to a different conclusion. The first technique works best with drivers, managers, and any manager in the sales arena—aggressive and forceful people who appreciate assertive, take-charge types of people. Analytical, amiable types of people and lower keyed managers seem to respond best to the second technique.

The message is the same but the manner in which the candidate presents it is how the two versions differ. The first technique takes immediate control of the conversation and the second technique encourages candidates to ask a number of questions *before* they make a presentation about themselves. You can decide which one you think you should use. However, don't decide this based on what *you like*; choose the one that best fits the kind of manager you are interviewing with.

Successful Interview Technique Number One

You walk into the interviewer's office or interviewing environment. You are rested, refreshed, and prepared. You sit down and lean forward a bit. After you share a few ice-breaker comments, you pull out a legal pad and pen to take notes, you hand the hiring or interviewing authority your résumé (*even if he or she already has it*), and state:

PHASE 1

"Mr. or Ms., I'm here to share with you why you should hire me. First of all, I am [ten or twelve descriptive adjectives to explain your work ethic]: _____

_____."

Transition Phrase No. 1

"And here in my background is where these *features have been benefits* to the people I have worked for _____."

PHASE 2

"I am presently [or most recently have been] at [name] company. I have functioned there in the capacity of: _____."

(continued)

You give a thorough description of exactly what you did, how you did it, whom you did it for, and how successful you were—in terms a high-school senior could understand. You then emphasize *how much you love the job and the company, the reason you have to leave or why you left*—in very positive terms:

"And before that, I was at [name] company. There, I functioned in the capacity of _____."

You give a thorough description of exactly what you did, how you did it, whom you did it for, and how successful you were—in terms a high-school senior could understand.

You then emphasize *how much you loved that job and why you had to leave it* in very positive terms:

"And before that, I was at [name] company. There I functioned in the capacity of: _____."

Again, you give a thorough description of exactly what you did, how you did it, whom you did it for, and how successful you were—in terms a high-school senior could understand.

You then emphasize how much you *loved that job and why you had to leave it*, in very positive terms. You continue in this manner for at least three jobs, if you have that many. If you've had a series of short stints at jobs, like one year or less, you may want to go back further than three jobs.

Transition Phrase No. 2

"Now, tell me Mr. or Ms. _____, how does what I have to offer stack up with what you are looking for?"

PHASE 3

With the legal pad in front of you, you start taking notes on what the interviewer answers in response to your question and begin to ask other questions of the interviewer. If you do this correctly, one question will lead to another question, which will lead to another question, which *will lead to a conversation*, which is exactly what you want.

As the conversation progresses, the hiring or interviewing authority is going to tell you more of what the company is looking for in an individual. As the interviewer does this, you weave into the conversation any important information that *pertains* to the job that you can extract; you also expand upon the information about where you have been, what you have done, and how you did it in the second portion of your presentation.

As the conversation/interview winds down, when you feel the time is appropriate, you move into Phase 4.

PHASE 4

"Based on what we have discussed here, Mr. or Ms. _____, my_____ [background, experience, or potential]___makes this a good fit for both of us. What do I need to do to get the job?"

Then be quiet and don't say a word.

Now, the conversation may go off in a number of directions. If you have to, repeat your enthusiasm and interest in the position; you may have to push harder and repeat that you are an ideal candidate for the job and you have to know what you need to do to get it.

Let's analyze the script. Basically, it's: *Tell 'em what you're gonna tell 'em . . . tell 'em . . . then, tell 'em what you told 'em.*

Phase 1

What you say in Phase 1 is really simple. You state ten to fifteen basic intangible traits of a hard-working, successful, committed worker that you possess. In the final analysis, all hiring or interviewing authorities want to see is somebody who is going to possess the traits of a committed, hard-working employee. It is that simple. So, what you're doing in this phase is simply communicating that you understand what hard work is. You would be shocked and amazed at the number of people who go into an interviewing situation and just assume that the interviewing or hiring authority *already knows* that they are a committed worker. Remember that your hiring or interviewing authority is scared of making a mistake. This person is afraid of risk.

When you communicate the ten to fifteen intangible traits of a hard worker that you possess, it provides assurance in the interviewer's frightened state that you not only know what the traits of a hard worker are but also possess them. What I recommend here is stressing traits such as: hard worker; determined to go the extra mile; get up early, stay late; accomplished; passionate about your work; committed to the customer; love what you do; intelligent; great work ethic; and so forth.

I cannot emphasize enough that prospective employers hardly ever hear these words from the typical candidate. You are simply communicating basic attributes that every employer wishes he or she saw in every employee.

Transition Phrase No. 1

The transition phrase leading to Phase 2 of your presentation is, "Now, here in my background is where these *features have been benefits to the people I have worked for.*" This is a powerful phrase. You are using the terms *features* and *benefits*. It is implied that these *feature*s will be *benefits* to the hiring authority and his or her company. This transition phrase allows you to lead into an explanation of every job you have had, what you've done, how you've done it, and how successful you were.

You are doing their thinking for them! They don't need to ask that stupid question, "Well, tell me about yourself." (The worst question you can get asked.)

Phase 2

At this point, you are going to work backwards and give a short, but very thorough, description of exactly what job function you had, how you did, whom you did it for, and how successful you were, as well as—and this is very important—that you loved the job, and why, in very positive terms, you're looking to leave or why you left. The execution of this phase of your presentation is very important. There are clear key parts to this phase.

- *Explain your job function.* First, you need to you explain *exactly* what your job function is now or was in the past so that the hiring or interviewing authority understands *exactly* what you have done before. I can't tell you the number of times over the years that candidates have walked away from interviews thinking that they had done a really good job on the interview—only to have the hiring authority, in giving us feedback, explain that he or she really didn't understand what the candidate did (either in his present job or the jobs he had before).

  This happens because hiring authorities are just as nervous as you are in the interviewing process. They feel like they have to get a deeper understanding about you and your background in order to evaluate you. They usually have to do this with a large number of people. Most of the time in the interviewing process, when hiring or interviewing authorities ask a question, partway through your answer they are thinking about the next question, and then partway through that answer, they're thinking about the next question, and so forth.

On top of that, most hiring or interviewing authorities don't want to look stupid or ignorant. Like most people, they are uncomfortable saying, "I don't understand; could you explain it to me in layman's terms so that I really get it?" After all, they are the hiring authority. They are supposed to know and understand everything as the so-called authority. So, they will act like they know exactly what the candidates are talking about, and nod their heads in complete agreement and understanding as the candidates speak in terms foreign to everyone but themselves. Then, after the candidates leave, rather than admitting they had no idea what the hell the candidates were talking about, they will claim that these candidates' skills, experience, background, or personality aren't what they were looking for.

- *Explain why you want to leave your job.* Next, you need to explain, in very positive ways, why you are seeking to leave the company you're with now and why you left other jobs. I cannot overemphasize this point. You are going to weave into your explanation, along with what you've done and how you have done it, all of the positive reasons that you left the companies and the jobs that you had or the one that you are leaving now. If you bring up why you left in positive terms—even if it wasn't under the most positive circumstances (for example, you were fired)—the whole scenario has a tendency to be more palatable to a hiring authority.

  The reasons that you want to leave, and the reasons that you have left other positions, have to be very specific and as detailed as necessary. Saying things like, "It was a mutual understanding . . . it was just time to go . . . we grew tired of each other . . . management changed . . . the company was bought"—or any other broad generalizations—will not help you be successful in the interview. Remember that the interviewing or hiring authority is concerned about taking a risk. Nebulous, unclear, broad generalizations have risk written all over them.

  This is one of the many situations in the job-finding process where you absolutely need to see what you are communicating through the eyes of the interviewing or hiring authority. There is a tendency for all candidates to see the reasons that they're looking to leave, or the reason that they left other opportunities, only from their own point of view. What matters is how the hiring or interviewing authority is going to react to the reasons you give. If those reasons communicate risk, you're doomed.

This is going to take much thought and practice on your part. You always want to tell the truth, but you might have to put a spin on it, that, if nothing else, neutralizes any negative connotations. Do not think that an interviewing or hiring authority is going to see things from *your personal* point of view. Trying to justify your getting fired, or quitting on a whim, the awful environment you were in, the lousy boss, the lousy pay, the lousy CEO, your stupid peers, the "going nowhere" job, etc., will do nothing but hurt you.

- *Communicate your positive feelings about previous employers.* The third idea that you are going to communicate in the second phase is that you absolutely loved every job you ever had. You don't have to use the word *love* in every instance. But you need to communicate that you had a very positive experience with every job that you have ever had; that you learned a lot from each one; and that you really appreciated the people you worked for. You can communicate this by saying things like, "You know, I really love the organization that I work for now, but unfortunately. . . ."

    The point is that you talk positively in every way you can about the organization that you're currently with and every organization that you ever worked for. No matter how difficult the circumstances are or were, you have to put your present or previous employers in a positive light. Even if you were laid off or fired, you have to say something along the lines of, "Although I'm disappointed by not being there, I understand what took place from their point of view." Remember, employers identify with employers.

* * *

Both the second and third points in this phase of your presentation must never communicate an adversarial relationship between you and your current or previous employers. No matter how difficult the experience was or is with your past or present employers, you have to communicate a "we're all in this together" type of attitude.

In this phase of your presentation, you only need to go back three, maybe, at the most, four jobs and describe what I have suggested here. If you had jobs before that, unless they are germane to the position that you are applying for, you can lump them together by just saying something like, "Before that (meaning the third or fourth position back) I was in sales or accounting or engineering (insert your job area) for a number of firms."

At this point in the interview, you want to make sure that you don't ramble for so long that the interviewing or hiring authority gets bored. Stick to the high points in your background that are applicable to the job for which you are interviewing. It should not take more than five to seven minutes.

USE STORIES TO MAKE AN IMPRESSION

It's very important to weave in many stories about what you have done as examples of your successes. People love stories. People remember stories. People remember *you* when you tell them stories about your past. Stories bypass conscious resistance and preconceived notions. Stories, analogies, and metaphors about you that pertain to the hiring authority's need are absolutely the best way to be remembered. Of course, they need to be short (no more than 45 seconds), to the point, and, above all, pertinent to the opportunity for which you are interviewing.

"There're two things that never get boring, a person and a story and the story has to be about people.
    —G. K. Chesterton, English journalist and humorist

"Stories are more than entertainment. . . . They teach us the art of being human."
                                                                    —Anonymous

Storytelling experts tell us that there are six types of stories: "who I am" stories, "why I am here" stories, vision stories, teaching stories, value stories, and "I know what you are thinking" stories. It's not hard to come up with these types of stories in the interviewing process. They can be very powerful. I mentioned earlier about our candidate who had been born and raised on a chicken farm in East Texas. During the interviewing process he would talk about what it was like growing up on a chicken farm, how hard they had to work, etc. It was a great story. The candidate was chosen over nine other well-qualified candidates. The hiring authority told us that what made the difference was the candidate's stories about growing up on a chicken farm.

"Why I am here" stories could be about why you have to leave your present job or why you have left jobs in the past. Vision stories could be about what the company you're interviewing with might look like if it hires you. Teaching and value stories can be about the mistakes you've made in your career and what you learned from those mistakes. "I know what you're thinking" stories can explain why you had too many jobs or have been out of work for a long time *before* the hiring authority brings it up as a concern. Your *stories* will make all the difference in the world.

Transition Phrase No. 2

This is a transition phrase you use to get to the third phase of your technique. You simply ask, "Now, tell me Mr. or Ms. _____, how does what I have to offer stack up with what you are looking for?"

Phase 3

"He who asks the questions controls the interview."

—ANONYMOUS

When the interviewing or hiring authority starts answering your question of how you stack up with what he or she is looking for, take notes. When the interviewer stops answering that question, you want to have a prepared set of questions ready. Some questions that you may ask are:

- What are the most important qualities that a successful person in this position should possess?

- How would you measure the success of the last person who was in this job?

- Why was he or she successful? or Why was he or she not successful?

- In your opinion, Mr. or Ms. _____, what is the most difficult part of the job?

- Mr. or Ms. _____, how long have you been with the company?

- Why do you like working here?

- What is the most difficult part of your job?

- Where do you see the company going in the next five to ten years?

- As I was doing my research on the company, I found that _____.

- Could you give me your opinion about that?

- What is the biggest challenge that the company is going to face in the next five to ten years?

- I believe your competitors are doing _____. How does your company respond to that?

- How will you know when you have found the right person for this job I'm interviewing for?

- How would you describe the culture of the company?

- What do you, Mr. or Ms. _____, like most about working here?

- How many people have you interviewed for this position?

- Have you seen anybody who you felt was qualified to do it?

- Have you offered the job to anyone before my interviewing here?

I could go on and on but you get the idea. Ask enough questions to engage the employer or hiring authority in the conversation. You want this person to open up to you as much as he or she possibly can about what the company wants in the person it is going to hire. You then have a better idea of how to sell yourself into the job.

Now, the following is very important. As the conversation progresses and you write down some of the highlights of what the employer is looking for, you will reinforce the fact that you are a qualified, excellent candidate by *going back to some of the jobs that you had, or the job you presently have, and talking in even more specific terms than before.* As the interviewing or hiring authority is sharing with you his or her exact needs, you need to be able to relate exact experience, responsibilities, duties, and successes that you have had that specifically address the particular issues being discussed.

In the presentation you made (in Phase 2), you talked about each job that you either currently have or have had, your duties and responsibilities, and your successes. But you did it in a very broad, descriptive way. Now you are going to use the information that the interviewing or hiring authority is giving you and bring up examples in the job that you have now or the jobs you had before that specifically demonstrate your ability to do the job under consideration.

Whereas your initial presentation about your experience and background was detailed enough for the interviewing or hiring authority to understand what you have done, you now get specific about particular things that would be of value to the interviewing or hiring authority—based on the conversation that results from the questions you ask.

Phase 4

After the conversation has begun to wind down, and you can see that the interview is nearly over, you close the interviewer or hiring authority by stating that your background and experience fit what the employer is looking for, and you need to ask, "What do I need to do to get the job?" This is the hardball part of the interview. You are either a candidate or you're not, and you need to know right now!

Since I first recommended this in the first edition of *The Job Search Solution*, I've found from readers that this has been the hardest question for people to get used to asking. I have heard it from candidates, from radio callers, and from my own candidates—*after* I have instructed them to ask this question, even after they have agreed to ask it, even after they have practiced the question. They *did not* ask it, even when they knew they should. They ask stupid, soft questions like: "What is the next step?" "Where do we go from here?" "When can I expect to hear from you?" Blah, blah, blah! I know most people who are looking for a job are also trying to avoid rejection. They will even admit, "I know I should have asked . . . but it didn't seem appropriate." Or, "I was just too darn scared to ask . . . afraid they'd simply tell me I wasn't going to be considered."

Listen to me: No is the second-best answer you can get. More often than not, at this point in the interview most candidates are going to fear "No" so much that they avoid the rejection.

Interviewing and hiring authorities want to hire an individual who *wants* the job. I cannot tell you the number of candidates over the years who failed to ask this essential question in the interview and ended up being dismissed by the interviewing or hiring authority. I know that this is terribly unfair. But life is unfair. This is a part of the interview that truly is a contrived event. The truth is, there is no real way of knowing whether or not you really want this job right now. But, unless you ask for the job, you're never going to get beyond first base.

Whatever you do, don't fall into the trap of thinking, "Well, I'm not really sure that I want the job so, before I commit, I better think about it." Remember: While you are thinking about it, somebody else is getting an offer. *You don't have anything to decide about until you have an offer.* Asking the question, "What do I need to do to get the job?" takes courage. That's okay. But if you're serious about finding a job, you will use this question at the end of every interview, especially the initial one.

I will now provide a detailed example of how to use this interview technique, so that you can really understand this strategy.

Interview Technique One: Example

Background: John has been selling IT consulting services for sixteen years. He began his career with a large national consulting firm, starting out as an analyst and moving his way upward over a seven-year period of time to a managing director. He left there and went to work for a regional consulting firm as a selling-branch manager. After being there four years, the company was sold to another national company. Since then, he has been at one firm for two years and two firms for one year each. John's last four years have been very difficult owing to the economy and to challenges within the companies that he has worked for. He knows that these will be challenges for prospective employers.

The day of his interview, John arrives early. One minute before the interview, he takes a deep breath, relaxes, closes his eyes, and envisions himself performing well in the interview. He goes into the interview with a hiring authority, a regional manager for another midsize consulting firm that is somewhat of a competitor to the company that currently employs him. They break the ice with casual conversation, and even though the manager already has a copy of his résumé, John hands him one. John then states:

PHASE 1

"Mr._____, I'm pleased to be here and to share with you why you should hire me. First, you need to know that I possess all the skills of an excellent consulting salesperson. I am aggressive, assertive, get up early, stay late, don't take 'no' for an answer, and understand the ratio of calls to presentations to sales. I love to cold-call, and have taken a number of excellent sales training programs. I sell business solutions through technology. My clients see me as consultative, and that I'm there to help them "get" the right project for their needs—rather than "selling them" something they don't need. People like me. People trust me, I work independently and I have demonstrated success in every position that I've had."

There's a pause, as he looks him in the eye.

Transition Phrase No. 1

"Here in my background is where I can document that these features have been benefits to the organizations that I've worked for and therefore for you:_____."

PHASE 2

"I am presently selling SAP consulting services for Macquarie Partners. They are a boutique international consulting firm with revenues of about $100 million. I am responsible for a quota of $5.5 million and I manage the projects that I sell. I was the first person they hired in this region and have been there for 12 months. I

---

landed two of the largest accounts the company has ever had [*story*].They are a wonderful organization and I am 100 percent of quota year to date. My customers love me and would follow me to wherever I go.

"I'm working with the same group of people that I worked with at the job before this one, so it's almost as though I've been with the same group of people for the past two years. The company has made a strategic decision to devote most of its resources to a multimillion-dollar project the company landed in the Netherlands. The company has made it very clear that most all of its consultants/resources for the next 12 months are going to be devoted to that project and that the projects that I have as well as my pipeline are going to be put on the back burner. [*story*]

"I hate to leave them, because we have a very good relationship and the company itself is sound. Unfortunately, my clients need their projects done now and my earnings are based on our ability to do the projects and get them implemented. It's a tough decision, but I need to put my clients first.

"Before this position, I worked for Jupiter Consulting. This is basically the same group of people as Macquarie Partners, and Macquarie picked us up along with some of the consulting projects from Jupiter. Jupiter was a very small ERP project consulting firm with offices in Chicago, St. Louis, and Dallas. I was a salesperson for Jupiter and even though we didn't have quotas, I sold $3 million worth of projects the year I was there. The owner got cancer and sold all of his projects and contracts to Macquarie Partners. They are really nice people and the circumstances were really rather unfortunate. [*story*]

"Before that, I was at XL Consulting for two years. Again, I sold ERP projects in the state of Texas. The company had a very interesting model where the salesperson managed the project after it was sold. XL looked for a unique set of skills for both a tactical person who understood analysis and implementation, and also a strategic person who could sell. This is a great model, but unfortunately we were compensated for selling the projects and not for their profitability. I sold $2.5 million worth of projects. I loved the job and the people, but it was so difficult to both sell and manage the projects that I was limited in what I could earn. I eventually spent most of my time managing the projects rather than selling. I was paid a high base of $165,000, but I was never going to be able to make much more than $200,000 in a year because I had to spend most of my time managing the projects after I sold them. I left to join Jupiter, where I was strictly a sales guy and didn't have to worry about managing the project. *[story]*

"Before that, I was a regional partner for Trend Technologies. I left RCMG to join this organization. I had a lot of autonomy, as well as P&L responsibility. I was responsible for profitability of $30 million in sales a year for our branch with myself as a selling manager, two salespeople, and 22 to 25 consultants. We did mostly ERP projects and some staff augmentation. I had a base of $125,000 salary and earned $250,000 a year each year I was there because I was paid on profitability. It was a wonderful job and I made the most money that I ever made doing it. Unfortunately, the company was sold to a large, global organization and it was clear I was going to be back with the same kind of constraints that I left RCMG for. [*story*]

"I began my career with RCMG. I started out as an analyst, was promoted to an implementation consultant, and then to a project leader. I spent my last three years in sales and was promoted to managing director, where I had P&L responsibility. There were 35 people in the group, including consultants and sales and administrative personnel. Our quota was $50 million in sales and we were 122 percent of quota. We sold ERP consulting projects primarily in the retail vertical. It was a wonderful job in a wonderful company. I got a tremendously solid foundation there and am very appreciative to RCMG for all that I learned. I was the youngest managing director in the history of the company. The company was so very big, though. I could see a long-term career with RCMG, but there was way too much security and really not enough risk, which translates into reward, for me. I left to join a smaller organization where the risk and reward might be greater. RCMG was a wonderful place and I was able to get my MBA from the University of Chicago while I was there. [*story*]"

Transition Phrase No. 2

"As you can see, I've been successful at selling large, even small, complex software implementation projects. I began my career as a consultant, and made the transition into sales, as well as management. I've proven myself on all levels. I've been on my number and beyond just about every year I was in sales and management. I have a tremendous number of contacts with clients that would do business with me no matter where I was. My references are excellent. My previous employers, subordinates, and especially clients would all say very good things about me.

"I'm well aware that I have made too many moves in the last few years. I'm ready to make a long-term commitment to my next employer. I can't afford another short stint and I'm willing to do whatever it takes to ensure long-term success. Whoever hires me needs to know that I have to commit to a long-term relationship.

"Now tell me, how does what I have to offer stack up with what you're looking for?" [John takes out his legal pad and begins to take notes.]

This presentation took seven minutes. The hiring authority explains to John about the job and the company. John takes notes.

PHASE 3

After listening to what the hiring authority has to say, John asked the following questions:

- "I noticed in doing my research, and speaking with some of your clients, you have been very efficient in delivering the projects on time and under budget. Based on what I've found you have a higher degree of this kind of performance than most of us do. How have you been able to maintain that kind of performance?" [This question shows that John has done his homework. He has spoken to some of the clients of the company he is interviewing with and found one particular aspect of the firm that makes it good. Any hiring authority is going to love to answer this question.]

- "What do you think the biggest challenges of the position I'm interviewing for are?"

- "You have been with the company for ten years. That's a long time for a consulting business. What attracts you to the company . . . why do you stay?" [People love to talk about themselves. John is giving the hiring authority a chance to do that.]

- "What are the biggest challenges facing the company today?"

- "How would you describe your management style? The management style of the company?"

- "In doing my research I discovered that the last two people in this position have not been very successful. Can you give me your views on them?" [Again, it's obvious that John has done his research. Notice that John did not ask, "Why were they not successful?" He simply asks the hiring authority's views on their success or lack of it. Much more of an open-ended question than "Why?"]

I'm sure you get the idea that John is asking a lot of very good questions, showing that he has done his research and that he is knowledgeable. Notice that *none* of these questions is a "What can you do for me?" question. John wants to get the hiring authority to talk as long as he or she can about everything regarding the job and the company.

At the end of the interview, John moves to Phase 4.

PHASE 4

"Based on all that we have discussed, I am an excellent fit for your organization. I have sold, implemented, and even managed groups of people who do the same thing that you all have been successful in doing. I could be a tremendous asset in your company and significantly increase your bottom line. It would be a win-win for both of us. *What do I need to do to get the job?*"

The Positive Spin

There is much more to the story of why John is looking for a job. His run at RCMG was a good one. But it became obvious in his sixth and seventh year that, although he made director, he was never going to be a partner in the firm. In his last year at RCMG he had lost two major political battles and the guy who was promoted over him was a clear-cut adversary. It was very clear to everyone in RCMG that John's future was limited. In his attempt to "win" the two political battles, he very much alienated a whole group of folks. He was going to be eventually "eased out." He left before it got ugly.

John left RCMG and went to Trend Technologies. It was a direct competitor of RCMG's and John immediately started calling on some of the clients he had at RCMG. It was obvious that he was trying to "go after" RCMG's clients. RCMG, in an effort to protect itself, had to threaten both John and Trend Technologies with a lawsuit based on John's noncompete agreement. The threat never became reality because John agreed to back off from RCMG's clients. The threat of a lawsuit, however, caused a bit of tension between John and his new employer, Trend Technologies.

John performed very well with Trend, but he never developed a close bond between himself and the managing partners. Although they hired him from RCMG because of his knowledge of the clients, their previous cordial relationship, even if a bit standoffish, with their competitor, RCMG, became very strained to the point that the regional office of RCMG was doing everything it could to get "even" with John and Trend Technologies. Competition between the two firms got downright ugly, and the management at Trend began to blame John for the distraction of having to fight with RCMG. Egos on both sides became more important than business and even as late as the fourth year of John's employment, the whole thing was a "black cloud" that hung over John in the firm.

When the company was sold to a much larger organization, John decided to leave. He was recruited by XL Consulting. He didn't do very much research on the company and how it managed its sales and its business. He found out when he got there that the management of the company had really developed a "delivery" model of business where sales was a "necessary evil." John came into the company thinking that his sales approach would be much appreciated, but it wasn't. He felt that XL could have doubled the volume of sales if the company was more sales oriented. The firm turned down as many projects as it agreed to accept. The partners of the firm were all very happy with the size of the organization and the money they were earning and found no compulsion to grow the company much beyond what it already was when John got there. John's contribution was appreciated and acknowledged, but when he tried to accelerate sales and really grow the branch beyond where it was, he was literally told not to do it. It was clear after a short while that John's approach to consulting and XL's were very different and incompatible. John's initiatives were stymied and both parties were very unhappy.

John left XL abruptly and joined Jupiter Consultants. The company had been competing against him in a couple of situations. When XL became untenable, he simply picked up the phone and called the people he knew at Jupiter. They hired him immediately and he started selling for them. John did not know it but the owner of Jupiter Consultants was combating cancer when John joined. Even worse, there was infighting between the owner and his two sons, who were officers in the company. It was a real mess and John found out about it after he had been with the firm for only a month.

The infighting of the family became a phenomenal distraction and the company was standing still. John was basically a one-person sales branch who hired consultants to do their projects on an as needed basis. You had to give John credit for being somewhat ingenious. When he saw that Jupiter Consulting was going to be a dead end for his career, and that the company itself might even go under, he contacted the people at Macquarie Consultants and "brokered" a deal to get Macquarie to "buy" the projects he had sold for Jupiter. Since Jupiter was in such turmoil, it jumped at the chance to let Macquarie take over its projects. John got Macquarie to pay Jupiter a small transfer fee and John, as well as the consultants he had on the projects, became Macquarie employees. The clients were a bit uncomfortable with this, but it was better than Jupiter going under with them being left in the middle of unfinished projects. It took John a whole year to do this.

John's job at Macquarie is okay, but the company did sell a gigantic project to a worldwide firm based in the Netherlands. Macquarie is devoting almost all of its economic and personnel resources to the project. It's a good deal for the company but not a good deal for John. He's been told to "maintain" his sales volume of his one-man office, but not to grow it. John could sell more consulting projects, even to the clients he has now, but Macquarie simply doesn't want to do that. So, John is looking for a job.

Looking Closer at the Spin

In the interview, John has put a positive spin on just about everything that he's done. The fact that he's had two jobs in two years is a big red flag to most anybody he is going to interview with. He lumps the two jobs together and tries to make them as much of a two-year job with the same people as he can.

John was successful at XL Consulting but didn't do a very good job of finding out about their sales model before he got there. He was a risk-taking salesperson working for a very conservative group of consultants who considered sales as a "necessary evil." Trend Technologies was a good company and a good job for John. He made a mistake in being too aggressive about going after his clients at RCMG, so RCMG threatened a lawsuit. Although it never came about, John was perceived by Trend to be *too* aggressive and when RCMG took it upon itself, as a mission, to get "even" with John and Trend, John became a distraction within his own company. He got the reputation of being a "gunslinger" and everyone in the firm tried to distance themselves from him. Instead of having a bright future, he was ostracized.

John did fairly well at RCMG. He became the managing director. But when it was clear that he was not going to ever become a partner, he decided to leave. He often wonders what would've happened if he had stayed with RCMG. Looking back, his youthful ego might've gotten the best of him when he decided to leave.

The reason I mention all of this is to show you that John is presenting himself in as much of a positive light as he can. If he goes into an interviewing situation saying things like, "I should have never left RCMG" or "I was too aggressive in trying to steal RCMG's clients when I went to Trend," or "I didn't do my homework about the sales model at XL Consulting," he probably won't get hired. John is aware that he has had too many jobs in the last few years and he turns the "lemons" into "lemonade" by communicating that he has to stay for a long period of time in his next job. He's giving assurance to the hiring authority and minimizing the number of job changes. He tells some great stories—all true—that support his success.

Successful Interview Technique Number Two

This technique is for those people who feel more comfortable with trying to find out what an interviewing or hiring authority might be interested in before they talk about their experience. It seems to work best with analytical types of hiring authorities—that is, accountants, finance people, information technology folks. It works well with non-driver types of people like amiables and not sales-oriented people.

It isn't much different from the first technique. You ask the question, "What would you like to find in the ideal candidate?" before you talk about your intangible attributes and other experiences and background. It works like this:

You sit down in the interviewing or hiring authority's office, take a deep breath, and affect the pleasantries.

PHASE 1

As you put the legal pad down in front of you, you say:

"Tell me, Mr. or Ms_____, what kind of candidate would you ideally like to find?"

As the hiring or interviewing authority speaks, you take notes about what the individual is looking for in an ideal candidate. You may ask a number of questions, but the idea is to find out, in the employer's words, what's being sought.

PHASE 2

"If you will allow me, Mr. or Ms._____, I would like to explain why I would fit what you are looking for and how I could do the job. First of all, I am [ten or twelve descriptive adjectives to explain your work ethic]:_____."

Transition Phrase No. 1

"Based on what you said you wanted in a candidate, I would like to demonstrate where these features have been beneficial to the people whom I've worked for, in the light of what you need."

PHASE 3

I am currently [or most recently have been] at [name] company. I have functioned there in the capacity of : _____

_____.

Give a thorough description of exactly what you did, how you did it, whom you did it for, and how successful you were—in terms a high-school senior could understand. You then emphasize *how much you love the job and the company and the reason you have to leave or why you left* in very positive terms. Tell a story or two.

"And before that, I was at [name] company. There I functioned in the capacity of _____."

Give a thorough description of exactly what you did, how you did it, whom you did it for, and how successful you were—in terms a high-school senior could understand. You then emphasize *how much you loved the job and the company and the reason you left* in very positive terms. Tell a story, if appropriate.

"And before that, I was at [name] company. There I functioned in the capacity of _____."

Give a thorough description of exactly what you did, how you did it, whom you did it for, and how successful you were—in terms a high-school senior could understand. You then emphasize *how much you loved the job and the company and the reason you left* in very positive terms. Tell a story or two.

Continue in this manner for at least three jobs, if you have that many. If you've had a series of short stints at jobs—like more than one in the last year or less—you may want to go back further than three jobs.

Note: The only difference between this and the first technique is that you ask up front what the employer is looking for in an ideal candidate. With this approach, you might be able to be more specific about the things that the employer wants in a candidate in the descriptions of the jobs that you had.

The drawback to this technique is that the hiring authority may "drive" the conversation. You may not get the chance to make your presentation because the hiring authority is directing the interview. Use your own judgment.

Transition Phrase No. 2

Based on what you said you wanted, I'm an excellent match. What do I need to do to get the job?

I now provide a detailed example of how to use this second interview technique, so that you can really understand this strategy.

Interview Technique Two: Example

Background: Cheryl is an accountant. She has an accounting degree and sat for the CPA exam twice, but did not pass. For the past ten years she has been working for an $80 million parts-distribution firm in a suburb of Chicago. She worked for the company for six years and left to have a baby. She stayed home for a year with the baby, and then went back to work at the company for the last four years.

The firm is owned by a woman, and since it is a minority-owned firm, it gets a number of government contracts. Cheryl had worked for the firm while she was in college and, when she graduated, the company hired her. She reports directly to the owner. Over the last six months, the owner has asked Cheryl to keep two sets of books, which is clearly unethical.

Throughout the most recent difficult economic times, the owner has needed to borrow money from as many banks as she could. She is now in over her head, so she has demanded that Cheryl keep a fictitious set of books for the lenders. To make matters more complicated, the owner and Cheryl have become good friends. The owner treats Cheryl like a younger sister. She has been very liberal with Cheryl about her earnings, bonuses, and especially giving her plenty of time off to attend to the needs of her child. Cheryl's husband has been out of work for almost a year and they had been scraping by on Cheryl's earnings, even with the generous bonuses that her boss has been giving her.

Cheryl is appreciative of all the owner has done but knows that she could be held responsible for the owner's impropriety. She really doesn't want to leave the job, but knows she must. It is even harder because they are friends. Cheryl has been instructed by her boss to not share any of this information with anyone in the company or its external CPA firm.

To make matters even more complicated, the owner is well known and very respected in the business community. She has been written up as a model business in a number of local, state, and national publications, is a model member of the Chamber of Commerce, and is a tremendous supporter of women and minority businesses. Cheryl needs to leave but cannot discredit her company or the woman she works for and cannot afford to be embroiled in any kind of legal issues that "turning in" her boss would lead to. She can't afford to be out of work for any length of time, so she needs to find a job quickly.

Cheryl belongs to one accounting and finance association and began to call some of her fellow members to see if any of them knew of any employment opportunities. She also registered with a couple of recruiting firms. One of the people who used to work in her present company had moved to another much larger distribution firm and Cheryl had called him to ask if his firm had any accounting opportunities. That's how she got this interview. She simply tells the people that she is interviewing with that her firm is experiencing some financial difficulties and she needs to leave. She is not planning to tell anyone of her boss' activities.

She arrives early to the interview. She has done a lot of research about the company and the information she found was very insightful, especially in light of her own situation over the last six months. She is greeted by the controller, who is the hiring authority.

PHASE 1

"Mr. _____, I'm very pleased to be here. I've heard a lot about your company from my previous peer, Tom, who works for you. He says good things about your company, and I think I can bring a lot of skills, determination and hard work. Tell me, what would you like to find in a person for this position?"

Cheryl takes notes. The hiring authority states, "We'd like to find a person with an accounting degree and at least seven years of experience in either manufacturing or distribution. It is a very fast-paced department and there are only four of us in it. Over the last five years we've transitioned our software from QuickBooks to Great Plains Software, and we are now implementing an Oracle enterprise application. So I would prefer to find someone who is familiar with Oracle and, in a perfect world, someone who has implemented an Oracle applications system.

"We are a close-knit organization, and I report to the CEO, who is very demanding. He likes accurate reports, on time. He himself came out of the accounting and finance field before he became CEO and knows exactly what we ought to be doing. He is personable but not very tolerant of mistakes.

"The last person who was in this job did very well, but relocated to a different part of the country because of her husband's promotion. We are anxious to fill it, but don't want to make a mistake so we are willing to wait for the right person. [pause] "Tell me about yourself."

PHASE 2

Cheryl says:

"I am a hard worker and dedicated to my professional career. I get up early and stay late. I am very dependable and haven't missed a day of work in four years. I love accounting and I am known for being accurate and on time with my reports [*story*]."

Transition Phrase No. 1
"Based on what you said you wanted in a candidate I'd like to demonstrate the features I possess that have been of benefit to the people whom I've worked for, in light of what you need."

PHASE 3

"I'm presently at Babson Distribution. I work directly for the CEO and founder, Mildred Babson. I worked there during college in a number of kinds of positions and after I got my accounting degree Babson hired me as an accountant. I have been there for ten years, been promoted twice, and do the majority of the accounting for the company.

"Ms. Babson and the company have been very good to me. I love my job and am appreciated. I have progressed as far as I can in the organization and, because of its size I am not experiencing any personal growth or new challenges. Although I love the firm, I'm not growing professionally. I was responsible for installing Great Plains accounting software when we first got it a few years ago and we migrated from QuickBooks. I do not have any specific experience in Oracle, but I didn't know anything about Great Plains before we purchased it and installed it. I am very bright and I catch on very quickly. I graduated cum laude, while working, and have a minor in computer science. [*story*] An Oracle installation would be exciting and fun and, since I pick up that kind of thing very easily, I could really contribute.

"Tom, of your staff, and I worked together at Babson. He can attest to my diligence and ability to learn quickly and deliver reports accurately and on time. Ms. Babson is very demanding herself and, since I am the only full-fledged accountant in the firm, I was expected to get it right, every time. I'm very comfortable living under pressure."

Transition Phrase No. 2

"Based on what you said you wanted, I believe I'm an excellent match and would make an excellent employee. What do I need to do to get the job?"

The interview can go on with Cheryl asking questions.

Looking Closer at the Spin

Cheryl, if pressed, could bring up the financial insecurity of the firm. She got a little lucky because she doesn't have to worry about a reference from Mildred Babson, because the "internal" referral she got to the interview from Tom provides that kind of reference. She does not talk about she and Mildred Babson being friends and stays away from anything regarding the fact that she is being asked to keep a separate set of books.

There are some readers and some interview and career authorities who would claim that Cheryl could divulge the real reason she is looking to leave Babson. There might be *some* credibility to that idea. It is certainly reasonable to leave a company if you're being asked to cheat. However, having been in my profession since 1973, I can assure you that bringing this issue up will create more problems than Cheryl needs.

If Cheryl claims in an interview that she is being asked to keep two sets of books, there is no way a prospective employer can verify that. While it might be admirable for a person to say, "I'm being asked to cheat, so I need to leave," there is no way for her to prove that. Since Mildred Babson has a fairly high profile in the community, Cheryl's account of what's going on may not be believed. Bringing this issue up simply creates more problems that Cheryl doesn't need. If she sells herself in the right way, why she is leaving may not be a big issue.

What They Didn't Talk About

It's important to notice that both John and Cheryl *did not* talk about some of the things that they could have. It's important to remember to not just enhance the positive aspects of what you have done, but also minimize the risk by not talking about the negative things that might have happened to you. People often shoot themselves in the foot by thinking a prospective employer will *understand* the unfortunate or negative things that have happened to them. John could have tried to explain the issues at RCMG or the poor decision he made joining Trend. Cheryl could have tried to explain about her being asked to cheat.

Hiring authorities are very sensitive to any negative stuff. Over the years I've seen all kinds of candidates get into "true confessions" and try to justify all of the stupid stuff that they ever did, expecting empathy and understanding from a hiring authority. Don't make that mistake. Hiring authorities are looking for just as many reasons not to hire you as they are to hire you. Don't give them any.

Customization of Your Presentation

This whole process of presenting yourself as you is very simple. While there is some work involved in putting the presentation together, once you get the hang of it, it's very easy to keep going. You're going to give the same basic presentations to just about anybody you interview with. As you do your research for particular organizations, you will end up customizing your presentation when you know there are certain things that might be of value to particular employers.

For instance, Cheryl could have found out easily from her friend, Tom, that the hiring authority would be interested in her ability to upgrade or implement Oracle software. If you can find specific differentiators that you might have, you can propel yourself ahead of other candidates. This is one thing you want to do when you ask questions after your presentation. If you ask the right questions, you will be able to get more detailed information about what the employer might need and then you go back over your previous positions and emphasize your relevant experience.

Ending the Initial Interview

Once you and the hiring or interviewing authority have reached the end of the interview, you're probably going to get some idea of what the next steps might be. Don't be afraid to be assertive about pushing yourself into the next steps.

You may be surprised to discover that a lot of interviewing or hiring authorities are not sure of what the next steps might be. Most often, even though you have pushed for the next interview, a hiring or interviewing authority is going to say something like, "Well, we have a number of people to interview, we're going to complete that process and then we're going to set up second interviews."

This is a perfect time for you to again ask, "Based on what our conversation has been here, I would think that I would be in that group, would I not? So let's set up that second interview now." Then you pull out your note pad or calendar and ask, "When would be good for me to come back?"

You will probably still get from the interviewing or hiring authority the standard, "Well, we'll get in touch with you." Again, this is an excellent time for you to find out how you really stand, relative to the other candidates, by asking, "Well, Mr. or Ms._____, you must have some idea how I stack up with your ideal candidate or the others whom you have interviewed. Please tell me what you think."

This kind of questioning (and statements) will usually get you a good idea of how you stand. It is relatively aggressive, and it does not necessarily come naturally or easily. But if you practice asking these kinds of hardball questions, they will wind up becoming very easy for you.

If you don't get the chance to set a date and time for the next interview at the end of this initial interview, you need to ask for and get clarification of exactly what the next step might be. Most of the time the interviewing or hiring authority will give you an idea about what the next steps are, but most likely will not commit to your coming back, at least at this moment. Don't worry about this too much. Remember, I'm emphasizing *process*. Getting an answer as to how you stack up relative to the others is merely part of the process.

You may have to ask the question of how you stack up with other candidates in two or three different ways. "Based on the candidates that you have interviewed, do you think I'm going to be one of the finalists?" is a phenomenal question to ask. It takes lots of courage, and most candidates, unfortunately, don't have that kind of courage. You need to know how you stack up with other candidates and if you're going to get asked back. If you're not going to really be a contender, you need to know right now, so you don't waste your time and effort pursuing the opportunity. "No" is the second-best answer you could get.

Over the years, getting candidates to ask these hardball questions has been one of the most difficult things to do. Unfortunately, people don't seem to mind postponing rejection and refusal. It doesn't make sense. If you're not going be a viable candidate, you need to know that as soon as possible.

The Follow-Up Activity

The first thing you should do after the interview, when you get into your car or other transportation, is retrieve the notes you took during the interview and write down a summary of the interview on the form on the next page. Write down the high points of the interview: the major issues or topics that you spoke with the interviewer about. Summarize for yourself where you think your strengths are and where you think your weaknesses are relative to the interview. Write down your interpretation of the things that seemed the most important to the hiring authority and make sure that you understand them clearly.

Often, in the initial interviewing situation, we think we completely understand what a hiring authority is looking for, and we actually do not! The major reason you want to collect your thoughts immediately after the interview is so that you remember the important points; you cannot rely on your memory. It may be a two- to four-week period before the second round of interviews. You need to be able to refresh your memory with detailed notes.

The important issues and criteria for hiring may change as the interviewing or hiring authority interviews more and more people. It is not surprising that hiring/interviewing authorities become confused about the candidates whom they have interviewed. Likewise, I have had candidates become confused and remember the wrong issues and embarrass themselves during the second interview. So, take very detailed notes after every interview on the form that follows and use them. Keep them in the folder for that particular employer and refer to them, where appropriate, in your emails and letters. Keep them handy for when you go back to the follow-up interviews. Use them wisely and to your advantage!

FIRST INTERVIEW

Date _____   Interviewing company _____

Interviewing/hiring authority _____

Who did I interview with . . . a screener or interviewing or hiring authority?

How long was the interview? _____

Summary _____

What are the most important aspects of my background to the interviewing/hiring authority?

_____

What were the major concerns about my candidacy? _____

How could I have sold myself better? _____

What do I need to do to get to the next step? _____

Follow-up activity: _____ email? _____

Overall impressions and thoughts _____

Next steps _____

SECOND INTERVIEW

Date _____   Interviewing company _____

Interviewing/hiring authority _____

Summary _____

What are my strengths and weaknesses as a candidate? _____

What would be my impressions if I were in the hiring authority's shoes? _____

What do I need to do to get to the next steps? _____

How could I have sold myself better? _____

Follow-up activity _____

THIRD, FOURTH, FIFTH INTERVIEWS

Date _____   Interviewing company _____

Interviewing/hiring authority _____

Summary _____

What are my strengths and weaknesses as a candidate? _____

What do I need to do to get to the next steps? _____

How could I have sold myself better? _____

Follow-up activity _____

What questions should I be asking? _____

How can I better my chances? _____

The Immediate Email

You have the business card of the interviewing or hiring authority, handed to you at the time of the first interview. Immediately after the interview, or as soon as possible, you want to email the interviewing or hiring authority. You don't just want to thank the person for his or her time. More important, you want to reinforce all the reasons that you should be hired.

Every interviewing book in the world is going to tell you to send a thank-you to the interviewer. You would probably be shocked at the number of candidates who don't. One out of every seven or eight, even when they're coached by a professional, either don't do it or do it so late after the interview that it is ineffective. Of course, thanking someone for the interview is obviously important. But what is most important is that you reinforce the high points of what the interviewing or hiring authority said he or she wanted and restate where or how you address those issues better than anyone else.

The email needs to be short and to the point. Do not ramble about how much you appreciated the interview, how much you like the person, or how you appreciate the conversation. This letter is going to be read, like the résumé, in ten seconds. So this is what it should look like (remember to make it look like an actual letter):

Dear Mr. or Ms._____,

Thank you for taking the time to speak with me today regarding the position with _____. Your needs and my qualifications are compatible.
   You stated that you wanted someone who has:

• [Experience or attributes that the employer said were wanted]

• [Another experience or attribute the employer said was wanted]

• [Another experience or attribute the employer said was wanted]

   I have given a lot of thought to what we spoke about. I would like to reinforce the confidence you can have in me to deliver what you need.

1. When I was at [name] company last year, I [accomplished the first thing that you wrote previously].

2. When I was at [name] company, I [accomplished or proved the second thing you wrote previously].

3. And, when I was at [name] company, I [accomplished or proved the third thing you wrote previously] .

   I'm an excellent fit for you and your company. I would like to go to work for you and your firm. This is a win/win situation for both of us.

Sincerely,
[Your name]

When you reinforce what the interviewing or hiring authority said he or she wanted, you need to do it in quantifiable terms. State things that can be measured objectively such as percentages of quota, longevity on the job, grades in school, stability, being promoted consistently—anything that can be measured in a quantitative manner. Make sure that you address specific issues that the interviewing or hiring authority stated was of value to the company.

Follow-Up Phone Call

Once you have emailed the letter, you need to be aware that interviewing or hiring authorities, after initial interviews, have a tendency to move on to other things and don't think about the interviewing and hiring process as much as you think they do—unless, of course, their "pain" is extremely severe. Interviewing or hiring authorities will have a tendency to tell you things like, "Well, we'll get back to you in a couple of days," and then go on vacation for a week.

With this in mind, it is advisable for you to follow up with the interviewing or hiring authority two to three days after the interview with a phone call to check in and see how the process is coming along. Interviewing and hiring authorities have to at least act like hiring is a top priority. And sometimes it is. Hiring is something that everybody knows they should do with decisiveness and real business acumen, but they mostly don't. So, your call reminds them of the task at hand. It is often a timing thing. You may catch the person and, all of a sudden, because you have him or her on the phone, the person will make an appointment with you for a second interview. This is also a great time to ask about anything you might have discussed in the initial interview that you didn't fully understand or that you need further clarification on.

If you don't get the person on the phone, and most often you won't, you'll have to deal with voice mail. Even though I have a ton of experience in this profession, I'm never really sure of how many times to call someone back when the individual doesn't return the call. My best suggestion is to call until you get the person. You may say, "Well, Tony, don't I run the risk of irritating the interviewer and making the person angry and, therefore, he or she will not be interested in hiring me?" Well, my answer is that you have absolutely nothing to lose. After all, until you have a job offer, you really don't have anything to decide about.

Most hiring authorities don't intentionally think, "I'm not gonna call that sucker back. She's a schmuck and I'm not going to hire her anyhow." The truth is that their intentions to do what they are supposed to do are sincere, but the activity just doesn't get done. The process of hiring often just slips further behind in favor of other more pressing, less risky issues. So, a timely call, and many of them after that—if you have to—may put you on top of the list of potential candidates.

Now, after ten to fifteen days of calling an interviewing or hiring authority with no response at all, you might wind up with the conclusion that you should pursue other people and other opportunities. Never, never, never take this result personally and do something stupid, like calling the hiring authority and leaving a mean, sarcastic voice mail about what the person can do with the job and that you didn't want it anyhow. There is always a tendency to take perceived rejection personally.

Now, the odds are that if you have not heard from a prospective employer in a couple weeks, you were probably not on the list of candidates to be considered. But you never really know. Always leave the door open, so that if a prospective employer wants to still consider you, even after weeks or months have gone by, you could resurrect the opportunity.

You never know what might happen. I can't tell you the number of people whom I've placed over the years who have come in second or third in the hiring process and eventually wound up getting the job. The company hires somebody and, after a short period of time, it doesn't work out. They call the number two candidate and try to hire him or her. But this *won't* happen to you if you're a jerk to the hiring authority when you are told that you are the number two or number three candidate. Some years ago, I had a candidate who came in second place. The company was so impressed with his credentials that they considered him for another opportunity and hired him—seven years later.

Always be graceful, even if you were told no. You never know what might happen down the line.

10 Follow-Up Interviews: A Whole New Challenge

SO, YOU THINK BECAUSE you made it past the initial interview and have been called back for a second one that you're well on your way to getting a job offer and going to work? Wrong! Frankly, your quest has just begun. Now, it is true that you should be congratulated for making it past the initial interview; 90 to 95 percent of the time, candidates don't make it that far. But the race is far from over. In fact, I liken these next steps in the process to the playoffs in sports. The regular season is competitive and entertaining to all; you have to go through it to get to the playoffs. And, it is true that the initial interview stage was necessary for you to get to this level of the interviewing process. But once you've gotten through the initial interview, the competition really heats up—you've made the playoffs.

The people who write books and articles about finding a job rarely, if ever, enlighten people to the fact that interviews beyond the initial one are most often a very different experience from what you expect. That is because most of the people who write these books and articles don't really find people jobs.

Most candidates simply assume that subsequent interviews beyond the initial interview are going to be just like the initial one. I've even had candidates over the years call me after an initial interview and actually say, "Tony, I got the job. They're having me back for a second and third interview."

> "No wonder I wasn't doing well in interviews after my initial ones. I had no idea of the difference." —Cindy L., Portland, Oregon

Candidates often have no idea that the subsequent interviewing process is most likely much more difficult and treacherous than the initial interview. Most candidates aren't ready for the kind of intensity and complication that goes on in the follow-up process. The intensity, depth, and complication in this part of the process are much less predictable than any other stage in the interviewing process. This chapter presents the top ten mistakes candidates make on subsequent interviews, and then surveys the later interview process, including telephone interviews, group interviews, and other forms that this part of the job search process assumes. Here are the tips that will help keep you on track, moving toward that job offer.

The Top Ten Mistakes Candidates Make on Subsequent Interviews

1. *Thinking that because they have been invited back, they're going to get hired.* Subsequent interviews are simply steps in the process. Managing the steps at this stage is different from handling the initial interview.

2. *Treating subsequent interviews the same way they treated the initial interview.* Although the basic presentation of yourself is the same, subsequent interviews need to be "customized" and refined.

3. *Not knowing how many other candidates are being moved to the next step and what their backgrounds are.* Interviews beyond the initial interview are like the playoff season in sports. The competition is keener. Candidates have to get a really good idea about how many other candidates are being moved to the next level and what their backgrounds are. Successful candidates will need to find out where their perceived weaknesses might be compared to the other candidates. In other words, "How do I stack up to the other people I'm competing with?"

4. *Not soliciting the help of the initial interviewing authority in "promoting" them to the next step.* Before subsequent interviews, a candidate should meet with, at least over the phone, the initial interviewing authority to find out everything there is to know about the subsequent interviews. The candidate should ask about how many interviews there will be and, more important, who the interviews will be with. Knowing the background, interviewing style, and as much detail as possible about the people who will be conducting the subsequent interviews is essential.

5. *Failing to understand how the subsequent interviews might differ from the initial interviews.* Asking the initial interviewing or hiring authority questions like, "What will be the main focus of the subsequent interviews? Over and above what I communi-

cated to you in the initial interview, what more will these interviewing authorities want? Based on our initial interview, what are the strengths that I should highlight or weaknesses that I should augment in the subsequent interviews?" Get the idea? Candidates can't assume that subsequent interviews are like the initial interviews.

6. *Not researching the company and the position as well as the people doing the subsequent interviewing in even more depth than for the initial interview.* Since candidates now have a better idea of what the company might want in hiring someone, they should do more in-depth research about the job, the interviewing and hiring authorities, peers, and anything else that might be pertinent. Know your target!

7. *Not making some kind of "going the extra mile" effort in subsequent interviews.* I encourage candidates to develop 30-, 60-, and 90-day plans as to what they would do in the first 90 days of employment and pass them out to the interviewing authorities in subsequent interviews. I have some candidates create PowerPoint presentations on themselves and their ability to do the job and use them in subsequent interviews. Any kind of activity or effort that will set the candidate apart from the other candidates in subsequent interviews is great.

8. *Starting to relax and forgetting that it's in the subsequent interviews where most excellent candidates get eliminated.* A good candidate recognizes there are many reasons to interview better and work harder in subsequent interviews than he or she did in the initial interview.

9. *Neglecting to get the support of the subsequent interviewing authorities.* This means asking every interviewing or hiring authority and subsequent interviewer if they're going to endorse you to be hired. Candidates need to ask every subsequent interviewer after the initial, "What do I need to do to get the job?" and "Will you support my candidacy over the other candidates?" It is crucial that you get "buy in" from the people with whom you interview. You want them to commit to supporting you as a candidate.

10. *Not realizing how crucial subsequent interviews are.* Candidates have to interview better than they did on the initial interviews; they also must be aware that subsequent interviews are not the finals. These are the "playoffs." They need to be taken seriously because they lead to the finals.

Today's Hiring Environment

We have just come out of the greatest recession in the history of the United States since the 1930s. For now and the near future, all companies are going to be very, very careful about everything they do, especially hiring. This is the seventh recession that I have been through, and every time we come out of a recession, I have noticed that, for quite some time, hiring authorities are simply *afraid* of many things—the economy, foreign competition, and, most important, hiring the wrong people.

You need to know that the people you are interviewing with are operating as much out of the fear of making a mistake as they are about the vision of hiring the right candidate. When the economy is strong as it was in 1996 to 2000, and from 2003 to 2008, companies would interview and hire with the attitude of, "Well, if it doesn't work out, we'll just hire someone else. No big deal." Companies were going strong, profits were high, and the economy was strong.

After we came out of each recession that I have seen, companies, and the people in them, became more cautious about hiring people. They are *afraid* of hiring the wrong person. This fear dictates that they try to "ensure" a successful hire by being more and more careful about whom they hire. They want to minimize their risk.

This means that they are going to have more and more interviews of candidates they might be interested in hiring. It means that the interviewing process is going to be elongated. It means that they are going to scrutinize every candidate with more care than they ever have before. It means also that they will suffer *paralysis by analysis*. A hiring process that used to take three to four weeks now takes eight to ten weeks. Hiring processes that used to involve three or four interviews with the candidate now may take six, seven, or even nine.

It is counterproductive to complain about this environment. As a professional recruiter, I can absolutely assure you that no company is going to get a better candidate, and therefore a better hire, because it has nine interviews of the candidate instead of three. Even when companies ask me and I explain that this kind of activity isn't going to do them any good, they still do it. They don't want to make a mistake. They think that if they elongate the hiring process involving more and more of their managers, the interviewing process will ensure a careful, successful hire.

So just be ready for a ridiculously elongated interviewing process, with people who probably have absolutely nothing to do with the job you are interviewing for. I had one interviewing authority just this last week saying to one of my candidates, "I have no idea why I am interviewing you. I have nothing to do with the job you applied for. I guess the management here wanted to get another 'set of eyes' on you."

What to Expect

You absolutely must be aware that the follow-up interviewing process is going to be very different from what you experienced in the initial interviewing process. You're going to basically sell yourself in the same way, but there are going to be a greater number of variables in this process than there were in the initial interview. Just be ready and know that it is a brand-new day and a brand-new process. Just because you made it past the initial interview, *you can take nothing for granted*. Be prepared for playoff intensity because now it's all on the line—and just as in the playoffs, you have to bring your "A" game and ratchet it up tenfold.

Remember, I stated that the interviewing process was a staged and contrived event. Well, the reason that most organizations involve so many people in the hiring decision is to *spread the risk*. Yes, you read that right. Corporate America will tell you that the reason so many people interview a candidate for a job is that the more people involved in the decision, the better the decision. Employers say they want to make sure of the candidate's qualifications, that he or she can do the job, that everybody likes the person, and so forth. But the truth is that no one individual wants to take on the responsibility of making a hiring decision and having to personally live with the possibly bad consequences. People in the hiring process are so afraid of making a mistake that if they do, they want other people to share the responsibility for the screw-up.

When the First Interviewer Is Not the Hiring Authority

If your initial interview is conducted by a third party or simply an interviewing authority, and you make it past this person to the second stage of interviewing, you are most likely one of the safest candidates to be interviewed. The interviewer who does not have hiring authority is usually going to screen out far more candidates than he or she screens in. This person is going to look for more reasons a candidate *should not* be considered than reasons the candidate *should* be considered. As I've stated before, these people don't want to look bad.

Recently, I worked with a candidate who was eliminated by the internal HR department interviewing authority because he had been out of work for two months. The interviewing authority was given overall instructions by the ultimate hiring authority not to consider people who were out of work. The particular candidate that I was representing, though, had an exceptional track record in pretty much the same business as my client. After the interviewing authority eliminated my candidate for being out of work, I called the hiring authority directly and explained the situation. Not only did this get the candidate an interview, but he was subsequently hired.

Once the interviewing authority has told you that you're going to be promoted to the next step in the process, you need to be sure that you get this person's support for future interviews within the company. Do what you can to get the person to promote you throughout the process. The way you do that is to simply ask if he or she will help you in every aspect of the subsequent interviews. In fact, it doesn't hurt to simply ask in this fashion, "Mr. or Ms. _____, I really want this job and am convinced that I am the best candidate you could hire. I would like you to help me as much as you can through the interviewing process."

Even if you have to suggest meeting a second time before you go on the subsequent interviews, you want the authority to "load your shotgun" so that you perform well in the rest of the interviewing process. You want to ask this person about the backgrounds of everybody you will encounter, what their positions are, how long they have been with the organization, what their role might be in the interviewing process, and so forth. The more you get this third-party interviewing authority to help you, the better off you are.

When the First Interviewer *Is* the Hiring Authority

Studies have shown that successful hires are just as likely if *only* the hiring authority is involved, as opposed to several people being involved in the process. In fact, one study I read documented that in certain industries and professions, it's actually better to have only one person, the hiring authority who is responsible for the position, involved in the interviewing process. But nobody is ever going to be able to convince corporate America that companies are just as well off when one person does the interviewing and hiring as they are when several people are involved in the process.

This is a much easier situation to deal with than when the interviewing authority is not a hiring authority. When the hiring authority does the interviewing, he or she takes on long-term, personal responsibility for the decision. Most of the time, this person is going to be responsible for not only hiring you but also contributing to your success or lack of it in the job. This person's reputation is really on the line.

When hiring authorities decide to move candidates up in the interviewing process, they are getting other opinions in order to protect themselves. Since hiring is a personal thing and these people have a personal, vested interest in whoever is successful in getting the job, they are likely to help you as much as they can. It is important that you ask this person how many people are being interviewed; how you stack up against the other people who are being interviewed; whom you are going to be interviewed by; the perception the hiring authority has of these people; how long the process is going to take; what the people involved like and don't like; and anything else you can glean from the hiring authority.

Once the hiring authority tells you that you are going to be promoted to the next step, it is not a bad idea to request another meeting with this person so that you can get as much information as possible about the other people you will be talking to. A hiring authority wants to hire someone who goes the extra mile and wants the job.

Multiple Interviews—Watch Out!

Mark my words, and you better remember this: *The more people who are involved in the interviewing process, the more difficult it is going to be to get hired.*

I am constantly amazed at the number of interviewing authorities above the hiring authority who have a completely different idea from the initial hiring authority about what kind of candidate should be hired. You would think that once an organization decided it needed a particular type of individual, all the people involved in the hiring decision would be reading from the same page and have some consistent idea among them about what kind of person they ought to hire. Unfortunately, most of the time this just isn't the case.

We recently had the vice president for a company interview one of our candidates. The VP was going to be the direct supervisor of the candidate. He liked the candidate so much that he made a date to play golf with him (which he did), take the candidate and his wife to dinner along with his wife (which he did), and meet with him a third time to prepare him for a visit to the corporate office (which was part of the interviewing process).

The VP told us that the candidate was absolutely perfect for the job. The candidate took a day off from work and woke up at 4:30 in the morning to catch a 7 a.m. flight to Chicago. He rented a car, drove two hours outside of Chicago, and arrived at the corporate office on time. Two executive vice presidents took him into an office, and after a 20-minute interview explained to our candidate that they had changed the parameters of what they were looking for, that he wasn't right for the job, and that he was going back to the airport and back to Dallas. They spent $3,000 on airfare and wasted people's time simply because they didn't communicate with each other. Don't ask me why this stuff happens, it just does. As I said before, people will generally act human. Don't even try to figure out the rhyme or reason. Just be ready for it.

In the past few years, I'd say the average number of interviews that you'll go through to get hired is four. This is especially true if your initial interview is with a screener. It's a good idea if you are called back for a second interview to find out how many interviews there will be in the process. I have experienced as few as one and as many as nine or ten. I had a candidate not too long ago who was interviewed five times here in Dallas, then flown to Atlanta for a corporate visit. She was interviewed by five senior managers, then flown back to Dallas. A week later she was asked to go back to Atlanta for a few more interviews. She flew back to Atlanta and interviewed with the same people she interviewed with the week before, who asked her mostly the same questions they asked her the first time. The candidate, upon her return to Dallas, told me that she was not interested in working for the company—and by the way, this was a multibillion-dollar firm. Before I could tell the managers that she was not going to pursue the opportunity because they were so indecisive, the hiring authority called me to tell me that they just weren't quite sure of her ability to do the job. Go figure!

Time Is Your Enemy

The longer the interviewing process takes, and the more people who are involved in it, the less likely it is that you—or anyone else, for that matter—will get hired. There is no normal time period that is standard for the interviewing process. I have experienced interviewing/hiring processes that took fifteen minutes and I have experienced ones that took eighteen months, and some that started but ended with no one being hired.

The time it takes to fill a position and for an interviewing process to run its course usually depends more on the level of "pain" that an organization or hiring authority has than the level of the position. An executive vice president's position would probably take longer to fill than an entry-level accountant simply because there are fewer executive vice president candidates than entry-level accountants; but, again, it really depends on how badly a person needs to be hired.

> **Key Point**: One of the issues you're going to have to deal with in the interviewing process is the paradox of urgency.

The paradox of urgency states that "every interviewing and hiring authority absolutely, unequivocally, urgently has to fill his or her position—someday." Most interviewing or hiring authorities whom you will interview with will act as though filling the position that you are interviewing for is the most important thing they can be doing, that it is their number-one priority, and that they are going to set everything aside until they're successful at finding the perfect candidate.

An interviewing or hiring authority must act as though there is a sense of urgency in filling the position and interviewing you. This person needs to act as though hiring is a high priority. It is not uncommon, though, for the priority of hiring to ebb and flow over a long period of time. (How would it appear if the hiring authority who was interviewing you said, "Look, we appreciate you coming all the way over here today to interview and appreciate the time that you've invested, but hiring you or anybody else is not a real high priority. We'd like to talk to you anyway just to see if you are a perfect candidate.")

You cannot afford to get emotionally wrapped up in what interviewing or hiring authorities tell you they're going to do. They will tell you that you are the best candidate that they have seen (until the next one comes along), and you then never hear from them again. You can't control what other people do; you can only control how you react to it. Just don't get excited one way or the other because time frames in the hiring process are dubious issues.

We have a rule around our place, called "Tony's ten-day rule." It states that, if an employer and the candidate don't take some kind of action after the initial interview to move the interviewing process forward within ten working days of the initial interview, the probability of the candidate being hired decreases 10 percent for every day after those ten days. So, if there isn't any substantial activity of an employer getting back to you within the first ten working days after the initial interview, continue to pursue the opportunity, but don't expect many results.

The second guideline, and this is an overall broad guideline that can be applied to many, many things in the interviewing and hiring process, is to *have no expectations*. Go after every opportunity you can as though it was the last opportunity on earth. Prepare well. Interview well. Sell yourself as hard as you can ever imagine. Just don't have any expectations for anything. In other words, focus on the process and don't worry about the results.

Again, interviewing and finding a job is one of your highest personal priorities. However, it is just one of the many priorities within an organization running a business. Hiring or interviewing authorities aren't intentionally rude or unprofessional. They, too, are subject to all kinds of factors that you may not know anything about. People in this situation don't intentionally lie—they just end up lying some of the time. You can't let yourself become overly upset or distracted by it. If you are pursuing enough opportunities, none of these things should affect you. When the hiring authority tells you he or she is going to call you back but doesn't, if you have enough other opportunities to pursue, it won't matter. Remember, it's numbers, numbers, numbers.

Also remember the "fear factor" on the part of hiring authorities and their companies. The fear of making a mistake is paramount in their minds. You know as well as I do that when people act out of fear, they are often irrational. So just expect it. Also, be ready for the fact that the higher up the hierarchy you go in the interviewing process, the less knowledgeable the interviewing authority is about the job you might be trying to obtain. The higher up the ladder you go and interview with people who are far from the day-to-day functions of the job you are applying for, the more likely you are to talk to people who don't know or, at least, aren't sure what the qualifications for the position should be.

A Success Plan for Follow-Up Interviews

The strategy for follow-up interviews is not far off from the strategy that you used in the initial interview. To a certain extent, you're going to do exactly what you did in the initial interview—with a couple of added steps to give you the advantage. The process, again, is so simple but most people don't think to do it.

Collect All the Information You Can

When you get a call from the interviewing or hiring authority whom you interviewed with in the first place to tell you that you are going to come back for a second interview, you need to ask a number of questions that are very important to the success of your subsequent interviews. If you get a call from someone other than the interviewing authority you initially interviewed with, you must call and talk to that person with whom you interviewed. Get out the notes you took after the interview, review them so you can ask any clarification questions, and then ask the following questions:

1. "Mr. or Ms._____, I'm excited about coming back and speaking with you all about the position we discussed. Can you please share with me what the whole process will be?" Even if you were told what the process would be in the initial interview, you want to take notes and get an exact and detailed idea of what all of the next steps might be.

2. "Please tell me what is Mr. or Ms._____, the next person that I'm speaking to, like as a person? What is his or her role in the interviewing process?"

3. "What does this person look for in a candidate?"

4. "Based on what you know about me, where am I going to be strong or weak in the eyes of Mr. or Ms._____ ?"

5. "If you were me, what are the things from our initial interview that I need to emphasize in my interview with Mr. or Ms._____?"

6. "Is there anything in my experience or background that I should emphasize or elaborate about to Mr. or Ms._____?"

7. "How many people are moving up in the interviewing process?"

8. "Mr. or Ms._____, in this next interview, I was going to present myself to Mr. or Ms. _____ , in the same way that I presented myself to you. Can you give me any pointers on how I might be able to present myself better as a candidate?" This is a very important question because it will give you insights into the next interviewing authority.

9. "If you were to personally rank the candidates that Mr. or Ms._____ is going to talk to, how would you rank me?" You hope that the interviewing or hiring authority will be honest with you and tell you how you rank with the other candidates. But most interviewing or hiring authorities don't have the courage or guts to tell you exactly how you rank. So, they're usually going to say something like, "Well, we're calling back three or four candidates and you are one of them."

10. If the interviewing or hiring authority actually tells you exactly how you rank with the other candidates, and you're not ranked number one, then you need to ask, "Then, please tell me, Mr. or Ms. _____, what do I need to do in order to become your number one candidate?"

11. If you are told that you are the number one candidate, then you need to say, "That is great to hear, Mr. or Ms._____, what, in your opinion do I need to do to continue to be the number one candidate?"

12. If you are told that you are one of a number of candidates being considered, then ask, "Mr. or Ms._____, what in your opinion makes me a unique candidate and what do I need to do, in your opinion, to get the job?"

13. "Mr. or Ms._____, do I have your support in getting this job?"

14. "If it were totally up to you Mr. or Ms._____, would you hire me for this position?"

   If the answer is yes, then you ask, "Great, what do you think I need to do to get the next interviewing authority to feel the same way?" If the answer is no, then, "What are your concerns?" If the answer is "maybe, depending upon what the other people think," then ask, "What are my strengths and weaknesses that you think I should emphasize or shore up with the next interviewing authority?"

15. "If all goes well with the next interviewing authority, are you going to recommend that your company hire me, Mr. or Ms._____?"

The reason that you want to ask all these questions is that it does absolutely no good to get to the second, third, or fourth stages of interviewing without knowing exactly how you stand or what you need to do to get the job. By asking these questions, you get the initial interviewing or hiring authority on your side of the fence. You are asking the person to support you as a candidate and you want him or her helping you as much as you possibly can. You will notice that I recommend asking the person to support you as a candidate in two or three different ways.

These last questions work very well. Unfortunately, most candidates don't like asking them because (1) it takes a lot of courage, and (2) they are afraid of rejection. Don't fall prey to this. As I've said before, "no" is the second best answer you can get. And if you are still a candidate, by asking these questions, you know how you stand. Knowing that empowers you in the next set of interviews.

Keep Doing What Is Successful

Once you go to the second and subsequent interviews, you are going to ask every interviewer who promotes you to the next stage all of the same previous questions after the interview.

Many people get to a second, third, or fourth interview and think that since they have gotten this far they have a lock on the job offer. They relax in their intensity, alter their presentation, and basically quit selling, thinking it's a done deal. *Not true!* At each succeeding interview, you should present yourself in exactly the same manner as you did with the initial interview. If your system is working, don't mess with it. You should only alter your technique based on what the immediate interviewer might tell you about the next interviewer.

If the initial and subsequent interviewing authorities make suggestions about your presentation, make sure you alter your presentation to accommodate their ideas. Keep in mind that if an interviewing authority promotes you to the next stage of the interviewing process, he or she has at least stated that you might be a viable candidate. If you ask the right questions as I have suggested, you'll not only get that person's support, but you will get his or her input and suggestions on how you might be able to interview successfully up the ladder.

If you don't get any substantial suggestions or input, the only way you should alter your presentation in the second and subsequent interviews is this: Instead of asking, "What do I need to do to get this job?" at the end of the interview, you should ask the interviewer this question: "Mr. or Ms._____, I believe that I have the kind of experience that you are looking for in this opportunity. I believe I am the most qualified candidate you can interview. *Do I have your support? Will you recommend that I be hired?*"

If you ask any question other than this, it's too easy for a second, third, or fourth interviewing authority to say something like, "Well, it's not really my decision, I'm going to leave that up to Mr. or Ms._____. It's really his [or her] decision." If you ask the previous question, you acknowledge that the decision might really belong to someone else, but that the person you are now interviewing with does have a say in who gets hired. You are not asking the person to hire you; you are asking the person to *support* you.

If the interviewer insists that it isn't really his or her decision, you need to say something like: "Well, Mr. or Ms._____, your company must think very highly of your opinion or I wouldn't be interviewing with you. I need to be sure that I have covered all the questions about my candidacy with you and that I have your support. If I have answered all your questions, are you going to recommend that I be hired?"

Note: These are blunt and to-the-point closes. If the interviewing authority dances around them in any way and will not give you outright support, you had best be aware that you probably will not get his or her support. On the other hand, you may get the person's support but still not get the job. In many instances, interviewing authorities up the ladder may not really choose a candidate to be hired, but they can say no. The idea is that you are being more aggressive and more assertive than most candidates will be.

Follow Up

Once you have completed the second, third, fourth, and so on interview, follow up with emails, letters, and phone calls, if appropriate. I would not recommend calling an interviewing authority whose job is to simply "gut-check" or provide another opinion in the interviewing process unless you bonded with him or her really well. You *do* want to phone the actual hiring authority and ask him or her about the decision. The more aggressive and assertive you are about selling yourself and closing on being the candidate who should be hired, the better off you are. You can be pushy, assertive, and confident without being obnoxious. Follow your gut, but don't be afraid you will lose the opportunity because you are too aggressive.

Since the first edition of *The Job Search Solution* appeared, these assertive questions have prompted a lot of comments and emails that they might be too bold. These usually come from people who aren't successful in the interviewing process. So my question is, "Which is more uncomfortable, asking these bold questions or continuing to have to look for a job?" On the other hand, I've had hundreds of emails, letters, and calls from people who, as they say, "got the guts to do it," and it worked almost magically. All it takes is practice.

Some Interviews Are Worse Than Others

Okay, so we've covered the basics of handling follow-up interviews. You've got to gather support for your candidacy and as much information as possible on those you will be interviewing with as you move on. You want to keep focusing on your presentation, which presumably is working, and tweak it as necessary, based on suggestions of interviewers along the way, to make it even better. But all follow-up interview situations are not equal. Now, let's take a close look at a few interview situations that can really throw you for a loop—if you don't watch out.

Telephone Interviews

In the days when companies are trying to be more economical, they will often have you speak to people in corporate or a distant manager via telephone interview. As with the videoconference or Skype interview—or any other, for that matter—there is not much you can do. Review what I said earlier in this book about telephone interviews (Chapter 7). Try to get as much coaching as you possibly can about the person whom you will be speaking with and what the person's interests or concerns might be.

Be prepared for a "surprise." It isn't uncommon to have these things postponed, have the interviewing authority "forget," or be caught off guard when you are told to call him or her.

Videoconference and Skype-Type Interviews

Over the past few years, these things have become more popular, especially with the advent of technology. But the truth is, the technology *does not make you look good*. In fact, as with video résumés, unless you have the God-given gift of being attractive in front of the camera, this technology can hurt you rather than help you.

The technology is used by the hiring authority's supervisors or other people who need to interview you in a far-off place. So, rather than pay for your travel there, they use videoconferencing and/or Skype. Just remember a few things if you're going to be interviewed this way. First, practice and see what you look like with these media before the interview. You are going to be shocked at how *bad you look*. Your face is going to look bigger than it really is, your hair is going to look awful unless you have it cropped very short, your coloring will be made indescribable, and your glasses, if you wear them, are going to make you look like a gangster.

So here's what to do. Get a haircut. Men, if your hair is the least bit hanging over your ears you're going to look like a hippie (if you're not old enough to remember what that looks like, Google it). Women, pull your hair back. Take off your glasses, even if you can't see. Do not wear a white shirt or blouse because they cause glare. Wear a light blue shirt. Let's hope the technology will get better, but it is not uncommon, depending on how good your Skype connection is, to have your head look like an egg. Speak slowly and distinctly because even with the most sophisticated videoconference equipment sometimes the video and audio will "stutter" and freeze moments at a time.

Practice will really help. But be prepared to be challenged. There isn't much you can do. You can't refuse them, but you can make the best of it.

The Group Interview—Really Watch Out!

Unfortunately, except in sales situations, the group interview in no way resembles anything else that goes on in business. I hate these things. The idea is to see how a candidate responds to a group setting. The candidate is brought into a room in front of three or four (I have seen as many as nine) people, and he or she is asked several questions. More often than not, this kind of interview becomes somewhat of a forum for personal, political strategizing among the people who are giving the interview.

Once you find out that it is going to be a group interview, you should ask the previous interviewing authority everything you need to know about the people and the situation. There is not much you can do about the group interview except prepare yourself to be ganged up on. If you get into the interview and there are more than three people interviewing you, be prepared for a lot of political undertone. At the least, it isn't easy to establish personal rapport with three or four people at one time.

The best way to deal with a group interview is to get involved in *telling stories* that support the attributes you have applied to yourself. It is likely that in a group interview, especially if it is more than three people, you are going to be addressing people who are drivers, analytics, kinesthetic, auditory, and/or visual. The best way to deal with all those types of people in the same environment is to tell stories.

Remember, stories bypass conscious resistance to the listener's own biases. In the previous chapter, I wrote about the power of stories. Remember, too, that Christ told stories to the masses. Aesop wrote stories. People ask themselves, "How would I react in that situation?" They identify with a storyteller, especially if you're telling a story about yourself. They work especially well in a group interview setting.

Immediately after the group interview, make notes about all the people you spoke with and what their individual questions, issues, or concerns were. Do not rely on your memory. Take notes immediately, while things are fresh in your mind. You want to follow up with each member of the group in the same way as you followed up with the initial interviewer. If you can, try to remember specific issues that each interviewer discussed or brought up. That way, in the email or phone call, you can customize your communications.

The Corporate Visit—Really, Really Watch Out!

For some management and sales positions, a visit to the corporate headquarters is often a common, required practice. Companies send candidates for a corporate visit for the same reason that they have multiple people interview them: *to spread the risk*. It isn't much different from when you interview with two, three, four, or five people in a local organization. You have to plan, be prepared, and get as much information as you can about the people you will meet at corporate headquarters.

There are a couple things to note. First, rarely does a company send more than one, maybe two candidates for a corporate visit (unless, of course, the corporate office is close and it isn't very expensive to send people there). Usually, if the corporate visit requires a $3,500 to $4,000 plane ticket and a day of everybody's time, it isn't likely that more than one or two candidates are going to be sent at a time. If, however, one of the original candidates is not hired, then other candidates can always be sent.

When local hiring authorities send one or two candidates for a corporate visit, they are essentially telling corporate that they would be comfortable in hiring any of the candidates they send up for those kinds of interviews. Whatever you do, though, don't take that for granted. I have known many organizations that insist on a corporate visit by almost every candidate they hire simply because they don't trust anyone outside of corporate to be able to make the right decisions.

Be prepared to interview with people who, unfortunately, are going to have a say in your hiring, but really won't have anything to do with your job, should you get it. This is done so that the company can have enough people interviewing you to make it look like the corporate visit was really of value. Rarely does the corporate visit involve interviewing with only one or two people. It looks rather silly for a corporation to spend $3,500 to $4,000 to get you to go to corporate to talk to only two people. So, the company loads up your day with a number of people who probably won't make any difference in the job you are interviewing for. However, since you were there to talk to them, they will have a say in whether or not you are hired.

There are going to be two or three key people whom you really need to impress with your candidacy when you go to a corporate interviewing visit. The rest probably shouldn't be talking to you at all, but for appearance's sake, they will. Unfortunately, you are going to have to impress them and sell them just as well on your candidacy as the two or three key people. After all, if they're going to interview you, they're going to have something to say about you. As I stated before, I've had many instances where my candidate got to the corporate visit and interviewed with two or three people who even made the statement: "I don't even know why I'm talking to you. I don't really have anything to do with the job you're being interviewed for, but I'll do it." My advice is that since anyone who talks to you could say no to your candidacy, treat every one of them as though they were someone you really had to sell and impress.

Unfortunately, over the years I've seen quite a number of candidates eliminated because of a no vote from someone in the corporate office who had nothing to do with the job and should not have even been involved in the interviewing process. And for no other reason than just to prove that he was important, he said no to the candidate. That's the way corporate politics often goes.

Local hiring authorities do have some say in the game when they send you to corporate headquarters. But that doesn't mean you're going to get hired. Most candidates believe that if they are being sent for corporate interviews, they've "got the job in the bag." Don't assume anything! Metaphorically, all you are is on third base. You still have to make the effort to get home and score. Absolutely nothing is certain. So, don't let it go to your head.

Here are a couple of points of advice about corporate visits.

- Try to arrange your trip so you arrive the day before your interview. It is not uncommon for flights to be delayed or canceled. I've had numerous instances where a candidate was instructed to fly to the corporate office the morning of the interviews, go through a number of interviews, and then fly out late that afternoon or evening. If the flights in the morning are delayed or canceled and you either don't make it all or are late, the whole day is usually a mess. I had one instance recently where the candidate was supposed to fly to the corporate office and weather canceled all of the flights on the day he was to go. The company reorganized the day of interviewing for the next week. The candidate got on the plane to fly out, sat on the tarmac for two-and-a-half hours, and the flight was canceled because of ice and snow. (Yeah, we even get that in Dallas, Texas, from time to time.) The company never arranged another corporate visit and simply hired another candidate.

- Before the trip, confirm the schedule for whom you are supposed to speak with. Showing up without knowing what the plan or schedule is will keep you in unnecessary suspense. Make contact with someone in the corporate office before your trip so that you can coordinate with the individual regarding any problems that might come up. I had a candidate a few years ago who was flown for a corporate visit—to the *wrong city*. You read it right; he was flown to the wrong office of the company he was interviewing with. When he got there and started asking for the people he was supposed to be interviewing with, he was told that this was a branch office and that the corporate office was 140 miles away. The only real "contact" he had was here in Dallas, and that guy was gone for the day, traveling himself, and couldn't be reached. The candidate finally reached the people he was supposed to be interviewing with and ended up driving to the corporate office. He had only half of the interviews one day, stayed overnight, and had the other half the next day. Needless to say, it was a mess and he didn't get the job.

So, if you are sent for a corporate visit, be prepared for the unexpected.

Lunch or Dinner Interviews—Really, Really, Really Watch Out!

As you can tell, I definitely don't like these things, either. Most people are not very good at mixing risky business events (like an interview) with social events that involve meals. I would certainly recommend trying to avoid them, but you may not have much choice.

The reason I don't like them is that I have seen candidates lose the opportunity to be hired, when they were the best candidate, because of poor performance in a social situation. So you say, "Well, Tony, we're all social beings and if a person doesn't have the social graces to perform well at a lunch or dinner, he or she may not have the ability to do a job." You may be right. But the truth is that the interviewing process is already an emotionally distressful experience. When you couple the distress and uneasiness of interviewing with having to be graceful in a social setting, it's very hard to do.

If the interview meal cannot be avoided, then there are a few things that you need to remember. First, watch your darn table manners. Slouching over your food, ordering the wrong kinds of food, talking with food in your mouth, or eating sloppily will kill you in a lunch or dinner interview. I have to admit that I am blown away by some of the poor manners that I have seen from both individual candidates and employers over the years. I've had candidates with fifteen to twenty years of excellent experience, MBAs from the most prestigious schools, and track records that were astounding screw up interviews at lunch or dinner because their manners were so appalling. There is no excuse for this.

Second, never, ever drink alcohol in an interview setting. I don't care if your interviewing or hiring authority sits there and proceeds to get sloshed. Don't you drink. In an interviewing situation, you have to be as mentally and emotionally sharp, congruent, and grounded as you possibly can be. You can't afford to let anything impair your thought process.

Order your food after you see what your host is ordering. Don't appear to be taking advantage of a "free lunch" by ordering something on the high side of the menu. Let your host lead the way and follow suit. Either order something on the same level that he or she has ordered or something of lesser value. Stay away from ordering messy foods, such as barbecue or spaghetti. Stick to simple foods that you can cut into small pieces before you put them in your mouth. In an interviewing situation, you are going to be doing most of the talking, especially if you are being asked numerous questions. Stay away from things that you have to pick up with your hands; even sandwiches can be a mess in some restaurants. Pieces of meat like a small steak or a chicken breast are perfect foods to order in an interviewing situation because they can be easily cut.

Also, it is preferable to eat a little something before you go on an interview that is going to involve a meal. Appearing ravenous or even hungry when you're trying to carry on an interview is very distracting. Order small amounts and eat slowly.

When your spouse or date is invited to a social dinner with the spouses or dates of the hiring authorities, you really need to be on your guard. These kinds of social engagements can be very nice, but they have the potential to be disastrous. Whether we like it or not, our spouses reflect on us, and they can be either a positive or a negative reflection. I have experienced all kinds of unfortunate consequences because of a spouse or date who screwed up the social interview for my candidate. I've had spouses of male candidates drink too much, tell dirty jokes, even flirt with the hiring authority—in front of his wife, no less. I also have had male spouses of female candidates get into arguments with their spouse at a dinner interview, dominate the interviewing conversation, and, in one instance, inform a hiring authority that he would not let his wife go to work for the company.

The spouse of a candidate who is being considered for a job needs to realize his or her role in the interviewing process. We're all judged by the company we keep. Many businesses have lots of social interactions with their customers. Most social engagements with customers or clients will involve an employee's spouse. So, it is not uncommon for an organization to evaluate candidates not just on who they are but also on whom they marry. I had one situation years ago where the wives of the president and three executive vice presidents literally voted on the candidate and his spouse. Yes, the wives of the president and executive vice presidents voted on whether or not the candidate *and* his wife should be hired. My candidate and his wife lost the election, which is why I remember it so vividly.

One issue to remember in the social interviewing situation is to always ask people about themselves. People love to talk about themselves. It's their favorite subject. It is amazing how thoughtful, intelligent, wise, and professional you will appear in a social setting if you let most people talk about themselves. And if you know how to master this skill, you are!

Social interviews can be treacherous. I had a candidate a few years ago who took his "fiancée" to a dinner with the CEO and his wife. It became obvious during the dinner that my candidate was living with this woman, but they were not married. At the end of the dinner, the CEO made it very clear that he thought the candidate was living an immoral life and that there was no way he would hire anyone who was living with someone else, unmarried. The CEO's attitude was that if a person didn't respect the bonds of marriage, there were very few things that the candidate would respect.

Other Social Events—Really, Really, Really, Really Watch Out!

Keep in mind that a golf game or a tennis game might be an integral part of the interviewing process. Remember, you are not yet a part of this organization—you are still being interviewed! When you are involved in a social gathering of the organization, if you are not yet hired, you run a big risk of being eliminated because someone, who probably has absolutely nothing to do with hiring you, isn't impressed with you and voices that opinion to a hiring authority.

Regarding the social events like picnics, Christmas parties, birthday parties, and so forth, if you don't believe they are the essential to your being hired, gracefully decline the invitation and say that you have other plans. I can't tell you the number of times that I've seen candidates, their dates, spouses—and, even in a couple of cases, their children—screw up the candidate's opportunity to go to work in the company because of the way they behaved at a social function that had absolutely nothing to do with the hiring process.

I know one CEO who invites the candidates to play golf with him. His purpose is to see if the candidates—even women candidates—dress appropriately for his very exclusive golf club. He also wants to see how they interact with him and his management staff. And, most important, he wants to see if they "fudge" on their golf score. His attitude is that if they would cheat on their golf score, they would cheat him. Another one of our clients over the years invites the candidate to lunch and asks the candidate to drive. He wants to see how clean the candidate keeps his or her car. You can laugh all you want at these rather odd ways of judging candidates, but that's reality.

Collateral Materials

Now, this stuff can actually be fun. And done the right way, can land you the job. Collateral materials are additional "proof" that you are a phenomenal candidate and better than any other candidate the company may be interviewing. These can be special presentations, like PowerPoint presentations or documents that are *delivered by* the candidate at the beginning of or during the interviewing process. Once you get the idea, there are probably endless numbers of things you can use to prove you are a great candidate. Some of the collateral materials that I've seen used in the past few years are:

- *30-60-90 Day Plan:* Darryl S. was a graduate of one of the military academies. He drew his analogy of what he would do in the first 30, 60, and 90 days on the job as if he was a commander in the military. Creative and brilliant! He presented this plan in the second round of interviews to the three people that he met with, which included the vice president. (Although 30-60-90 day plans are oriented toward sales, I have seen them used for just about any kind of position—administrative assistant, accounting, finance, IT, engineering, etc.)

- *PowerPoint Presentation:* Michael P. designed and developed an impressive PowerPoint presentation titled "Roadmap to Success: Strategy Plan" that showed step-by-step what he would do if he was hired by the company. He made this PowerPoint presentation to the executive committee of the company.

- *Talking Points:* Tim C. handed a list of his "talking points" to all of the people he interviewed with, either individually or as a group. This was simply a list of the points that he wanted to be sure to cover in the interview that made him stand out from other candidates. A hiring authority is likely to remember something like this specifically because they are on a sheet in front of him.

- *Business Proposition:* Don T. was applying to a company that sells workforce management software. His business proposition statement for the company was simple and to the point: *Performance-driven organizations leverage their workforce to realize a higher return on investment, increased productivity, decreased operational costs, improved customer and employee retention, and a host of other benefits. By employing key workforce management practices, companies are able to reach a higher level of employee performance that leads to increased profitability.*

- *Psychological assessment:* Jim L. had a psychological assessment done by a major retained recruiting firm. He used it in a number of interviews to show that he had received a "top grade" assessment.

- *Sales process summary:* Jim K. was applying for a job as national director of sales. He spelled out in detail exactly what kind of sales process he would use if he were hired.

Other examples of excellent collateral materials I've encountered that can be used to your advantage include:

- Intelligence tests that show the candidate is smart

- Stellar performance reviews (present or previous positions)

- Customer/client recognition letters

- White papers or articles that the candidate has published

- Project reports that the candidate completed

- Portfolios of design or art samples (usually used in artistic or design types of interviews, but I've seen architects, engineers, and even IT people use them)

- Business proposals

- Published strategies that the candidate developed for previous employers

- Personal business and philosophical statements

- Independent/consulting assessments of the candidate

- Personally profiles

- Personal mission statements

You really set yourself apart from the other candidates when you walk in and pass out to the people in the room documentable "proof" that you are a great candidate or you make a PowerPoint presentation on why they should hire you. Some of these, like previous performance reviews or personal business mission statements, can be part of a résumé or information given in an initial interview. Things like PowerPoint presentations or 30-60-90 day business plans are probably best used in follow-up interviews.

Now, this kind of thing takes practice, but it is absolutely killer. Be sure to practice how you present this stuff to an individual or a group. It does absolutely no good to have an excellent PowerPoint presentation unless you deliver it just that way. Get it?

Remember, This Is the Finals

"Never let the fear of striking out get in your way."

—BABE RUTH

You are now in the finals. You're not going to get any other chance. You either win or you lose. It's just that simple. *Whatever you do, play to win!* Go after these opportunities to interview with everything you've got. Leave it all out on the floor, as they say in basketball.

But equally important, don't get overly cautious and play not to lose. Often in the interviewing process, when candidates get into the final interviews, they have a tendency to start operating out of fear of loss rather than the vision of gain. They start to become too careful about what they say and do in the interviews. They start reading into every question they're asked and every interview that they have. They start thinking, "Boy, I've made it this far, I'm really doing well. I really want this job. I really don't want to screw it up. I hope I don't screw it up, so I'll just be careful and not run the risk of making a mistake because things are going so well." Then the candidate proceeds to be completely different from the interviews that got him or her this far, and the candidate starts interviewing out of fear of loss rather than vision of gain.

Dance with what brung ya! Don't tighten up or change strategies. Oftentimes when candidates have "nothing to lose" in initial interviews they give lucid, smooth, and confident interviews. When, after two or three interviews, they start thinking "Oh, my God, I really have a shot at this. I don't want to lose it," they start tightening up, start over-thinking everything, and totally destroy the manner and the confidence they had that got them to the point. Play to win and don't think about losing. (Besides, if you followed my teaching, you have a number of these opportunities available to you at the same time and you don't have to focus on just one opportunity.)

If You Need to Take a Test

Let's spend a few moments on the subject of testing. This would include all kinds of psychological, aptitude, and intelligence tests. Since 1973, I have seen candidate testing ebb and flow in popularity. Believe it or not, it seems to ebb and flow depending on the economy. Testing of job candidates can become very expensive, so it is one of the first things that companies stop doing when the economy gets difficult.

Be prepared for what I call the *paradox of testing*. Every company that has ever used testing as a part of its selection process is going to tell every candidate that, at most, the testing accounts for only 25 percent of the final decision. Don't believe a word of it! Whatever kind of test is used, from grapho-analysis to psychological interviewing, is a qualifier that you must pass with the minimum standard arbitrarily set by someone or some group in the organization, or you aren't going to go further in the interviewing process. Whether hiring authorities or companies will admit it or not, the test becomes a binary, black-and-white, proceed-or-go-home qualifier.

So, when a hiring authority tells you something like, "Oh, by the way, we have some psychological (or aptitude, or skills, or intelligence) testing you need to do as a candidate, but don't worry about it. Everybody who comes to work here has to take it and it doesn't really account for much more than 10 percent (or 25 percent, or 50 percent) of the decision," don't believe a word of it! Testing becomes the gate that has to be passed through before you can be considered as a viable candidate.

Testing objectifies the hiring process. When supposedly objective tests decide on your viability as a candidate, no hiring or interviewing authority involved in the process of hiring has to have her butt on the line, has to take a stand on your candidacy, or has to run the risk of being the only person who likes you and wants to hire you. Now, a hiring authority is still going to have to make a decision in choosing someone to be hired. But the convenient thing about testing is that it also functions as a cover-your-butt issue. If hiring you turns out to be a mistake, but you did well on the company's battery of tests, the hiring authority can turn to everyone else and say, "Well, she did well on the testing!" It is just another way of passing the buck of responsibility. The tests become a qualifier, screening out tons of candidates so no one person has to, and it's convenient and easy.

Please don't tell me that testing is stupid and it doesn't work. Part of my graduate studies—admittedly forty years ago—included extensive studies about testing. I can make the case that testing will never measure passion, commitment, focus, and, in general, "heart," the real things that separate a top performer from an average one. But, as you know, the people who manage companies don't really care what you or I think. If somebody sells a company on the idea that any kind of testing will help it hire better people and the company invests thousands and in some cases hundreds of thousands of dollars in this testing, it's going to use it—no matter what.

Does the testing work? Well, it certainly creates an environment of homogeneous people. Being included or eliminated in the interviewing process by a testing procedure is just as valid or invalid as any of the other crazy reasons by which you may be included or eliminated. And it's like the old joke of the guy who snaps his fingers to keep the pink elephants away. Since he keeps snapping his fingers and no one sees any pink elephants, this system works. If companies never hire anybody who doesn't do well on whatever kind of testing they have, they never really know how valid it may be.

My gut—and it is only my gut—tells me that the companies that use any kind of testing don't have any more or less success or turnover than companies that don't. But, hey, what do I know? They ain't asking me my opinion, and they don't care. If they invest in testing, claim that it gets them better employees, and so on, then I guess it does. (I worked with a company five or six years ago that hired a CEO. It had had a succession of three CEOs in three years—all miserable failures. The company hired a candidate of mine, and after a couple of weeks on the job she was given, the company discovered that she hadn't taken the company's testing. She was given the tests, and the tests indicated that she would not be successful. Well, the company certainly couldn't let her go over that, so, as with a lot of stuff that goes on in businesses, nobody said a word and just let it be. She was not only one of the most successful CEOs the company ever had, but grew the company 115 percent in four years. When the company was sold, she and the major stockholders made millions of dollars. The company is now a division of a major corporation, and, guess what—it still uses the testing to qualify candidates before hiring them. Go figure!)

How to Take Tests

First, whatever you do, don't bitch and moan to the prospective employer that testing is a lot of nonsense. In some cases, it very well is, but if a prospective employer does it as a routine part of the selection process, your opinion isn't going to matter. If you voice your negative opinion too much, you'll be eliminated for that reason alone. So, just decide to take the test in stride and resolve to do the very best you can. And, don't say something stupid like, "Oh, my God, I'm absolutely awful when it comes to tests." This may be true, but for goodness sake, don't tell that to a prospective employer.

Second, before you go to take the test, get lots of rest, eat a good meal, and relax. Do the very best you can. Look at it as a challenge. Take it in stride. Trying to prepare for it is hard. Do not be overanalytical and agonize over each answer, nor be flippant about the answers that you give.

While not as prevalent as they used to be, there are still some companies out there that test candidates with a face-to-face interview with a psychologist or psychiatrist. If this kind of thing is involved in your interviewing process, approach it the same way as you would approach a paper-and-pencil or computerized test. Be thoughtful of your answers. Be consistent in your answers and, for goodness sake, don't try to read into every question what the interviewer is trying to get at. That's a losing proposition. Don't become belligerent, challenging, or argumentative with the interviewer.

No matter what you do, no matter what kind of test you're given, whether it be multiple interviews with the psychologist or psychiatrist, written essays, multiple-choice, intelligence, character, or personality tests, do not try to outguess the test! Don't sit there and ask yourself, "What are they trying to find out when they ask that question?" because if they're trying to find out "that," then I will answer "this" so that they will think "that" of me, you're finished! You can't outguess them.

If you do this you are going to be given a computerized test, psychological test, or the like, you might want to go online and practice with tests that you can buy for yourself. Tons of intelligence and psychological tests are available on the Internet for very reasonable prices. Some even give feedback and corrective advice. Studies have shown that practicing some kinds of tests makes you better. You're not likely to be able to do this with psychological or personality tests, but you certainly can with math or intelligence tests. So, practice when possible.

Drug Tests and Physicals

Drug tests and physicals are part of the hiring process for many companies. I can address these in one short, simple sentence: *You cannot avoid them and you cannot argue with the results.* If a physical is required, you probably already know what the results will be. If you have any physical problem that will be discovered, it is best to ask the hiring authority before the exam what criteria are being used and what the concerns are on the part of the hiring organization. Physicals are most often done in relation to the particular job that the company has in mind. These kinds of tests are supposed to be related to the job function. Executive-level physicals, for insurance purposes, may not be technically legal. But, legal or not, if you refuse for any reason to take the physical, you will probably be eliminated as a candidate.

I have never known an organization to retest or reconsider hiring a candidate who has already been turned down for failing a drug test. Nor have I heard of a company that will consider hiring a candidate who refuses to take the standard drug test. We had a candidate a number of years ago who claimed that a drug test would violate his religious convictions! Oh, boy! We also had a candidate a few years ago—a very professional one, I might add—who, after she failed a drug test, claimed that it really wasn't her fault, that her brother had thrown a bag of cocaine at her, it burst and she accidentally inhaled the cocaine and therefore failed a drug test. We can certainly give her high points for creativity, but she still failed the drug test and didn't get hired.

Look at the list of mistakes I presented at the beginning of this chapter. You now are so much better prepared than 95 percent of the job candidates you are competing with.

11 How to Prepare Yourself for the Interview— and the Toughest Interview Questions

I'VE SHOWN YOU HOW TO GET INTERVIEWS—the key to your job search—and given you a basic script to follow during the initial interview to sell yourself through to additional interviews. I've also given you pointers on how to handle those subsequent interviews. In this chapter, I'm going to show you how to overcome underlying obstacles that can cost job candidates during the interview itself. Your dress, body language, and delivery are important because they set the overall tone for any interview. However, the critical measure here is your mastery of the art of answering interview questions.

> "Until I heard you discuss it on your radio program yesterday, I really thought I knew how to answer interview questions. I never imagined that I was a 'risk' to a prospective employer." —John T., *The Job Search Solution* radio caller

Dressing for the Interview

It's ridiculous that I even have to cover this, but it never ceases to amaze me how people don't know how to dress for an interview. Just the other day I sent a candidate with twenty solid years of excellent consulting experience, working with top Fortune 500 firms, earning $250,000 a year, to an interview. She dressed in what the employer considered to be "a sun dress and sandals." She claimed her outfit wasn't that bad, and that she wasn't dressed inappropriately. Yes, she wore a sleeveless dress with thin straps connecting the back to the front, but it was comfortable for a Dallas summer. And she wore designer shoes, even if they looked like sandals. Oh, brother!

So, get this. For *all* business interviews, you should look like a very conservative banker: dark suit—navy blue or dark blue, maybe gray or charcoal gray—and a white shirt or blouse, conservative tie, modest blouse, conservative business shoes with black or blue socks, neutral skin-tone pantyhose for women. Unless you're twenty-five years old and interviewing with a dot-com company, you need to dress this way for every interview you go on. Even if you are overdressed, do it anyhow. It's much better than being underdressed.

This also means no sport coats, double-breasted suits, short-sleeve shirts, and nothing other than a conservative tie—no polka dots, loud ties that have pictures of baseballs, footballs, basketballs, ducks, geese, fish, etc. In short, no casual dress, no big jewelry, no cleavage, no short skirts (don't give me this garbage that you aren't sure how short a "short skirt" is), no gold chains around your neck or on your ankle. Also, no smells—bad breath, body odor (it's amazing I even have to write this, but equally amazing are the number of people who have these problems and don't rectify them for interviews). This also means no perfume or cologne. And cover your tattoos. Don't wear a hat or a Mickey Mouse watch. Remove the tongue or nose studs. Don't have stars painted on your fingernails, or any one-day-old facial hair. (In fact, I don't really like facial hair at all—many people will tell you they don't trust people with beards.) This is an interview, not a date.

People will give me this nonsense that the business climate has changed and that things are a lot more casual now. Look, there are sixteen to forty-three qualified people who can be interviewed for every job. If you want to run the risk of being eliminated because of poor taste in dress, I guess that's your prerogative. And you can justify it if you wish. But just remember that you are at a big disadvantage if you don't dress appropriately. Dressing conservatively is rarely a risk!

Body Language

My experience has been that in at least 50 percent of the cases in which an interview goes poorly, it begins to go poorly on the part of the candidate because of his or her body language. Many hiring authorities, during the interviewing process, don't help with their body language, either. And there is a tendency to take on the body language of the person with whom you, as a candidate, are interviewing.

One good way to build rapport with an interviewing authority is to assume the basic posture that the person is assuming in the initial stages of the interview. If the person crosses his or her arms or leans back in the chair, it isn't a bad idea for you to cross your arms and lean back in the chair, at least in the first few minutes of the interview. As the interview goes on, however, you want to present yourself in a more open, direct, and assertive manner. It is important that, for the majority of the interview, you have your feet planted flat on the floor, your arms are open (at your side or on the arms of a chair), and you lean forward just enough to make good eye contact with the interviewing authority.

Another pitfall is coming across as too animated and nervous. This kind of thing happens when the candidate is too intense. He or she leans forward almost to the point of being in the interviewer's face, speaking loudly, nervously, and quickly, and waving his or her arms to emphasize a point. Being enthusiastic is one thing, but being so animated that it puts people off is another; that certainly isn't going to win friends and influence people. Invading the other person's space isn't a good idea.

Remember: If your body language isn't appropriate, your words may never be heard. I have known too many candidates who, over the years, have blown interviews because they simply didn't practice interviewing. I've never figured out how people will spend literally hours figuring out answers to some oddball interview questions, most of which they will never be asked, and not simply practicing their interviewing techniques, especially their body language. Practice, practice, practice.

Delivery

Along with body language, you need to be certain that you communicate your answers with enthusiasm, focus, and a high degree of confidence. Most people, especially in the beginning of interviewing cycles, are scared. I can't tell you the number of accomplished professionals I've interviewed over the years who mumbled when they talked, didn't look people in the eye, spoke in a monotone, and seemed distracted and uninterested, when in reality, they were scared.

You need to communicate decisiveness, confidence, enthusiasm, and conviction with every answer. *Remember*: If your delivery isn't effective, you will never be heard. Practice, practice, practice.

The Top Five Mistakes Candidates Make in Answering Interview Questions

Check yourself to see if you've done these things in the past, and make sure you don't repeat them.

1. *They don't understand or think about what the employer is asking from the employer's point of view.* Candidates don't stop and think if the employer is asking, "Can I do the job? Do they like me? Am I a risk? (. . . and what kind?) Can we work the money out?" Candidates have to realize from what point of view the employer is acting and answer accordingly.

2. *They answer interviewing questions from their point of view.* They try to justify things like being fired, being out of work six months, getting laid off, etc., from their own point of view. They try to explain that they are right and they were wronged by someone else.

3. *They start answering the questions before they clearly understand them.* People are so nervous in an interviewing situation, they start answering a question before they really understand what's being asked. There's nothing wrong with asking the hiring or interviewing authority to restate a question for you to get a better understanding of it.

4. *They adopt an "I think great on my feet!" attitude.* They will think, *I'm not worried about answering questions. I will do fine at ad-libbing the answers.* This kind of attitude leads to disaster. No matter how well a person thinks on his or her feet, the interviewing process is more sophisticated than it has ever been. Ad-libbing won't hack it.

5. *They don't practice.* You've got to practice answering questions to the point where you're prepared for just about any interview situation. Answering questions well takes a lot of practice and preparation! The candidates who prepare well for interviewing questions get the offers.

The Art of Answering Interview Questions

Most of the literature (both books and hundreds of articles about finding a job) addresses the kinds of questions that a person needs to be prepared for in an interviewing situation. In fact, some books devote the majority of their pages to providing answers for traditional questions that you will get in an interview. It is a very good idea to have answers to most of the traditional questions, but what I am going to do for you is provide the *underlying rationale* for all of the questions that will be asked. If you understand these underlying reasons, you will understand the art of answering interview questions.

Every question that you will be asked, in every interviewing situation, can be categorized under four subjects. If you understand the four subjects, then your answers will be a natural outgrowth of your understanding. The four subjects that all interviewing questions fall under are:

1. Can you do the job?

2. Do we like you?

3. Are you a risk?

4. Can we work the compensation out?

Look and sound familiar? Yes, it is that simple.

So, let's begin. Here, I will present a number of the most frequently asked questions in interviewing situations and categorize them under each of the four topics. When you catch on to why these questions are being asked, knowing how to answer them will be very easy. I will set the stage for the answer to each question in light of the subject category it falls under; after a while, you'll be able to figure out your own answers very easily. (As an exercise, at the end of the first three sections, I'll ask you some questions and allow you to answer them.)

Can You Do the Job?

John calls me after his interview.

JOHN: It really went great. They really liked me and I like them.

TONY: How long was the interview?. . . and did you communicate that you could do the job?

JOHN: It lasted about an hour and a half. I met with three different people. And of course I can do their job. It's obvious from my background and my experience that I can do their job.

TONY: Okay . . . but how do you know that?

JOHN: Well, we discussed some of what I did. We don't have to worry about that—it's obvious from my résumé that I can do their job. I've done exactly what they want done in my last two jobs.

Conversation with the client:

TONY: Troy, how did it go with John today?

TROY: Well, Tony, we really liked him, but after he left, the three of us got together and found out that none of us was really sure of exactly what he did at the Lancet Company. We're not sure of his track record and what he actually did there. As a matter of fact, we all walked away very impressed, but when we put our heads together to discuss all the candidates we found out that none of us really knew what he had done before and if he could do our job.

Your other two candidates weren't as personable, but it was clearer in their interviewing that they can do exactly what we want done. We'll keep John on the back burner.

Here's the lesson: John did not make it clear to everyone that he was capable of doing the job.

The answer to this question—whether or not you can do the job—accounts for 20 percent of the hiring decision. You say, "Wait a minute . . . are you telling me that my ability to do the job amounts to only 20 percent of the hiring decision?" Yes, that's exactly what I'm saying. However, it is the *first* 20 percent of the hiring decision. It is a threshold you have to cross before you get to any of the other questions.

Most authors who write about finding a job have never been in the position of listening to anywhere near the number of hiring authorities that I have. Most hiring authorities are going to *tell you*—and me, and anyone else who'll listen—that a candidate's ability to do the job is the most important assessment they need to make. That is the party line, and they're going to stick to it. But I have seen thousands of candidates who were minimally qualified, if not totally unqualified, get hired. And those thousands of hired candidates were offset by the thousands more qualified candidates who were *not* hired.

The reason this happens is that successful candidates are the ones who can communicate and convince a hiring authority of their ability to do the job well enough—just well enough to get hired. The rest of the successful interviewing process centers on the other three questions. The mistaken *assumption* that most candidates make is that it is obvious to everyone else that they can do the job. As John expressed, "Why of course I can do the job . . . any idiot can see that!" But this assumption is the Big Mistake! The hiring or interviewing authority *doesn't know that!*

The very first thing a candidate needs to do in the interviewing process is to make clear to the hiring authority that he or she is capable of doing the job. And the best way to do this is to demonstrate to the interviewing or hiring authority that you have done a similar job very successfully in the past. It is *your* responsibility to make it very clear to a hiring authority that you can do the job you are interviewing for. And it is likely that you are going to have to s-p-e-l-l it out in very, very clear terms . . . that the person will understand.

The questions you are going to be asked will be "What did you do?"–type questions. The interviewer is trying to discover your skill level or, in some cases, your potential.

There are going to be only four or five *factual* aspects of your work history that will either get you to the second interviewing stage or will eliminate you from consideration.

- *"Tell me about yourself and your last few jobs."* If you've developed and used the presentation I provided in the chapter on initial interviewing, you will not need to be asked this question. You will have already answered it in the presentation that you gave about yourself. However, if you haven't given your basic job history and you need to answer this question, it is the perfect time to begin your presentation as I've outlined earlier.

- *"What kind of job are you looking for?"* In other words, "Is what you're looking for the same thing that I'm looking for?" If you have done your research, you will know exactly what kind of position you are interviewing for. If not, then the answer is, "I'm looking for a position that is going to help make a company better and challenge me based on my experience and background."

- *"Describe in detail your last two positions."* Even if you did a good job with your presentation on the last two or three jobs you had (what you did, how you did it, for whom you did it, and how successful you were), you still may get this question. Give exactly the same description that you gave in your presentation, maybe with a little more detail. Be sure to precede your answer to this question with, "I really loved that job."

- *"What was the most difficult part of your past two jobs?"* Whatever your answer is, you need to say, "Even though that was the most difficult part of the job, I met the challenge every time." Then communicate in appreciative, upbeat tones the hardest part of the job. You can even add something like, "Meeting that challenging part of the job made me a better person."

- *"What are you looking for in a job?"* Obviously, you need to respond to this question with an answer that has something to do with the job or position for which you are applying. Make sure that you say something along the lines of, "I've enjoyed the challenge of learning in just about every job I've had."

- *"Describe the best job that you've ever had and why it was so much better."* Whatever you describe, make it similar to the position for which you are currently interviewing. A great way to precede the answer is to say, "You know, there have been some wonderful aspects to just about every job I've had. I have really loved all of them, and they are all 'best' for different reasons."

- *"How do you define success?"* Simple answer: "When I contribute to a successful organization, I am successful—we both grow. Growing as a person through the growth of a company and the people I work with is my measure of success." Then perhaps relate a *story* about how successful you were in your last one or two jobs. Remember, people love stories.

- *"What is your greatest accomplishment in each of your last three jobs?"* Be sure to tell a story about the best accomplishment you had in each job. Whatever attribute was associated with the accomplishment; it needs to be supported by a short, interesting story. (Practice one, two, or three stories that you might use throughout the whole interviewing process.)

- *"What made you choose to become a_____?"* It doesn't matter what job title fills in the blank. You need to be able to say that you always had an inclination or a passion for some aspect of your profession. Maybe you had a mentor, parent, or teacher who modeled the kind of profession that you got into. Whatever you do, do not communicate that you stumbled into your profession, it chose you, you couldn't find anything better to do, or you figured it was as good as any profession.

- *"What would be your ideal work group? How would you define a 'good-fit' work environment? Do you work well with other people? Do you prefer to work alone or with other people? Do you require and appreciate lots of supervision? Do you work best with large groups or small groups?"* Any questions related to working alone or with others, in large or small groups, need to be answered with something like, "Well, I've had the good fortune of being able to work in all kinds of different environments. I have worked well alone and with others, in relaxed work environments and in tension-riddled work environments, in big groups and in small groups. I find that, fortunately, I am adaptable and work well in just about any environment."

- *"Describe the situation in your last one or two jobs where you made a mistake. What was the mistake and how did you rectify it?"* Be ready for an "in hindsight" type of answer. Give the example, but highlight what you learned from it. Have one or two of these kinds of stories available for this question when you get it.

- *"What are the things that you find most difficult to do? And how did you deal with them?"* If you are an accountant, engineer, a technical person (or anybody who is analytical or kinesthetic), the answer should center on what your personality is not. For instance, if you are an accountant or an engineer in an organization, you would say that the most difficult thing you have to do is operate in a sales function. If you are a salesperson, then you would say that the most difficult thing you have to do is operate in an accounting or engineering function. This may seem rather obvious, but the answer is very safe.

- *"Why should I hire you?"* As soon as you hear this question, you should be ready to reply, "Because I can do the job, I'm a hard worker, people like me, I'm not a great risk, and we can come to a conclusion about money."

INTERVIEW EXERCISE 1

Prepare answers for the following basic questions. You're going to get questions like them over and over on interviews. (Where possible, your answers to many of these questions should describe when and how you were successful in the past.)

1. Can you walk me through a day in your current or most recent job?

2. Are you creative?

3. What do you know about the position you are applying for?

4. How do we know that you will be successful at this job?

5. What is the most recent business lesson you have learned and how did you learn it?

6. What specifically have you learned from the jobs that you held most recently?

7. What can you contribute most to our organization?

8. What do you know about our business? What is our business's biggest challenge or problem? What trends do you see in our profession or industry? What do you know about our competition? What do you know about our company?

9. Can you describe a difficult business problem that you had to deal with and how you handled it?

10. Where have you made difficult decisions before and what were they about? What makes you think you can handle this position?

11. Why did you apply to our company?

12. I don't think with your experience and background you are capable of doing this job. What do you think?

Do I [We] Like You?

Devin calls me after his interview:

DEVIN: Tony, it went great. I don't have exactly the experience that they're looking for, but we really hit it off. I had just a great feeling about it. They should hire me . . . I really want to work there.

Conversation with a client:

TONY: Mr. Foley, how did the interview go with Devin?

MR. FOLEY: Tony, of all of the candidates you sent us, he's probably the least qualified. We think he has enough skills to be able to do the job—but barely. But, man, he just fits into our company so well. He's about our age. We all have kids about the same age he has. We have the same kind of hobbies. Heck, he even goes to the same church that one of the guys here does.

We are going to have him back to really assess his skills, to be sure that he can do the job, but we're pretty excited about him. The others you sent were really good, but this guy's special.

Devin got hired two days later.

Once a hiring or interviewing authority has established the first 20 percent of questions like "Can you do the job?" the next really big question is, "Do we like you?" These questions account for 40 percent of the hiring decision. Most people don't like to hear this and even argue with me about it. But the truth is that none of us hire people whom we don't like. Hordes of qualified candidates do not get hired because they aren't as likable as other, less qualified candidates . . . like Devin.

I've never met a candidate, no matter how qualified, who wasn't hired without being minimally liked by the company and the hiring authority. Unless you're in a very scientific or analytical position where you have minimal interaction with other people, your being liked by the people you are going to work for makes a very big difference in your being hired.

So what does this mean? It means that if you're not already an affable, somewhat enthusiastic person who interacts well with people, you'd best practice being that way for interviews. The first rule of thumb is to appear energetic, engaging, and attentive, leaning forward in your chair. And after you've answered the questions below, smile and be sure to ask people about their favorite subject—*themselve*s. Then listen to what they have to say, respond enthusiastically, and ask more questions about their favorite subject—*themselves*. Interact based on what they say and then ask them about their second most favorite subject—*their kids*. Listen enthusiastically, be responsive, and then ask them about their third most important subject—*their company and their job*.

The "Do we like you?" questions can have a tendency to get under your skin. So the way to prepare for them is to either use the answers that I've given here or come up with your own, but practice them with your coach. Many candidates, who aren't particularly "people people," will complain that this kind of thing shouldn't happen, that it's not fair. They complain that hiring authorities ought to focus on the candidate's ability to do the job rather than being likable. "That shouldn't be that important," they tell me.

Even interviewing and hiring authorities will never really admit that liking the candidate is that important. They will claim that this kind of thing doesn't matter that much. Don't buy it! Most employers will not admit to being that fickle or influenced by someone's personality. But it is true. So, here are samples of "Do we like you?" questions:

- *"Are you a leader or follower?"* Simple answer: "Well, in certain situations I am a leader and in certain situations I am a follower. I can be both." Then reinforce this answer with stories, if necessary.

- *"What do people like most about you? What do they like least?"* Things like being a team player, getting along well with others, dealing well in tense situations, volunteering when you don't have to, perseverance, communication skills, and so forth always work well. Being a perfectionist, wanting to see things done right, assuming control when no one else steps forward, or correcting coworkers when they've done something wrong work well as things people don't like about you (but employers do).

- *"What are your three greatest strengths? Three greatest weaknesses?"* Strengths should be easy for you to come up with. Weaknesses are always difficult. What works well is saying things like, "Well, I'm very impatient with myself . . . I often expect the same passion and commitment from the others that I tend to have . . . I'm working on becoming a better listener." Make sure your weaknesses can also be viewed as strengths. Ask your coach to help you with these because you are going to get this question or something like it.

- *"What do you like and dislike about your present (or last) boss?"* This question has nothing to do with your boss; it has to do with how you express what you think of him or her. Badmouthing your present or previous bosses or company is the kiss of death. Have something positive ready to say and tone any criticism way, way down. You can begin by saying, "We didn't always see eye to eye," and go on to describe a situation where you disagreed with your boss. Tell a story.

- *"How do you handle criticism?"* How you react to this question is as important as your answer. If you look startled like a deer in headlights, you will be communicating the wrong idea. Just expect to be asked this question and immediately respond by saying, "I really do appreciate constructive criticism; feedback is the breakfast of champions."

- *"Do you ever lie?"* This is another catch-22 question. The best thing to do is admit that you do lie in some rare instances when telling the truth has no consequences other than to hurt someone's feelings. For instance, you might say, "If I'm invited to a social occasion that I really don't want to go to, I will say that I have other plans. I guess, technically, that is a lie, but I see no sense in hurting other people's feelings by telling them that I don't wish to socialize with them." Then shut up. If the interviewer probes your response, simply say, "It is important to be truthful in every business dealing. I think lying is basically wrong and should only be used in situations as the last graceful alternative where the results are inconsequential."

- *"If you knew then what you know now, how would you change your life or your career?"* This is a really good question and you need to have a really good answer for it. You should mention things that might be obvious. For instance, if you have not completed your degree, you might say that, looking back on it, you would have finished your degree. If you have had a couple of very short jobs on your résumé, you might say that if you knew then what you know now, you wouldn't have taken those jobs. You should discuss any obvious mistake or misstep in your career; admit to it, and add the fact that you have learned a lot from the mistake. You might also add in summation, "The important thing, for me, is that I've learned from every mistake I've ever made and, fortunately, I haven't made the same mistake more than once. I know I will make others, but I'm going to make the best of what I learn from them." Do not say that you wouldn't change a thing because, even if it's true, not many people would believe you.

• *"What is your definition of success? Of failure? And how do you rate yourself in these two categories?"* This is a loaded question that has no correct answer. But try something along the lines of, "Well, success for me is the constant pursuit of a worthy goal where I am personally growing and economically providing for myself and my family. The only definition of failure, for me, would be when people quit trying and give up. Failure is not an option for me. I'd rate myself as 'constantly striving' and I don't think there's a number for that."

INTERVIEW EXERCISE 2

Prepare answers and review with your coach! (Think! Be reasonable! If you didn't know you, how do the answers sound? Rewrite your initial answers if you have to.)

1. What are one or two things your present or previous coworkers *dislike* about you?

2. What makes you mad?

3. How do you make your opinions known when you disagree with management or your boss?

4. Rate yourself on a scale of one to ten.

5. How would others at your current or previous jobs rate you on a scale of one to ten?

6. What makes you better than any other candidate I can hire?

Remember, when it's your turn to ask these kinds of questions, you should ask people about their most important subject—themselves.

Are You a Risk?

Discussion with client after my candidate interview:

TONY: Tom, I spoke with Jon, whom you interviewed this morning. He was absolutely thrilled and would love the opportunity to come back and speak with you all. What did you think of him?

TOM: Tony, he couldn't have nailed it any better. His background, experience, and personality are exactly what we're looking for. He is unquestionably the best candidate that you've sent us in the past three months, and God knows, I'm sick of interviewing. I had absolutely no idea it was going to be this hard to find someone. I like him so well, I had my boss interviewing, because he happened to be here in our office today. And the truth is, he loved him, too.

But Tony, in spite of the fact that we loved him, this guy has had three jobs in three years. He's got "risk" written all over him. The executive vice president would go nuts if we tried to hire this guy. He'd say something like, "What are you thinking, Tom? I don't care how good this guy is, he's had three jobs in three years. How long do you think he's going to be with us? . . . one year! Don't even consider it. He's a ridiculous risk and I thought you were smarter than that."

Since 1973, I have never met a candidate who thought he or she was a risky hire for a company. The truth is, every hire is a risk. There is actually no way of knowing if a new hire is going to work out. No one can predict the future. If you've gotten anything from this book so far, you realize that especially in today's business environment, hiring authorities are more afraid of making a mistake than they have ever been before. This happens every time we come out of a recession, and it's going to be this way for some time.

As I've mentioned, companies are hiring more out of fear of loss than they are vision of gain. They are afraid of making a mistake. Just like Tom, they are afraid of looking back on an employee who turns out to be a bad hire and having their supervisors say, "Couldn't you tell this person was going to be a mistake. He or she had too many recent jobs, had been out of work for six months, had been fired, was the president of his own company," and on and on.

The answer to "Are you a risk?" accounts for 30 to 40 percent of the hiring decision, depending on the economy. If candidates are easy to find, it amounts to 40 percent. If candidates are harder to find, it's closer to 30 percent. But it is still a big issue in the hiring decision. Now, most people are going to argue the dickens out of this. Most hiring authorities are going to deny it. They are going to say, "Oh, no, we hire people recognizing their upside potential." B.S. They are worried about how they will look if the new person they hire does not work out. They don't want to look bad, and they are so afraid of looking stupid that they are going to actually *look* for reasons why you, as a candidate, won't work out.

There you have it. Don't let hiring authorities kid you by telling you that they are very comfortable with taking risks on people, that they'll hire "outside the box," that their supervisors totally trust them in their hiring expertise. It is a lie. If they are so good at hiring and their company believes in them so well, why do you, as a candidate, have to go through umpteen interviews? If the hiring authority were so damn good at hiring, he or she would be the *only person* you'd have to interview with! These authorities may have to personally interview you two or three times, but if they were as good as they say, they are they'd be the only one to make a decision.

The reason you need to know that being a risk is so great a part of the hiring decision is that you need to recognize what kind of risk you might pose to a prospective employer and offset the risk in the interviewing process.

Here are some issues that spell R-I-S-K to a prospective employer: too many recent jobs . . . been out of work for a long period of time (no matter what the reason) . . . being the president of a company . . . own your own company . . . want to change careers . . . been a consultant . . . getting back into the workforce after being out of it for a while . . . coming off maternity leave . . . being with too big a company . . . being with too small a company . . . being a married woman of childbearing age . . . having been fired . . . having been laid off . . . earning too much money . . . not earning enough mone . . . having small children (for a woman) . . . being a single parent . . . being in management and willing to take a step back . . . and the list goes on.

As you can see, *everyone* is somewhat of a risk. That is the point. You need to be aware of what *your* risk factors are and offset them in the interviewing process. We're going to discuss some of these things and how to deal with them. Just remember that in today's business climate, with hiring authorities afraid of hiring the wrong person, you have to reassure them that whatever issues there are in your background or experience, they are not going to get in the way of you being a good employee.

These are going to be the most difficult questions you will be asked. They're going to encroach on your character, your judgment, and the quality of your decisions, both personally and professionally. The real question imbedded in this subject is, "What kind of risk are you?" And along with that, "Am I, as a hiring authority, willing to run the risk and put my reputation on the line with this person?"

It's a trade-off. A hiring authority wants to minimize his or her risk but get as many benefits as possible from hiring someone. With every risk you present, you have to offset those risks with the benefits you can provide.

Most candidates don't recognize the risks that they present to a prospective employer. In fact, many things that a candidate thinks are positive attributes might very well be a big liability to most employers. For instance, most people who have owned their own business or been the president of the company think that that these are great reasons for why they should be hired. Trust me, they aren't. Most hiring authorities are afraid of people who have owned their own business or run a company because they think that if they hire them they will come into their company and tell them how the company ought to be run. Their attitude is, "Well, if you were so good at running a business, why are you interviewing with me?" So, if you've been the president of your own firm and you're being compared to four or five other candidates, it is likely that those four or five other candidates have *one less risk factor* than you do. It's that simple.

You better analyze and know what the risks are that come with hiring you.

• *"Why do you want to leave where you are?"* or *"Why did you leave your last position?"* This is one of the biggest "What kind of a risk are we taking?" questions you will be asked. The answer to this question is one that will either effectively end the interviewing process for you or enhance the rest of the interviewing process. The key to this answer is to be as non-self-oriented as you can make it. An interviewing or hiring authority will assume that you will leave the company somewhere down the line for exactly the same reasons that you are leaving where you are now or you've left the last position. Employers identify with employers.

Being currently employed and looking to leave when you have been employed by that company for a relatively long period of time—say, five years or more—and you are looking to leave because you are not growing personally or do not have the opportunity to grow beyond your job is a better reason to be leaving the position than new management coming in and not liking you. You have to be truthful in this answer, but you also have to spin it so that you communicate a good business reason for yourself and for a future organization.

Again, saying anything negative or disparaging about the company that you are presently with, or have left is not going to do you well. Anything negative about the people whom you were working for or have worked for will shoot you in the foot. If the hiring authority and hiring company have a tremendous amount of "pain" (that is, they really need to hire somebody or they are desperate to fill a position), they are less likely to care about why you are looking to leave or why you left your last employer. So, if you sense that the need to fill a position is great, you don't have to be quite as concerned about how analytical they will be with your answer to this question.

However, few organizations are so desperate to fill a position that they are not going to carefully analyze the answer to this question. Whatever you do, you have to communicate that you like your present job and the present organization that you work with. You are leaving simply because you are capable of doing more for an organization and therefore growing both personally and professionally.

Your answers should be along the lines of "Well, I really love my job, I really like the people I work with, and I appreciate everything the organization has done for me. However, the organization is in the process of being sold (is under new management . . . has been contracting for the past few years . . . because of its size, it isn't going to grow, and so forth) and I am personally stymied in my professional challenge and personal growth. I can stay in the position that I am in, and I am not threatened, but for the next few years, I'm not going to be able to grow beyond the job I'm in now."

If you communicate self-oriented answers like, "I need more money or I want a better title or I'm going nowhere in my present firm," you'll be dead in the water.

- *"You sure stayed short periods of time in your last three jobs. What's wrong?"* The obvious fear behind this question is that, if you are hired, you will stay at this job for only a short time. Your answer has to be one where you do what is called in sales "changing the base."

  The answer goes something like this: "While you are correct that I've had three very short stints in my employment, there are two things that are very important. First, I realize that someone like you is going to look at this as a liability. I don't like it any better than you do; in fact, it has really concerned me. I made mistakes in taking a couple of those positions, and if I knew then what I know now, I would never have done that. The truth is, however, that I really learned from the mistakes.

  "The fact that I've had three relatively short job stints is one of the very reasons I can guarantee stability. I cannot very well afford another short stint at a job, so I am being very careful about the job I take. Whoever hires me is going to get a passionate and committed employee."

  Caution: It does not do any good to try to *justify* two or three short jobs that appear on your résumé. That is a road to disaster. If you have this problem in your background, it will be one of the answers that you have to play down. Practice it.

- *"You've been the president of a company (or the owner of your own company). How do we know that you know how to work for someone else, or that you will take direction?"* This is the underlying fear and concern that all employers have when it comes to hiring someone who has been the president of an organization, run an organization, or owned his or her own company. The idea that the highest manager of an organization would actually work for someone else scares companies.

It is hard for most presidents or company owners to work for someone else. It's an emotional adjustment that is difficult to make. However, it has been done and it can work. The answer to this question is really simple, "Well, you know as president of an organization [or owner of a company], I worked for a lot of different people and I answered to the entire company. I answered to customers, employees, the government, the IRS, my attorneys, my CPAs, insurance companies, vendors . . . and very often, my spouse [laugh]. We all answer to someone. Even your president or company owner answers to someone. I have never met a good leader who couldn't work within any organization, and be part of a team, as well as be a good follower.

"The truth is that we are all really *self-employed*. In reality, we all work for ourselves within an organization. The organization is simply a group of people working with and for themselves. Someone in the organization signs the paycheck, but the truth is that it is earned by the diligence of each individual. That is the way I've approached business when someone else signed my paycheck or when I was responsible for signing the paycheck. In this opportunity, I may not lead the organization, but I still work for myself. My future earnings will be dependent upon how I perform. In this case, the only difference is that someone else will sign the paycheck."

- *"This position is one or two levels below the ones you have had in the past. How do we know we won't hire you and then in six or seven months someone calls you with a position like that and you leave?"* To hire somebody and then have the person leave, for whatever reason, is a great fear for most employers. Other candidates may stay a short period of time and then leave for all kinds of reasons, but the issue of having held higher positions is so glaring, in the onset of the relationship, that the hiring authority is very afraid.

  The wrong answer to this question kills more opportunities for candidates than probably any other question that can be asked. You need to really think about whatever answers you are going to come up with and put yourself in the shoes of the interviewing or hiring authority. Ask yourself, "If I didn't know me as I do and I was being compared with a number of other equally qualified candidates, how does my answer to this question make me look?" If the answer to this question makes you look like a dedicated, committed, reasonably well performing employee, who for good business reasons is looking for a job, you'll be fine. If your answer does anything less than that, you're dead in the water.

So, here is your best answer: "Mr. or Ms._____, in every company in which I've ever worked, I've always started out at a position one or two levels below what I eventually attained. I realize exactly what I'm getting into with this job and the opportunity that you have outlined for me. I have no intention of wasting anyone's time, money, or effort, especially mine or yours. I wouldn't be trying to get this position if I didn't think that it would be challenging, gratifying work and that I wouldn't have a really good future with this organization. In the past, when I have been in the lower-level positions with the companies in which I worked, I would get calls from time to time about interviewing at other organizations or other companies for higher-level positions. But I was very happy where I was. I enjoyed the work, I was challenged and, frankly, the compensation followed my being happy, content, and challenged in the job."

- *"Were you fired? Why were you fired?"* If you follow the script that I have recommended about presenting yourself and each job you had (how you performed and why you left), this question may never come up. But, if it does, you must not communicate any kind of emotion or anger.

  I strongly recommend that you *do not* answer this question with something like, "It's the best thing that ever happened to me. It was a blessing in disguise. The job wasn't working out, anyhow. The job just wasn't for me." These kinds of answers have a tendency to come across as flippant and arrogant. The employer thinks, "Well, if getting fired was such a blessing, or the job wasn't working out anyway, or the job wasn't right, why did you keep the job?"

  I hope that if you were in a position to be fired, you got your most recent organization to lay you off rather than fire you. The difference between being fired and being laid off connotes an adversarial discharge for cause in the former case and an involuntary, at least on your part, separation, usually for economic reasons, on the part of the company that let you go in the latter. There is less stigma in being laid off. Different companies have different policies regarding what they will tell a prospective employer about why a person was terminated or laid off. The terminology may not be important to your previous employer, but it is very important to your future employment.

  If the last organization you were with formally states that you were laid off rather than terminated, you can honestly look the interviewing or hiring authority in the eye and say that you were laid off. It is important to say something along the lines of, "I really loved that job and the opportunity it afforded me. I learned a lot from those people and the time I spent there was gratifying."

Being fired is tricky, but you obviously have to face up to it. It is rare for an employee to do well in a company for two or three years and then suddenly become a bad employee. So, the longer you had been on the job that you were ultimately terminated or fired from, the easier it is to say, "I really loved that company and I was there for a reasonably long time. I performed well, but there came a time for us (the company and me) to make a change." Looking the interviewer in the eye, you can then quickly follow up with, "And before that, I was at _____ company, where I performed very well."

Answering this question, when you have no other choice but to admit you were fired, *takes more practice than probably any other answer you will ever give in an interviewing situation.* Practice! Practice! Practice!

If you were fired for cause (and you're pretty sure that a prospective employer is going to find out that you were fired, rather than laid off), the best thing to do is to explain exactly what happened, in your opinion. You shouldn't criticize or denigrate your previous employer. Communicate the idea that although you don't agree with your former employer's decision, you respect it. In order to overcome the situation where you were fired for cause (and there is no way around having to talk about it in the interview), you are going to have to counter being fired with excellent references.

You may say, "Tony, how can I get good references from a company or individuals who fired me?" Well, you can do two things. First, find some individual at the company you were fired from who will, on a personal basis, speak to a prospective employer about what you did, how well you did it, and, at least, provide a personal reference that might offset a formal negative reference. In other words, you are going to counterbalance and neutralize the negative reference.

Second, you must have a plethora of positive, glowing references from previous employers whom you worked with before your last job. Being fired, or let go, just doesn't have the same negative impact if it doesn't stand alone.

• *"If you could start your career over again, what would you do differently?"* This is a trick question. Whatever you do, don't go overboard about all the mistakes that you made and what you would've done much differently. Something along the lines of "You know, I've been fortunate, I haven't made too many mistakes in my career and I sure learned a lot from the ones that I made. There aren't many career choices or decisions that I would change." Then have ready some rather innocuous mistake you can own up to and describe what you learned from it.

INTERVIEW EXERCISE 3

Carefully prepare your answers to the following questions and review them with your coach:

1.   Where do you see yourself five years from now?

2.   How does this job fit into your career goals?

3.   How much time did you take off last year?

4.   Have you ever had personal financial difficulties?

5.   If you inherited a lot of money, say $2 million or $3 million, what would you do?

6.   If a personal commitment conflicts with a business emergency, what do you do?

7.   How long will you stay with us if you are hired?

8.   How do I know that you will stay with us for a reasonable period of time to be effective?

Can We Work the Compensation Out?

Believe it or not, this question accounts for only 10 percent (or at most, 20 percent) of the hiring decision. Most people think that these are some of the most difficult questions to deal with in the interviewing process. In my opinion, if all of the other questions about being able to do the job, being liked, and being a risk are answered, even reasonably well, the questions about money and compensation are easy to deal with. In fact, the answers to these questions are merely an outgrowth of all the previous ones. The more an organization would like to hire you, and the more you would like to work for the organization, the easier it is to work out the compensation. So, the better you sell yourself, the more likely the organization is to compensate you fairly. I discuss negotiating in Chapter 16.

Always associate compensation with performance in the job. This means that every time you answer a question about compensation, you tie it to performance. Your mantra needs to be, "If I perform well, the compensation is going to take care of itself."

The reason most folks think that this is a difficult group of questions to deal with is that compensation is a common denominator. Of all the things you could discuss in the interviewing and job search process, money is the most relative and consistently comparative issue. That is, $100,000 with benefits is $100,000 with benefits (although benefits might vary a bit), whether you're with a big company, a small company, or self-employed. People often focus on money, especially before they interview, simply because it's the only relative common denominator that they can go by. The reason this accounts for only 10 percent of the hiring decision is that, if all of the other questions in the interviewing process are satisfactory, the compensation usually works itself out. And as I tell candidates all the time, you can't reject an offer that you don't get. If the compensation isn't right, simply don't take the job.

- *"What are you currently earning?"* Or *"What were you earning most recently?"* This is a simple question and requires a simple answer. Just share with the hiring or interviewing authority exactly what you have been earning or currently are earning. Whatever you do, don't inflate the numbers. If you are in sales, do not extrapolate the best month that you ever had and annualize it. If you are asked for a salary history, give it accurately. Over the years, I have had many employers ask this question during the interviewing process, and then after a person is hired, call the person's previous employer to verify his or her earnings—only to find out that the candidate lied. The person is then almost always terminated.

  Over the last few years, many companies have started asking for copies of candidates' W2s or tax returns to verify the money they had been earning. I've even had candidates ask me, "Is that legal?" Of course it is! There are lots of illegal questions, but this isn't one of them. Many candidates think that this kind of question is an invasion of privacy. It's nothing of the kind. It's a reasonable request and, the bottom line is, if you don't provide them, you won't get hired. You can complain all you wish, but it isn't going to change a company's procedure.

  Our organization has quite a number of candidates eliminated every year because they embellish what they earned in the past. The hiring authority asked them what they have earned or the question is asked on an application. The candidate writes down what he or she *wants* the employer to believe and before the company goes to hire the candidate it asks for a copy of the last three years' W2s. When the candidate cannot come up with them, because it would prove that he or she lied, or the forms are produced and there is no resemblance to what the candidate has said they have made, the candidate is eliminated. So, if you're asked about what you have earned in the past, you need to be able to prove it. Don't complain, it's reality.

- *"What kind of money would you like to earn?"* You should have some idea about the salary range for the position that you are interviewing for. However, your stock answer in a situation like this is, "Well, I'd like earn as much as I can, commensurate with the service that I give. I am just as interested in a fulfilling and challenging position as I am in the money I want to earn. What kind of money for this position did your organization have in mind?"

Always discuss money in conjunction with the relationship it has to the job. What this communicates is that you are just as interested in doing a good job as you are in the money you will receive.

- *"You have been making $_____ and the money that is associated with this position is significantly less. How do we know that you will be happy?"* In this situation, you have to find out exactly how much of a difference there is between what you have been making and what this particular position pays. If you've been out of work for any amount of time, the truth is, at this point you are making absolutely nothing.

  No matter what the difference between what you have earned in the past and what the company is paying, your answer to this question needs to be something like, "Well, I realize there is a difference between what I have made [or what I am making now] and this position. However, I have found that if the opportunity is right and I am able to perform at my best, the difference in the money isn't as important as the quality of the job and the opportunity."

- *"What is the most money that you have ever made?"* Bragging about making a lot of money will never help in negotiations. If you made an inordinate amount of money several years ago—and many people did, pre-recession—I would recommend not even mentioning it. Again, the answer to this type of question needs to center on not just what you've earned, but also the challenge of the job opportunity itself. Try saying, "There have been a few years in which I've been fortunate enough to be with organizations where bonus earnings were sizable. But I realize that those are very uncommon. I am more interested in the opportunity, the challenge of the job, and the potential. If those things are taken care of, my earnings will reflect my performance."

- *"What do you consider most valuable: a high salary, job recognition, or advancement?"* Again, combining earnings with job performance is the most important thing you can do. Say something like, "Well, I have found that the better job I do, the harder I work, recognition, advancement (and, especially, money) usually take care of themselves."

- *"What kind of benefits are you expecting?"* In the past few years, benefit plans, especially in the health insurance arena, have skyrocketed in cost—particularly for companies with a hundred people or fewer. So, there is no such thing as standard benefits. Many organizations have drastically reduced their benefit plans for their employees. The purpose of this question is to find out if there is going to be a great deal of difference between the kind of benefits that you have had before and the kind of benefits that might be offered with this company. So, answer something like, "Benefits, like money, to me are not as important as the company, the job, and the professional challenge. I will certainly take the benefits package into consideration if an offer is made, but right now those kinds of things shouldn't be an issue."

Other Interview Question Types and Situations

Aside from the four above-mentioned question types, there are a couple of questions you might encounter, and here's how to handle them.

Early Questions About Money

Any questions you are asked about money during the interviewing process before you get to the final offer need to be handled gracefully—in effect, postponing them until the final stages of the job offer. Once you get to that stage, you have established yourself and the value you can bring to the organization. The greater the value you establish for yourself, the more money you will be able to negotiate.

Remember: Always discuss money in relationship to the value you bring to the job.

Illegal or Inappropriate Questions

With the majority of companies in this country having fewer than one hundred people, it probably won't surprise you that some hiring authorities just don't have any idea about what is legal and what isn't. Some will simply ask inappropriate questions, thinking that they're trying to help both you and them. Again, I repeat: Most hiring authorities in the United States just aren't very professional. They might be good at what they do, but they're lousy when it comes to interviewing and hiring people.

Interviewers who ask illegal and inappropriate questions usually do so out of ignorance. However, some people's egos cause them to ignore the law and ask whatever they damn well please. There are better ways to handle these questions.

Many of the following questions are illegal and the ones that may be technically legal seem very inappropriate.

- How old are you?

- Are you married?

- Are you single or divorced?

- Does your spouse work?

- Do you have small children?

- Can you work long hours with your family commitments?

- We have a lot of women (men, whites, blacks, Hispanics, Vietnamese, Asians, Christians, Jews, Muslims, etc.). Will that be a problem for you?

- Where were you born?

- What country are your parents from?

- What is your religion?

- Do you go to church?

- What is your race?

I happen to disagree with the experts who will tell you flat out that, in an interview, you don't have to answer certain questions, especially ones that are illegal. I'm going to tell you to do what you think is best. I'll be the first one to tell you that illegal and inappropriate questions are completely out of line. However, if you really need the job, the legality or inappropriateness of any question is probably way down on your list of priorities. Getting a decent offer is more important.

Even if you think that the hiring or interviewing authority is aware that what he or she is asking is illegal, it may not be a good idea to say, "That is an illegal question and I don't have answer it," or "That is an illegal question and I won't answer it." This kind of answer will challenge the hiring authority and will probably eliminate you as a candidate.

You may want to consider answering the question, depending on the context in which it is asked. If you feel like someone is asking your age, or if you were married, because the person will probably use that information to eliminate you from consideration, then you might say something in a startled, surprised but very *kind* manner like, "Oh, goodness, I didn't know you could ask that question, but . . ." Then answer the question in a way that you think is appropriate.

You might also answer the question with a question, such as, "How does the answer to that question have an impact on my performance of the job or my ability to get it?" This is a very nice way of saying, "That's an illegal question. It has nothing to do with my ability to do the job, so I'm not going answer it." If you feel that the question is being asked out of genuine interest and in sincere empathy—as in a casual conversation after a formal interview—feel free to answer it in any manner that you wish.

Again, follow your instincts and answer these questions in whatever way you are comfortable doing. I don't think it's good to get defensive or stern about the fact that these are illegal questions. Depending on how badly you need a job, you may have to overlook some inappropriate questions, but *you need a job*. Don't let it get in the way. If you think it is appropriate to set someone straight about the illegal questions, feel free to do so. Just don't get your nose out of joint over it. If the questions insult you, don't go to work there.

12 Overcoming Employer Biases That Can Keep You from Getting a Job

THERE ARE MANY THINGS that can hold you back in your job search that would seem to have little to do with your ability to do the job in question. These hindrances fall under the general category of *employer biases.*

Employers may have biases against hiring candidates who have been let go by another employer, who have been out of work too long, who want to change careers, or who have had too many jobs. They may even have unstated (and illegal) biases against hiring older people, women, or minorities. As a job candidate, all you can do is face these kinds of employer biases head on and deal with them as positively as you can. The best solution is to keep knocking on lots of doors, presenting yourself to as many potential employers as possible, and pressing for the right door to open with a good job opportunity.

> "All my friends told me that my age would work against me in my job search. Since I never had trouble finding a job before now, I just didn't believe them—I thought I was different. It's like starting all over. It's depressing. It isn't right and it isn't fair. I am so frustrated. I really need your help." —Joe S., Sarasota, Florida
>
> "I've been out of work for six months. How can these employers hold this against me? Don't they understand that there is a recession? It's unfair. How do I deal with it?" —Mary, *The Job Search Solution* radio caller

These are typical questions I receive and they involve employer bias. Let's go through some of the more common employer biases.

Fired or Laid Off?

Yes, you can find yourself being discriminated against because you were fired or laid off. This can represent a big red flag of liability to most employers. The difference between being fired and being laid off is significant, however. You are going to have to work hard to overcome the stigma of being fired. You are much better off if you can communicate the idea that you were laid off instead.

The Situation

Let's hope that, if you were in a position of potentially being fired, you got your most recent organization to lay you off rather than fire you. Most companies, rather than create a picture of an adversarial bad employee, would rather lay you off than fire you. Unless you were fired for a very serious cause, such as embezzlement or sexually harassing a coworker, most organizations will be amenable to stating that you were laid off.

There are some situations in which a prospective employer is going to more easily understand your being let go or fired. A total change in management, the buyout of a company, or a large downsizing are all acceptable reasons for someone to lose a job. And if your ex-boss gives you a good recommendation, you're in good shape.

What to Say

Chapter 11 took this matter on in relation to the interview questions, so you should review that section as well. As I've said, avoid true confessions and trying to justify what happened from your point of view. You will never win a job that way. In fact, how you present the whole situation of being fired is more important than what you say. You need to practice your presentation over and over again so that you can disassociate yourself emotionally from the actual firing.

Be humble about being fired; it also doesn't hurt to take on some of the responsibility. Say something like, "You know, looking back on it, I would've done a little better about getting those reports to my boss in a more timely fashion," or "Looking back on it, I realize how much pressure my department was under to perform faster than we did."

Remember that you can overcome just about every unfortunate situation regarding why you left your last job if you can establish enough *value* for being hired. In other words, if the benefits of hiring you outweigh the liabilities and risk in hiring you, how you got there won't matter.

Most employers these days are more understanding about being laid off than they were a few years ago. When the economy was strong, it was harder to understand people being laid off or let go. After all, most hiring managers had stable jobs and it was hard for them to appreciate someone who didn't. Well, since this last recession, no one is immune. Most everyone is or was looking over his or her shoulder, wondering who will be next. If you are in this situation, you are still going to have to explain yourself, but folks are a little more tolerant today than a few years ago.

Out of Work for Six Months or More

You were laid off or fired, or you quit your job a while ago—a lot longer time ago than you want to admit. You are really hurt and surprised at having to look for a job, and you thought you would take a little time off to get over the immediate emotional strain. Besides, you really hadn't taken much time off over the years, so . . .

The Situation

It was summertime (or spring, or winter, or the holidays) and you really hadn't spent much time with your kids or your spouse in a while, or you hadn't visited back home (your family, your cousins, and your old friends), so you thought you'd take a little time off. Or, you had some savings and some money in your 401(k), so you thought, "We can live on that for a while." Or, the house needed painting, and once you started painting you thought, "This would be a great time to build onto the house." You lost your job in September or October, and you decided that since nobody does any hiring around the holidays, you'd just take some time off and wait until after the first of the year. You had a friend who had a friend who had a friend who thought there might be an opening in her company in two or three months and you might just be the perfect fit, so you waited . . . and waited . . . and waited, but the job never came about. Since the kids are only little once, you decided to stay home with them so you could really create a great bond with them, and one month led to another and that was six months ago. You always wanted to take time off and see America, so you did.

Problem is, the emotional and mental spiral downward began with the best of intentions! And the problem you have created is at least twofold. First, you now must convince a prospective employer that you are *not* a risk! A prospective employer is going to look at what you have done—or should I say, what you haven't done—for the past six, nine, or whatever months. The prospective employer is going to think, "If this person can afford to be out of work for the past six months, how do I know that if I hire him or her, that three to four months into the job he or she won't just decide to take another sabbatical and leave? I don't think I can afford that!"

The second problem you've created for yourself is that the longer you postpone looking for a job and go unemployed, the harder it is and the longer it is going to take for you to be successful in finding a new job. This is because the mental and emotional downward spiral often creates mild to severe depression. And when people are depressed, they don't interview very well. The longer you go without making a plan to find a job and executing that plan, the harder it is to do!

I don't care what any professional or career counselor or psychologist or psychiatrist—or your mother or your spouse—might tell you, taking any extended period of time off to "clear the cobwebs from your head" and emotionally get used to the idea of looking for a job—by doing any of the things mentioned previously—is nothing but stupid.

When people take an extended period of time to begin looking for a job after they have lost one, they begin to make all kinds of mental and emotional excuses as they spiral downward. They start saying things like, "Well, you know, I passed up a job better than that three or four months ago, so there's no reason for me to take that job." Or, "Well, I always thought that I could call my friends and I knew they would hire me."

A few weeks leads to a few months, and then the person starts thinking, "What's really wrong with me?" Then the unemployment runs out and the savings run out and the 401(k) runs out, and the person begins to panic. And this panic may very well lead to depression. Then the person begins to think, "I'll never find a job"—even if he or she is not taking any action to look for a job. People in this state start telling themselves and their families that "the economy sucks," "we have come out of the worst recession since the 1930s," and "there are no jobs out there." And the whole thing becomes a self-fulfilling prophecy.

If you are reading this before you have hit that sixth-month wall of quasi-depression and confusion, and haven't gotten to that self-fulfilling prophecy of "there are just no jobs out there," *don't* keep doing things that are going to lead to postponing the activities necessary to look for a job. *Start today to work the process of finding a job!* Whatever you do, don't let this downward emotional and mental spiral happen.

If you find yourself mentally and emotionally mired in the sixth-month syndrome, there is only one way to get out of it. And that is to take massive action by beginning to manage the process of finding a job. You cannot postpone it any longer. You have to start reading inspirational and motivational books, listening to inspirational and motivational tapes, and stop reading the newspaper and take all the actions I have recommended. Start at the beginning of this book and throw yourself into the job-finding process.

What to Say

You now need to figure out what you're going to say to a prospective employer when he or she asks you why you've been out of work so long. If in any way, shape, or form you communicate the idea that you could afford to take the time off so you did, you are going to give the employer the idea that you could take another six months off—and it won't bother you one bloody bit. But it will definitely bother him or her. You won't get hired. You are just too much of a risk.

So, you need to say something along this line: "I had no idea how difficult it was going to be to find a job. When I lost my last position, I took a few weeks off and then started to look around and interview fairly casually. I ended up pursuing a couple of opportunities that I waited on way too long. *(If you can be specific about names of companies and names of opportunities, and names of the people whom you were talking to, it adds more credibility.)* I hadn't changed jobs in several years, and, unfortunately I didn't know how difficult the process would be. I've been earnestly looking for a job by proactively going after interviews for the past two months. I am in the cycle with two organizations but I do not have any offers at this moment. Looking back on it, I've miscalculated how difficult the job market was. I thought it would be easier. I have to go to work. I need to feed my family. I'm an excellent worker." And then you start selling yourself in the way that I have recommended.

Admit that you miscalculated the market and communicate that you have been (for the past couple of months) interviewing your butt off, that you can't afford not to work, and that you need to be hired, preferably by the person with whom you are speaking. Communicate that you are not a risk, that you can't afford to take off extended periods of time, and that you are a passionate and committed worker.

As with many of the other challenges in this chapter, if you create enough of a value for yourself in the eyes of a prospective employer, he or she really won't care how long it has taken for you to look for a job.

Note: If you *really* want to take a few days or a week to clear your head, immediately after you lose your job is the time to do it. But first make a plan for your job search. This plan will give you the emotional comfort that you are ready to go to work on going to work as soon as your short break is over.

You've Had Too Many Jobs

I discussed this issue to a certain extent in Chapter 11, when I addressed how to answer the question of, "Why have you had so many jobs?" This issue is as much a concern about minimizing risk as anything else.

The Situation

One of the biggest fears that most employers have is to hire someone and then not have it work out—for whatever reason. It makes them look bad and no one wants to look bad. So, if you had two or three jobs in the last three or four years (it really doesn't matter in what profession it has been), there is going to be a concern that you've had too many jobs.

If you have had three jobs in three years, a prospective employer is going to assume (or be afraid) that you will stay on the job for only one year. Suffice it to say, you will never win this argument.

What to Say

The key to answering this question successfully is not so much to offset the concern as it is to counterbalance and neutralize it. Since you know that you are going to get the question (if you don't, the interviewer is going to think it), you should bring up the question and provide the answer to it *before* the interviewer or hiring authority asks it.

In fact, as you begin to make your presentation the way I suggested in Chapter 11, you should begin by saying something along the lines of: "Unfortunately, I know that I have to overcome the fact that I've had too many jobs in the past few years. I know that it appears to be somewhat of a risk, and I don't like it any better than a prospective employer would. However, I really learned a lot at each one of those positions. One of the very reasons that I should be hired by an organization like yours is that I can't afford to make a mistake and I plan on being in my next position at least five to seven years." Then go on and explain every job you had in the detail that I suggest.

If you have had a long stint of employment before the previous two or three short stints, it's a good idea to remind the interviewing or hiring authority how much you are looking for long-term employment. It is also a good idea to admit that one or two of the positions you had were mistakes. Say something along the lines of, "If I knew then what I know now, I probably wouldn't have made that decision."

In fact, one of the best ways to deal with any glitches or issues regarding your number of job changes or anything that might appear a distraction on your resume is to *admit* that you made a *mistake*. There isn't anybody who doesn't make mistakes in business, and it's amazing how understanding interviewing and hiring authorities might be when you explain that, looking back on your decision . . . it was a mistake.

Do be careful, though, because if you start explaining more than two or so mistakes as poor judgment, it would be too easy for the interviewing or hiring authority to decide that it's better not to hire somebody who makes "poor business decisions." Have very good explanations as to why you made the mistake and, whatever you do, don't blame someone else.

Blame yourself: "I didn't investigate the financing of the company as well as I should have and it ran out of money" or "I didn't realize at the time that I went to work there but the company was in the process of being sold" or "The person who hired me, who was also my immediate boss, left the company a couple of months after I was hired. Unfortunately, the new managers who were promoted did not have the same vision and plans that their predecessors had. I was not really a part of their group and since I wasn't hired by them I was identified with the previous managers. It was awkward for all of us and I ended up leaving. Had I known there was going to be a management change like that, I wouldn't have taken the job."

Do not get defensive and pissed off at anyone and try to *justify* the mistake you made by saying something stupid like, "Well, you can't blame me. The screwballs lied to me . . . and anybody in their right mind would do what I did." Remember, employers identify with employers. You made a mistake; admit it—and take the blame for it!

You have to ask yourself, "How does my instability appear to a prospective employer, and if I were in his or her shoes, what would I think?" As I said before, whatever you say will be used against you. Remember to always reinforce the fact that you loved the previous jobs and appreciated all of the people—and you learned a heck of a lot.

The very best way to overcome any concerns about your previous employment or any challenging aspect of your candidacy is to prove the value of hiring you over anyone else whom the employer could interview. Along with this, you should have some really solid references that will substantiate your stability.

You Want to Change Careers

At least four or five times a week, our organization encounters well-educated, well-trained, well-experienced professionals who want to change their careers. Their attitude is that since they have been even reasonably successful in one endeavor, they can automatically be successful in another. They look around and see people in other professions and have a tendency to think that, for one reason or another, it would be a better place for them. So, they want to change careers.

The Situation: You're Thinking About It

In the boom cycle, when there are fewer people and more jobs, experienced people are hard to come by. Since some companies have a difficult time finding experienced people in what they specifically do, they are willing to take as close to like-kind experience as they can get and train those people. That is why some people at different times appear to have an easier time changing careers than others. The opportunity to change careers was easier in the boom economy because hiring organizations did not have much choice. They had to hire people who didn't have any experience in what they did and train them. They could afford to hire people who weren't immediately productive, train them, and not be concerned about their immediate contribution.

In a more difficult economy, however, there are lots of very qualified people available on the market and companies are watching their bottom-line profits more carefully. When earnings are harder to come by, the whole concept changes. Hiring organizations need to find people with as much experience in what they do as they can get because those people need to be contributing almost immediately to the bottom line. Companies don't think they can afford to wait around for someone to catch on to what they do. Everyone must be able to pull his or her own weight immediately. This, coupled with the fact that there are many more experienced people available in the marketplace, allows a company to be very selective in its hiring and pretty much find exactly the kind of experience that would be best.

What this means to you is that just because you think you would like to change careers doesn't mean that it is going to be feasible to do it. On top of all of this, you have to take into account the value you bring to a hiring organization when you have no track record in what it does. Why is an organization going to pay you the kind of money that you've been making doing one thing, or in one profession, to perform in a position or function that you have either absolutely no, or very little, experience doing?

So, to change careers you're most likely going to have to make it a good business deal for a prospective employer—worth the risk involved in taking on someone without proven experience. You'll have to say something along the line of, "Look, I've been a successful accountant for the past fifteen years, but I want be a real estate appraiser. I'm working on certifications. I'm willing to go to work for half of what you would normally pay an appraiser. I am willing to start out at the bottom and work my way up. I am a good employee. I will make the risk worthwhile for you."

There is always the option of owning your own business. This book is not about that approach, but it is a feasible option. There are tremendous amounts of entrepreneurial and franchise opportunities available in U.S. business. (Did you know that one of the industries that has created many millionaires from scratch in the United States is the dry-cleaning business? It certainly isn't exotic and it has its problems, but it can be extremely lucrative.) Owning one's own business, especially a small business, in the United States is a lot more difficult than most people think.

The Situation: You've Changed Your Mind

If you have already changed careers and are looking to get back into a profession in which you had previous experience before your most recent career change, you are experiencing the same difficulty that those people who want to change careers are experiencing.

A few years ago, I had a candidate who, after spending fifteen years selling software, bought a chain of retail dry-cleaning stores. He was very successful and had the chance to sell the stores at a sizable profit. He really didn't like all the business problems he encountered in the dry-cleaning business, so he wanted to get back into selling software. He had a hard time even getting interviews, let alone job offers.

First, he didn't have any recent contacts or recent track record in the software business and second, all of the other candidates he was competing with did. Although he had a tremendous track record up until he went into the dry-cleaning business, there were too many other candidates out there, especially in this market: ones who weren't as great a risk. Prospective employers would say things like, "Well, Tony, if he really wanted to sell software, why did he get out of it?" Or, "Well, Tony, we can't run the risk of hiring this guy even if his track record was good, because, after a year or so, he may decide to do something else entrepreneurial. And the last thing we need is for someone to get into the job for a year or so and then leave."

The success that a person might have in returning to a profession or career that was interrupted by a completely different profession or career will depend on timing. If the economy is in a boom cycle and the ratio of candidates to job opportunities is low, then the hiring organization has to take the best candidate who is available, even if his or her experience might be two or three years old. But, if the economy is like it has been in recent years—where the ratio of qualified candidates to job opportunities is high—competition is very keen, so the hiring organization can take fewer risks.

How can you overcome the fact that you're changing or have changed careers? Knock on lots of doors until you find someone who will accept the risk!

Reentering the Workforce

Coming back into the workforce after a period of time away can present special problems. There are many situations that can cause you to leave the workforce for a time. Here's a short word about each.

Retiring

Since the recession of '08 hit, tens of thousands of people who were living off their retirement incomes found that they couldn't do that anymore. Many have decided to get back into the workforce. Whatever you do, during the interviewing process *do not* bitch and moan and complain about how badly the economy has treated your retirement and about the fact that you have to go back to work. No one likes a whiner, especially whining about "poor me." Almost every businessperson has been through difficult times over the past years, so shut up about yours—they don't care.

If you're going to reenter the workforce after trying to retire simply say, "I tried retiring and not only was it boring but my 401(k) and retirement also went to the dickens. I *have* to work another eight to ten years. Now, here is where I have been a good worker in the past. . . ." Don't say any more than that regarding your retirement. The longer you talk about your plans that went awry, the more the hiring authority is going to think you will only work for a short period of time and if your investments rebound, you will leave.

And by the way, don't expect to go to work at anywhere near the money you might have been earning before you retired. If you can get back into a business or job that you know something about—that is, something you did before you retired—you might get lucky with your earnings. Many hiring authorities will consider someone hiring someone with solid experience in the field, but they'll want to hire him or her at a "bargain." So, be ready to negotiate realizing that you don't have a lot of leverage.

Childbirth

It's ridiculous to try to avoid this issue if this is why you are returning to the workforce. So don't try to come up with some cockamamie idea as to why you've been out of work for three or four months if you've recently given birth to a child. What most employers are interested in knowing is that you have dependable *child care*, preferably by a family member. The biggest issue a hiring authority is concerned with is your being absent from work because of the baby. Even with child-care centers, if the baby is sick, the baby can't be left, and you have to stay home with a sick child.

All of this runs through the hiring authority's mind. In today's work environment, the workforce is still very lean. The last issue a hiring authority wants to deal with is a group of other workers complaining about your being home with a sick child. Just be aware of this.

Make a simple statement that you are returning to the workforce after the birth of a child, reinforcing—*without being asked*—that you haven't missed any work in a number of years. Or saying, "My mother cares for the baby while I work," will make all the difference in the world. Don't say any more than that. Don't spend time talking about your three other children, or how much you love kids, or how you'd rather stay home but you have to work. Keep it a simple statement and move on.

Going Back to School Full Time

Many people think that because they've gone back to school and have completed their undergraduate degree or gotten a master's, they're going to automatically be able to get a better job than they had. They often claim that they will also make more money. Don't bank on it.

I have discussed in an earlier chapter the myth of the MBA, but the same thing holds true for people who *don't* have a baccalaureate degree and believe that getting one will help them get a better job. Having a baccalaureate degree simply opens up *more* opportunities to people because some organizations (mistakenly) require a baccalaureate degree. As with an MBA, no one is going to be able to prove that the baccalaureate degree makes people better employees.

A new degree is nice to have, but in itself it isn't going to get you a better job. Don't expect that all kinds of opportunities are going to open before you because you have a new degree. In fact, your being out of the workforce while getting the new degree may force you to have to go to work at a job one or two steps *below* the job you had before. Many people who lost their jobs owing to the bad economy figured that this would be a great time to go back to school full time, especially if they could afford to do it. I'm glad you have a new degree, and I hope you learned a lot, but don't think you're going to get some splendid job because of it.

Divorce

Many women are forced to go back to work following divorce, after being stay-at-home moms. The biggest challenge they are going to have is not so much needing to look for a job as making sure they don't communicate "poor me" and tell true confessions about their divorce settlement.

Stay away from this pity party. Simply state, "Due to my divorce I have to find full-time employment." Then move on as to why you are a good employee. Try to communicate that the divorce took place as long ago as you can possibly stretch without lying, and don't discuss the details—*at all*!

I had a very well-qualified candidate a year or so ago who went through a divorce after ten years of marriage. It was pretty devastating for her, and she had a tendency to want to tell people all about it when she interviewed. I explained to her that talking about it was a very bad idea and, no matter what, she shouldn't do that. Just state the situation and move on. I got her an excellent interview. The hiring authority was a women who had recently gone through a divorce, and when the subject came up, the hiring authority got my candidate talking about how she had been "done wrong." They compared notes, so to speak, and my candidate reported back to me that it was a great interview because the hiring authority really understood her situation.

When I followed up with the hiring authority, though, she communicated to me that there was no way she was going to hire my candidate. She liked my candidate's background and experience, but wouldn't even begin to consider somebody who was distracted by a divorce and *going through the same emotional strain that she was*. Get the lesson?

Death of a Loved One

Having taken time off to tend to the care of a dying relative, a parent, a spouse, or a child is totally understandable. And the sudden death of a loved one, especially a spouse or a child, is devastating; leaving one's job to deal with it is understandable. But sooner or later, a person wants to return to work.

The important point is to be able to let the hiring authority know that you're beyond the emotional strain of the event, that you've recovered, as much as anybody can, and that you're ready to go to work. Then, as with other emotionally dramatic issues, deal with it in one or two sentences and then *drop it*! "It was a devastating experience and emotionally very difficult, but I have now learned to deal with it and need to get on with my work. I'm a great employee."

The Kids Are Grown

Many employers love it when somebody's kids are grown. Those of us who have raised kids know that it's the hardest job in the whole world, especially for stay-at-home moms. Even though it is true, it is not a good idea to say something like, "Well, anybody who can raise my kids can do anything."

Most hiring authorities, even though they might have raised kids themselves, don't equate the (difficult, grueling, mysterious, miraculous) raising of kids to the job they need done. So, don't go there. Simply state, "Now that the kids are grown and gone, I'm free to focus on work without being distracted." Many employers will find this to be a good reason to hire someone.

Extended Personal Illness

To begin, let's hope the illness is not something that might recur. I've had some candidates over the years who tried to come up with another excuse as to why they had been out of work other than an extended illness, if that was the case. Don't do this. If you get hired and the hiring authority finds out—and he or she will—and then you are out of work for an extended period of time for a reason different than you gave, it will not put you in very good light.

If you have been out of work for a personal illness, explain it directly and to the point. Let's hope you are able to state that the problem is well behind you, you are fully recovered, and it won't stand in the way of you being a good employee. If it is a relatively catastrophic illness, like cancer that is in remission, make sure you let the hiring authority know that you have your own health insurance policy. (If you don't, get one.)

The big issues that the hiring authority is going to be concerned with are first, your being at work all of the time and second, the impact you may have on the company's health insurance program. Smaller firms that provide employee health insurance (and there are fewer of them every day) can be adversely affected by people who come into the program with special needs and end up being a drain on it. Now, no employer in its right mind is going to explain this to you during the interview, but the thoughts will be there, and the company won't hire you if it believes you are a long-term liability. And don't give me the "that's illegal" stuff—it might be, but the company is going to do it anyhow.

Again, don't dwell on any issue like this. State the issue and then explain why you are going to be a good employee.

Full-Time Care for a Family Member

If you had to take a break from work to care full time for an elderly parent or grandparent, or a spouse or child, you should state the situation and then explain how the matter has been resolved. Obviously, if your parent has passed on, it's clear the matter has been resolved.

Employers aren't going to be as concerned about what the situation was as they are that the problem might recur and cause you to either miss a lot of work or leave the job. A child who has fully recovered from illness, or a parent or grandparent whose dementia is so advanced that he or she has had to be put in a home with twenty-four hour care, has clear resolution. Be sure the hiring authority understands that and then move on. Just don't dwell on it or complain about it.

Relocation of the Spouse

If you are looking for a job because your spouse had to relocate to a new city, you need to make it clear that you intend to stay in that city for a very long time. Even though the average job in the United States lasts only two and a half to three years, a hiring authority is going to wonder, *Well, if his wife gets transferred again within the next year or two, he'll leave.* Something like, "My wife has been transferred here and that is why we moved, but her company has assured us that the commitment here is long-term," will make sense.

Leaving Military Service

Ever since the Vietnam War, there has been a little concern by hiring authorities, when they interview wartime veterans, about posttraumatic stress disorder. I don't know how often these cases occur, but you just want to be sure that the hiring authority isn't concerned about it. You have no obligation to tell a prospective employer why you were discharged from the military. Now, a hiring authority may find out that you were discharged dishonorably, but unless you are specifically asked either verbally or on an application, you have no obligation to offer the details. If there was any medical issue surrounding your leaving the military, especially if it has been resolved, there is no need to mention it.

Also, stay clear of any kind of political discussion about any of the wars America— or any other country, for that matter—has been involved in. Your agreement or disagreement with any political conflicts has nothing to do with the interview. So, even if a hiring authority says something like, "Well, you know I don't think we belonged in Vietnam or we should be in Afghanistan," don't take the bait. Simply say, "It was my duty to serve my country, and I'm proud that I did." Then drop it. Start discussing your ability to do the job a hiring authority is interested in filling.

Relocating

Since our firm works primarily in Texas, and we have a more business-friendly atmosphere than most other states, we get hundreds of résumés weekly from people in other parts of the country who want to move here. If they are having a difficult time finding employment in California, New York, or Florida, they consider going where the economy is better and they can find a job.

With the economy as it is (and may be for the foreseeable future), companies are reluctant to relocate candidates from other parts of the country. Neither are they keenly interested in hiring people who are willing to relocate if they get hired. This is the case for the following reasons.

First, there are already lots of people in the area. Except for very rare types of positions and experiences, most hiring authorities believe there's plenty of talent right where they are. Even though they may find a perfect candidate somewhere else in the country, they say, "Well, surely there's somebody locally who can do this job." This may not be true, but they still think it: *With all the unemployed out there, we surely should be able to find someone without having to consider somebody who doesn't live in the area.*

Second, with the economy as it is, most firms don't want to take on the expense of relocating someone from another part of the country unless they absolutely have to. So you say, "Well, I'll pay for my own relocation." Fair enough, but the issue isn't just the expense of having to pay for your relocation, even though a prospective employer might tell you that.

Third, when the economy turns around and a job is easier to find in your home state, the company might feel that you will return, leaving the job it hired you to do. When the economy is slow and unemployment is high, employers tend to think this way. They don't want to go to the expense of relocating someone, or run the risk of having their new hire leave them to "go back home" in the future. In the early 1970s and early '80s, there were similar situations here in Texas. Our businesses were expanding, so lots of people moved here. Eventually, some stayed and some didn't.

On the other hand, there are times when an employer simply can't get its people locally. For a plastics processing company here in Texas, we searched for over eight months to find the person with the exact experience and personality needed. We finally found a qualified candidate in Ohio. Even in 2010, in the middle of a recession, the company hired him and, reluctantly, paid part of his relocation costs. This, however, was an exception.

So, if you live in an area where you can't find a job and you're going to have to relocate, go to that place and start looking for a job. If you can't move there and have to search from a distant location, know that this is going to be extremely difficult. We hear this all the time: "Gosh, I can't move to [Dallas]; I have a job where I am and can't move. But if I can line up a few interviews at a time, I can come for a few days or maybe a week." Alas, it doesn't work that way. Lining up "a few interviews" at a time is hard. In fact, getting one interview is tough enough; getting more than one is a bonus.

If you're set on relocating nonetheless, here are some recommendations:

- Be prepared to pay your own relocation costs for the place where you desire to live. Lots of companies did away with paying relocation expenses a long time ago. You may be able to negotiate this once you have secured an offer, but don't bank on it.

- If you live far away from where you're trying to find a job, take your physical address off the résumé. If you have a friend or relative in the proposed city, ask to use that address on your résumé. I've known candidates who rented P.O. box numbers in the desired city and had friends or relatives pick up the mail.

- Use the addresses of corporate headquarters in the body of your résumé. You can work for J.C. Penney and similar large firms in all kinds of cities. Don't worry if your cell phone does not have an area code that corresponds to the desired city; people keep cell phone numbers from place to place.

- Don't tell a prospective employer *before* you've interviewed that you are not in the area. Eventually you're going to have to explain to a hiring authority that you don't live in the area and that you need to relocate. But you're going to do this *after* you've had a chance to sell yourself.

In short, I'm not suggesting you deceive prospective employers; I am just telling you to remove potential barriers to getting interviewed. Concerns about relocation on the part of a prospective employer shouldn't be a bigger problem than if you were fired from the last three jobs or if your references are awful. Location may wind up being a deal killer, but you don't want the issue to keep you from getting the interview.

Dealing with Discrimination

So, you think there is discrimination. The blunt truth is, you're absolutely right. All hiring is discriminatory. The issue is that some factors used to discriminate are legal and some are illegal. No employer is ever going to admit to the illegal ones. Any selection process for just about anything discriminates in favor of some qualities as opposed to others.

In almost forty years that I've been in the employment profession, I have seen discrimination drastically change. For the most part, it has been for the better, but the issues and types of discrimination have changed radically. Some of it has to do with the globalization of businesses in the United States, some of it has to do with the immigration policies of the United States, and some of it has to do with the United States still being a model of the world's land of opportunity for those who want to work.

When I entered this profession, there was a lot more discrimination against women and minorities than there is today. We don't hear, "Don't send me a woman . . . or a black . . . or a Hispanic, or an Indian" anywhere near as much as we used to. We probably hear a little more age discrimination, in very subtle ways, than we hear about sex or race discrimination.

Discrimination, for all kinds of reasons, is always going to be with us. You're just as likely to be eliminated for lack of experience, or the wrong kind of experience, or salary considerations, or the kinds of things discussed elsewhere in this book as you are because of your race, religion, age, or gender. Just be aware that you might be discriminated against for all kinds of reasons. Move on!

If You're Over Fifty (or Forty or Sixty)

To start with, unfortunately, our society is youth-oriented. It has gotten better over the past number of years because boomers account for about 79 million of us—compared to only 49 million GenXers. It is an attitude that we can do nothing about.

When it comes to hiring, there is an unconscious cultural bias even by the majority of the hiring authorities who are boomers themselves. The majority of employers in the United States don't really care about age. But they do end up being concerned about some of the *problems* people who are near sixty and older might bring with them. Here are some of the blunt, real issues that employers are concerned about:

- *"I'd be hiring someone old enough to be my father or mother."* What this means is that hiring authorities are afraid that older candidates won't respect them, be subordinate to them, or want to work for them. The hiring authorities have enough to be concerned about without having someone appear to know more than they do. Mention that you have worked for many younger managers before.

- *"Older people are set in their ways."* Of course, this is a myth. There is absolutely no truth to it. The fear here is that the new employee would be doing things his or her way instead of the company way. You can demonstrate a number of different kinds of organizational procedures that you have learned in your years of experience. Say, "I find that being flexible has really helped me . . ." and then relate a story or two about how you were flexible in your way.

- *"We are a young group. Older people may not fit in here."* If you get that sense from a hiring authority, say something along the lines of, "I've been on a number of teams in a number of different kinds of companies. I've worked well with young trainees and senior people on their way to retirement. If you check my references you'll find that I've always been able to get along with everybody exceptionally well. 'Fitting in' is more of an attitude than a matter of age or experience."

- *"Anyone with twenty-five or thirty years of experience should be making much more money than we can pay and be further in their career. So, therefore, this person can't be very good."* This, of course, is a relative statement. Some people advance, some don't, for all kinds of reasons. But the perception is out there. It is a terribly misguided theory, but it is prevalent nonetheless. Let the hiring authority know that money is not as important as the quality of the work you do, and your experience has been that when you do good work that's fulfilling, the money usually takes care of itself. "Besides, the kids are grown and our expenses are very, very low. I simply don't need to make as much money as I've made before."

- *"An older person has to be overqualified for this job."* The matter of being overqualified can apply to any age. If a thirty-five-year-old was "overqualified," there would be a concern. Since the predominant numbers of people going down the career ladder are in their fifties, the overqualified experience appears to be an age thing, but it's not. Deal with being overqualified by explaining to a hiring authority that you know exactly what you're getting into and that you have never left jobs in the past because you were "overqualified" and you won't again. Being overqualified is more of a state of mind than it is a reality. "I wouldn't take a job if I felt I was overqualified—that doesn't do either one of us any good."

- *"Older people don't have the same passion, drive, and commitment as younger people."* Some feel that older people are looking more toward retirement than they are toward work. They have climbed the proverbial ladder, and they have plateaued. There is no way of disproving this, of course. Some have; some haven't. But there are also thirty-year-olds looking toward retirement; they just don't talk about it, lest they look foolish. Demonstrate the drive and passion you have for your last few positions . . . pretty simple.

- *"Older people don't have any energy."* People have energy or they don't. People who have energy have it when they are fourteen, twenty-eight, or sixty-eight years old. People who don't have energy don't have it when they are fourteen, twenty-eight, or sixty-eight years old. Make sure you have pep and energy in the interviewing process. Dress in today's fashion but don't be flashy.

- *"We want people on the upswing of their careers, not on the decline. We want them going up the ladder, not down."* Well now, everyone cannot be climbing the same ladder. And older people get promoted the same as younger ones do. Since most promotions are based on performance—or should be—what is the difference? Say that to a prospective employer.

- *"Older people are looking for security and a place to retire. We want aggressive risk takers who aren't afraid to fail."* This is another ridiculous myth. If there's anything that this recent economy has taught us, it is that no one's job is secure. Risk taking, like energy and passion, is either in a person's makeup or it isn't. It has nothing to do with age. No one can look for or find security these days.

- *"An older person will be asking for too much money for our job. If they are older and haven't made more money than this, something is wrong with them."* Earnings, especially in this recessionary market, have nothing to do with age. Ask Bill Gates when he made his first billion. But the perception is that people should make more money the older they get.

- *"Older people have more illness than younger people and our insurance rates are already sky high."* There is some validity to this comment. The older the workforce, the higher the insurance rates. Insurance programs are changing, and employers' options are becoming more flexible. Many employers are opting out of providing insurance for their employees at all. However, this still presents a challenge for employers, especially the smaller ones. So, lose weight, get in shape, and look fit. Talk about your exercise routine and what excellent shape you are in.

- *"Older folks don't have the stamina that younger folks do."* This just isn't so, but no one can argue it. Come up with three or four stories in which you demonstrate where you've dealt with a high degree of pressure—that is, deadlines, long hours, and grueling work. Also mention that in the past few years your ability to *focus* has gotten better. Point out that with experience you know how to separate the real important stuff from the seemingly important stuff. That takes lots of experience to learn.

- *"Our company culture is young. We party a lot together, and a fifty-year-old just wouldn't fit in here."* We don't hear this one as much as we used to a few years ago. Why? Because the majority of managers are now fifty or older. Ha! Being fifty years old (or older) looks pretty different when you're fifty years old or older!

These days, there is not as much bias about older job candidates as you might think. But you may be more sensitive to it because it is you, so you need to be prepared to face the issue. The reality is that being older or too experienced is just another consideration for employers, like a candidate having had too many jobs, not the right kind of positions or experience, and so forth. The truth is that to a prospective employer the amount and quality of your experience are relative and subjective things. Your age isn't.

If you sell your age and experience the right way, it can be one of your best assets. But, it really has to be sold in the right way. Here are a few tips:

- Stress your longtime experience; don't try to hide from it.

- Use plenty of stories during your presentation to show that you've seen a lot of things in your work life, dealt successfully with most of them, and learned from the rest. Describe how you've worked under lots of pressure, with lots of focus.

- Explain that you know what to expect from the job; you are not likely to be surprised by any aspect of it because you have experienced a number of jobs in a number of different kinds of companies. Remind employers that young "kids" have to learn on their nickel and it is much better to acquire the skills of someone who's already had tons of experience.

- Assure the interviewer that you want to work; you are not looking toward retirement.

- Where possible, mention things like your computer skills to show that you are not a technophobe, or a sport or activity you enjoy to show that you have energy and are not slowing down. Demonstrating that you have kept up your computer skills—using iPhones or iPads, taking technical classes, becoming certified in certain technologies, etc.—will show the hiring authority that you're inquisitive and interested.

- Don't talk about spending a lot of time with the grandkids; your physical ailments, e.g., your hip replacement or the seven stents that you have in your heart; your declining memory, eyesight, hearing and manual dexterity; the "good old days" when we used typewriters and the phones had dials; watching Joe DiMaggio, Yogi Berra, Mickey Mantle, Bart Starr, or Paul Hornung play; or the first television your family ever had. I'm sure you get the message. Don't *sound* old by talking about ancient history (more than 10 or 15 years ago). Talk about now and the future.

- Above all, emphasize how much value you would bring to the company and how much you would like to work for this employer. Joyce Lain Kennedy offers great advice about how to deal with this issue. She has been writing about careers for more than thirty years. Kennedy is one of the few career authors who write practical, real advice. Her research is impeccable. Her newest book, *Job Interviews for Dummies* (Wiley, 2008), has excellent advice on how to overcome age and overqualification bias.

Being a Woman

There is less discrimination against women than there used to be. However, it is still true that women, for the most part, have to work harder than their male counterparts. I am not here to justify why this is the case. But in the vast majority of companies in the United States, this is the case. Now, there are some professions where women are the majority, but if they compete in the normal realm of business in America, they simply have to work harder than men to prove themselves and to be recognized.

The cause of this inequality may be the stark reality that the majority of businesses in this country are run and managed by men. If you are a woman and trying to raise a family, as well as work outside the home, you have to be a superstar to do both jobs well. Most employers are aware of the difficulty in performing both jobs. It is a choice that a woman has to make, but being a wife and mother and "earner" is a phenomenal challenge. On top of that, the underlying standard that women are measured by in the business world is more stringent. Being a mother and wife are two of the most difficult jobs there are, and when you combine those with business opportunities, most women need to be superhuman. Being a working, single mother is, maybe, even harder.

Having said all that, it appears to me that women have to perform better and have a better track record than men in competing for the same positions. I'm not saying this is right or making an apology for this, but that is the way things are. I've often thought that women perform better than most men in equal jobs simply because they know they have to compensate for the perceived inequities.

If you are a woman reentering the workforce after raising children, you are going to run into the same challenge that any candidate would, having left business for a number of years then needing to get a new job. This has nothing to do with you being a woman. The same would be true for any man if he were out of the business environment for a number of years. What it means is that you are, to a certain extent, going to have to start over in your career. Just be ready for it.

One nice thing about having raised children is that you can use it as a *selling point* for your candidacy. "Well, all of my children are raised (or just about raised) and they don't need me home anymore. I don't have to attend to them when they're sick; they get themselves to school (or they are out of the house), so I am free to focus on my career and my job." And, frankly, anyone who has raised children knows how complicated it is just to get your child to eighteen or twenty years old.

If you are a woman of child-bearing age and you are asked if you have children, or if you intend to have children, or about your ability to work or travel because of children in an interviewing situation, (which, of course, is illegal), you probably won't get very far by being indignant and informing the interviewer that his or her question is illegal. You have to decide how you are going to answer these questions before they are even asked.

Many female candidates we have worked with over the years simply make it clear in the interview, before they are asked, that they have small children. They clarify that they have excellent child care and it hasn't inhibited them from performing well on the job. Many women have felt that it is better to offer this answer before the question is asked—to keep the prospective employer from wondering about their ability to be at work every day. They say something along the lines of, "You need to know that I have a small child who is ____ years old. But we have excellent child care and even when he is ill, I've not had to miss work." It's even better when the candidate can say, "I do have two small children, but my mother (that is, a relative who cares more than a hired child-care giver) takes care of the children and I've never had difficulty with them interfering with my work—even when they are ill." This comment keeps a prospective employer from having to wonder about that particular issue.

Some women don't feel comfortable telling a prospective employer that they have small children. It is their prerogative not to do so. But, if you don't feel comfortable in offering it to a prospective employer, you'd better be ready to suffer the consequences of the employer not being sure, and therefore not wanting to run the risk of hiring you because you may have small children.

You have to decide how you're going to handle this situation. But remember, the employer's concern isn't that you have small children, the concern is that you are going to be absent from work a lot because of small children. So that is the concern you have to address.

If You Are a Minority

If you are a minority of any sort, you're already familiar with the inherent prejudice and bias that many people have against others who are significantly different from them. Whether you're black, yellow, or brown, or any other kind of minority, looking for a job has this one added difficulty. I have observed that this prejudice toward American-born minorities isn't anywhere near as great as it used to be, but there is no denying that it still lingers on in some quarters.

I'm still of the opinion that American-born minorities have to be just a little bit better in performance and previous employment than the average white guy (if there is such a person). Again, it does absolutely no good to complain about the truth of this fact. And, I say the best way to overcome discrimination is to knock on lots of doors until the right one opens.

In some instances, being a minority can be an advantage. In fact, many companies consider it a tremendous bonus if they get an excellent candidate who is also a minority. However, interviewing and getting hired are still going to be a challenge. You are going to have to prove that you are a better candidate.

When you interview, you need to be sure that you sell yourself extremely well. You are going to have to practice your interviewing techniques and perform them better than most of the average candidates the employer is going to interview. If you stress your strengths, skills, and experience, most companies will be willing to give you a shot—at least to go further in the interviewing process.

In no way do I want to belittle the effects of racial discrimination, but I do feel strongly that in this day and age, most reputable companies want to hire the best candidate, regardless of race.

Being a Foreign-Born Minority

There is no getting around the fact that many foreign-born minorities are discriminated against. Even the generation that is born here in America of foreign-born minorities is discriminated against, especially if they keep native first names and surnames. I remember my grandfather telling stories about being discriminated against when he came to this country from Lebanon in 1899. He was Catholic and a foreigner, which certainly wasn't popular when he settled in Indian Territory, which became Oklahoma.

Because of technology, we have become much more of a world economy. Since 1973, I have experienced mainstream American businesses becoming more tolerant of foreign-born minority candidates. Like women, though, they have to perform better than other candidates. They are going to be discriminated against whether anyone admits it or not.

The matter of your name can be sticky, but I must address it here. If your name makes it obvious that you are of a member of a minority group or are foreign-born, you may want to consider changing it for résumé and interviewing purposes only. If you're uncomfortable doing this, don't do it.

We're all familiar with the studies done of two identical résumés, one with the name Sharonda and the other with the name Sharon. Sharon gets more interviews. So if your name is Janeka, Lee-Ron, Kareem, Kamal, Aadarsh, Dipti, Akbar, Abdul, Yan, Li, Mei-li, or Hala—in short, any name that immediately identifies you as a minority or as foreign-born—consider altering it on your résumé.

I'm trying to get you interviews so you can get a job. You don't want something on your résumé to keep you from getting those interviews, especially your name. I recently had a sales candidate with the first name of Kamar and a last name similar to Cole. It was obviously a Middle Eastern name. When he altered the name on his résumé to Kenny Cole, he increased the number of interviews he received. Interestingly enough, his nationality didn't hinder him at all once he got into the interviewing cycle; no one seemed to care.

Again, don't shoot the messenger! If you don't feel comfortable doing this, don't do it. Use your own judgment. Just remember that you don't want to be eliminated from an interview by what is on your résumé, if you can easily avoid it.

13 : Looking for a Job When You Have a Job

HERE'S A LETTER I RECEIVED from someone who bought the earlier edition of this book:

> "I thought looking for a job when I had one would be a tremendous advantage for me. I thought that since I was competing with so many people who were probably out of work, I'd look so much better to an employer. Boy, did I not understand. It took me almost a year to change. I started and stopped four times. It was really hard. For the last group of interviews, I studied your book again and reread that chapter on looking for a job when you have one. I sure must have missed it the last time. You are so right. Thanks. I was better this go around."
> —Stan H., Herndon, Virginia

First, let me dispel the myth that you are a better candidate, in the eyes of a prospective employer, if you are currently employed. Although most surveys will tell you that a currently employed candidate is supposedly a better one, it just doesn't work out that way from a practical point of view. The blunt truth is that 99 percent of the hiring authorities with "pain" in 99 percent of the companies in the United States don't really care if the person who relieves their pain is presently employed or not.

In fact, there are some kinds of positions where being employed—and therefore not immediately available to start a new job—might be a deterrent. Most organizations and hiring authorities will rarely admit this, because they want to appear as though they plan and execute on hiring people well in advance of the need, with forethought and exceptional business acumen. But they don't. In fact, based on my gut, 35 to 40 percent of the hiring that's done is begun when hiring authorities are downright *desperate*. Every business guru in the world teaches us to plan ahead—to interview well in advance of the need, well in advance of being behind the eight ball. I can't tell you the number of managers I've spoken with over the years who claim they interview and hire well in advance of their needs. And it's all B.S.

Hiring is an emotionally risky event and people don't like doing it. It's a pain. They'll claim they're good at it, but they're not. They'll claim that it is, next to making a profit, the most important thing they'll do, but they'll postpone it and avoid it until they absolutely have to do it. It takes focus away from the easier parts of their job. Most often when they hire they need someone yesterday. And they are interviewing and hiring for someone to start *tomorrow*.

So, you *aren't* a better candidate because you are employed. You may be harder to hire, and you may not have the urgency to take an offer because you are employed. But you aren't intrinsically a better candidate just because you have a job. (Conversely, you are not *less* of a candidate because you are unemployed.)

The simple economic and psychological comfort in having a job alleviates most of the emotional and psychological stress that is associated with finding a job *when you don't have one*. At least most people feel that way in the beginning of their job search. There are, however, a whole different set of emotional and psychological challenges that come with looking for a job while you have one. And those should not be underestimated.

First Considerations

I would hardly recommend that an individual quit a job in order to look for one, unless there were extenuating circumstances, such as following a spouse who is relocating or some other odd situation of that type. However, you will find that looking for a job while you have one is a lot harder than you think.

To begin, an employed individual who is looking for another job has the added difficulty of not having the same amount of time to devote to a job search. In most instances, it's going to take at least twice as long, if not longer, to find a job. In fact, you will find that if you are employed, *looking for a job is like having a second job*. It's really, really hard to do.

On top of this, if you have a job and are motivated enough to devote time, effort, and strain to finding a new one, you probably don't like the one you have. Unless your job is going away, or your company is, you may even *hate* your job. So, you have to make time to try to find a new job in a very rough economy while keeping one you hate. It isn't easy.

Why Do You Want to Change Jobs?

The first issue you have to come to grips with when you have a job and you think you need to look for a new one is the great question of "why?" People leave a job for very personal reasons, in the same way they take a job for very personal reasons. Over the years, psychologists and business analysts have concluded that the top five reasons why people leave their jobs are:

1. *Job Content*—People really don't like the majority of what they spend their time doing in a particular job.

2. *Level of Responsibility*—People feel like that they can do more and want to experience more self-fulfillment and personal growth in what they do.

3. *Company Culture*—People don't feel compatible with the personality of the company. They disagree with the company philosophy and approach to doing business.

4. *Dissatisfaction with Colleagues*—People discover personality differences or chemistry differences between them and the people whom they either work for or with.

5. *Compensation*—(Notice that this is the fifth reason!) People don't feel like they're compensated fairly for either what they are doing or for what they are asked to do.

After these top five reasons, there are numerous other reasons for why people want to leave the job, including:

- Lack of recognition
- Lack of teamwork
- Lack of support
- Lack of control
- Feeling isolated
- Lack of autonomy
- No compelling future

- Lack of feeling empowered
- Poor working conditions
- Lack of equity
- Poor management
- Unappreciative supervisors
- Stress

You need to analyze all these common reasons to be sure that you really want and need to leave the job you presently have.

On average, unless an individual has *at least three or four urgent, uncontrollable reasons* for leaving a job, the job search itself becomes too emotionally, mentally, and physically difficult, and eventually the candidate chooses to stay where he or she is.

The reason I bring this up is that often people want to change jobs on the whim of the moment. Abrupt changes in management or changes in pay scales, benefits, acquisitions, and so forth will cause employees to panic and begin looking for new jobs. Then, they find out that looking for a job entails a tremendous amount of emotional, psychological, and physical strain, and after a short-lived effort to change jobs, they decide to stay where they are. The immediate issue goes away or at least subsides.

So, carefully analyze the reasons you want to change jobs and make sure that these reasons will motivate you for the possibly long ordeal. Make sure, by the way, that the reasons you are looking to change jobs are *your* reasons and not someone else's.

Avoidance or Acceptance

The longer a person has been at a company, unless he or she is being forced out by downsizing, the company is changing hands, or the like, the harder it is for the person to emotionally get used to the idea of changing jobs. When people have been at their company for a lengthy period of time, they feel strong emotional ties to the company. They feel a part of a family. And in spite of all the obvious, blatant proof in front of them that they really need to change jobs, they don't really want to and they often will do everything they can to postpone or avoid doing so.

If you are in a situation where you are being forced to look for a job when you have one, and you feel emotionally tied to the company, you need to take extra care to come to grips with the reality of having to change jobs. You will eventually get over the emotional strain that this initially causes. You just cannot afford to have it come out in an interview.

Happiness and Attitude

A recent Conference Board survey found that 59 percent of employed people were disgruntled in their jobs and would change jobs if they could. They were disappointed in their earnings and felt that they were overworked and underappreciated.

I have experienced six recessions since I've been in this profession, and during every economic downturn I have seen this kind of poor attitude. When the economy is difficult, everyone from stockholders on down is disappointed. Profits are slim, companies are reluctant to hire, and they overwork their employees to gain productivity. Owners, managers—everyone feels overworked and underappreciated. Doubt, uncertainty, and fear are pervasive.

If you have a job, it's very likely that you are unhappy with it. Looking for a job is emotionally difficult enough. Couple that with trying to keep one you don't like and things are even more stressful. This kind of thing happens in every recession.

Keeping Your Job While Looking for One

When you have decided to look for a job while keeping the one you have, the first step is to become emotionally and psychologically prepared. You need to start planning and developing the process steps that I recommend. On top of that, you need to keep your job.

Once people have emotionally and mentally left a job, the sooner they physically leave, the better! The longer you stay unhappily attached to a job that you know you are going to leave for all kinds of personal and business reasons, the harder it is to keep the job and perform even on a mediocre level. So, ironically enough, once you have decided to leave the job you've got, you have to focus on it even harder to maintain a reasonable level of performance.

You cannot afford, under any circumstances, to have word get back to your current employer that you are looking for a job or you run the risk of being fired. Under no circumstances should you ever inform anyone you work with that you are looking to leave your company. There is a tremendous emotional side to most people—they want support through commiseration; so people complain about the company and their job together, and in a weak moment, some admit they're looking to change jobs. Dumb and dumber! I can't tell you the number of people we've run into over the years who took someone at work into their confidence, told that person that they're looking for a job, and eventually got fired when the word got to management.

I recently had two candidates who worked together as peers at the same company. They both decided to leave for lots of different reasons, and they came to see me—together. They were both upset with the company, the money they were earning, their job, and so on. In the course of two and a half months, one of them was promoted over the other and became the manager. One of his first activities was to fire his friend because he knew he was looking for a job.

I am sure there are literally thousands of stories like this. A downturn in the economy makes things even more difficult. Paranoia is not uncommon.

If your job search activities are discovered and your supervisors ask if you are looking for a job, you absolutely have to deny it! A number of misguided authorities are going to tell you not to lie and to sit down with your boss or bosses, explain why you are being forced—in your opinion—to look for another job, and try to work with them to rectify the situation. Don't let anybody kid you. Once you've admitted you're looking for a job, you're a marked person. If you aren't fired immediately, management is simply going to keep you around long enough to replace you.

Most of the time, if you are approached and asked whether you are looking for a job, your supervisors aren't sure. If they were absolutely positive, they'd probably fire you on the spot. Usually, they are fishing about your interviewing. Even if they are fairly sure, they may ask you about it just to keep you in check. You are now a traitor, an enemy of the state, and no longer the wonderful, upstanding employee you were before they suspected you were looking to leave.

You probably have a personal email address. Use it in your job search. Once in a while I've had candidates use their work email address in their job search. Dumb! Use common sense. Do not let anyone associated with your changing jobs—that is, recruiters, potential employers, and people who might help you find a job—ever email you at work.

Also, be careful in putting your résumé on a job board. In spite of what they promise, these boards are not as secure as they claim. Sure, they have means of releasing your name only with your permission; but most of the people who work with you, and most of your immediate managers, could recognize your résumé without your name on it. There is no way of knowing where your résumé might wind up when you send it out into cyberspace.

We had a candidate whom we placed a year and a half ago. She loved her job and was doing great. Her boss recently called her into his office and nervously asked her if she was looking for another job. He was pretty upset. She wasn't looking and was surprised to be asked. She asked him where he got that idea, and he stated that he had found her résumé on the Internet. It turned out that her résumé was still floating around cyberspace from a year and a half ago.

Going on Interviews

Interviewing is going to be the greatest challenge you will experience if you are currently employed. It will be a lot harder to find time to interview, unless you are in outside sales, and even then, if you travel, it is difficult. If you are in an office environment, getting out to interview usually takes a minimum of two and a half to three hours. There is a limit to the number of doctor, dentist, and school meetings for your kids that you can have before someone catches on to your interviewing. So, you need to arrange interviews for very early in the morning, 6:45 a.m. or 7:00 a.m., or early evening, 5:15 p.m., 5:30 p.m., or 6:00 p.m., or on Saturday.

One way to find time to interview is to see how much accrued vacation you have coming to you and use that time to take off for interviews. Do not take off large blocks of time, like two or three days, or one week, thinking that you will be able to spend that time doing nothing but interviewing. Interviews generally don't come that quickly or that easily; you can't line them up at your discretion. On average, you're going to have one, maybe two interviews a week (if you're lucky) and you are not likely going to be able to easily lump them into one day.

If your company will allow it, you might want to take a couple of hours off here, or a couple hours off there, and have them count against the vacation time you've accrued. Or, depending on the kind of job you are looking for, you might be able to arrange interviews on one morning or one afternoon and take that morning or afternoon off. At least by doing this, you won't feel as guilty and pressed as when you try to squeeze an interview in at lunchtime—or if you're late for work because of an interview that goes over the time that you have allotted. Interviewing on your time is much better for you mentally and emotionally.

It is also a good idea to inform an interviewing or hiring authority that you are either on your lunch hour or you have a time constraint about getting back to work, if indeed that is the case. Most interviewing and hiring authorities really understand that an employed candidate has to get back to work.

Dressing for Interviews

It has become very hard to dress for work and dress for an interview in the same way. People used to dress the same way for work as they would dress for an interview: dark suits, white shirts, conservative ties for men and suits and white blouses for women. Since business casual has become the norm at work, it is very difficult to show up on the job in a dark suit, white shirt, and conservative tie. The first thing that someone will ask is, "Are you interviewing?"

There are a couple of approaches you can take. The first is what we always called the Superman routine. (For those of you old enough to remember this concept, you know what it means; if you're not old enough to remember it, ask one of your elders.) You can have a suit in your car and, on the way to the interview, change (preferably not in a phone booth). Although this is a pain in the butt and most people hate the idea, it works!

Another idea that I recommend more and more is that, if you dress business casual at work, then have a nice sport coat (for a man) or a jacket (for a woman) in your car and wear it to the interview. Upon arrival, be sure to say to the interviewing or hiring authority something like, "You will have to pardon my dress. I normally wear a conservative suit to an interview, but we're business casual in my organization, and it is impossible for me to wear a suit at the office without broadcasting to everyone that I am interviewing. I hope you understand." Many of the people with whom you interview are going to be dressed in business casual. The ones who are not will understand your situation if you explain it in this manner. This seems like such a small thing, but it is really important.

Selling Yourself Aggressively in the Interview

The fact that you are currently employed is going to affect you most in this regard: You will be comparing the job that you presently have with an opportunity that you might consider. Now, a prospective employer certainly may have to take into consideration the fact that you're presently employed by giving you good business and economic reasons to leave your job, and accept the one that he or she might offer you. But, whatever you do, don't let the fact that you are presently employed *go to your head*.

You have to remember that you are competing in a difficult market with a lot of people who are very qualified. You may not feel that you have to sell yourself very hard, since you have a job and you might be making it a comparison, rather than having to find a job. However, a hiring authority doesn't know that and, what's more, doesn't care. A hiring authority cares about what you want only to the extent that he or she may get your services by employing you. Your goal is to get an offer. Whether or not you are employed should not have an effect on how aggressively and assertively you sell yourself in the interviewing situation.

The reason that you have to approach each interview this way is obvious: Your competition is approaching it this way. So, if you go to an interview with the idea of, "Well, I might be interested in changing and I might not. . . . I'll see if it's a better opportunity than the one I've got. Maybe I will and maybe I won't. After all, the job I have really isn't that bad," your competition is going to eat your lunch.

I had a candidate who was so comfortable in the job he presently had that he simply asked the hiring authority, "Why should I leave what I have and come to work here?" He asked this in the first four minutes of the interview. Bad move! He does have a great job and has been earning $500,000 or more pretty consistently. But the opportunity with my client was better, with a strong possibility of future ownership. The interview died right there. He didn't need to change jobs. But he should have sold himself well enough to give the client a reason to give him good reasons to consider a move. It is the candidate's responsibility to sell him- or herself, then see if the opportunity might be worth considering.

Giving Your Reasons for a Change

Make sure in your presentation that when you communicate why you are looking to change jobs, you relate your reasons for leaving to the five most prominent reasons people want to leave their jobs, as I've mentioned previously. When you don't have a job, it is obvious why you need one. However, when you presently have a job, the reasons you want to leave can eliminate you for consideration by an interviewing or hiring authority. If you tell a prospective employer that you are leaving your present position because, "Management is stupid . . . Idiots are running my company . . . I'm simply not making enough money . . . My husband (or wife) doesn't think I make enough money . . . I hate my job . . . It's just time to go," you won't do well in the interview.

I think you've probably caught on by now to the kinds of reasons you might give for leaving your job. Here are a few short scripts:

- "I really love what I do and the company that I'm with has been really great to me. But I have outgrown the function of my job. For the past two years I have felt underemployed. I am capable of doing so much more and I am not challenged in the position at all."

- "I love my job and the people I work with. However, the company culture has been very stagnant for the last few years, and I am limited both personally and professionally. I could be there for very long time, but I'm not challenged and there are no opportunities beyond the job that I have."

• "I love the company that I work for and the people I work with. But, for the past couple of years I have outgrown the level of people I work with. Because there is very little challenge in the job, I'm not likely to grow beyond this particular job. I am compensated fairly for what I do, but other than merit raises, which I have maxed out on, I'm not going to be able to earn more and provide for my family the way I want to. I'm capable of more, so I need to leave."

You have to provide very specific examples and stories that support any one of these scripts. This is *very important*! These statements are broad and general. After you make one, you have to provide a specific example. *This takes practice*! I have had hundreds of candidates over the years throw out ideas like this and then stumble and stammer with "umms and uhs" when I asked them to give me a specific example of what they mean. Have two exact, specific examples of how you have been affected—then drop the issue and move on. Continue to sell yourself.

Being Too Picky in Arranging Interviews

When you are employed, it isn't easy to make time for interviews. In fact, after the initial excitement of deciding to change jobs wears off (especially if you have to cram in a number of interviews that don't wind up being successful), interviewing becomes a real pain in the butt.

When this happens, there is a tendency to be overly selective about the kinds of opportunities you will interview for. You don't want to waste your time and go to the trouble of interviewing, especially when the first three or four haven't been successful, so you start to overanalyze what a job opportunity would be like before you interview. This is one of the biggest mistakes made by most employed job-seekers.

Candidates who have jobs will often make a decision about a prospective interview based on how it "sounds" to them or how they feel about the interview, the job, or the company before they physically interview. They tell me things like, "Well, I looked at their Web site and I don't think that is the kind of thing I want to do" or "Well I looked at the job they had posted on their Web site and it isn't something I'm interested in doing." Don't make this mistake. You want to go on any reasonable interview you can get. These jobs, companies, and the opportunities are completely different when you experience them face-to-face, compared with how you are probably imagining them.

There is no real way to evaluate a company or an opportunity unless you interview face-to-face. Don't kid yourself into thinking that you can "qualify" an opportunity over the phone by just hearing about it or reading about it on the company's Web site. It is also unfair to compare your present job with any potential job you may interview for until you actually get an offer. Now, you may decide after an initial interview that the potential opportunity for which you are interviewing is not as good as the job you presently have. If you are absolutely sure of this, then you should not continue that particular interviewing process.

When people don't make the passionate commitment to the long, difficult ordeal of finding a job (when they already have one), their job search sputters and eventually stops—until the pain of the job they presently have becomes greater than the pain of looking for a new one. And the longer the search sputters, starts, and stops, the harder it is to perform well on the job that you now have—and looking for a job becomes more frustrating.

Contacting Competitors, Suppliers, or Customers

Some of your best opportunities might be with your competitors, suppliers, or customers. If you are unemployed and you have no job to lose, it doesn't matter when you interview with them. However, if you are presently employed, you might contact these people (if you think that they might have a job opportunity for you)—very discreetly and carefully. Your biggest concern is that you may, for instance, talk to a competitor and have the fact that you're looking for a job get back to your employer.

In the case of a competitor, you may want to initially call a person one or two levels above the position that you might be interviewing for. You would tell the person that you are employed by one of their competitors, for instance, and you were thinking of a job change. You would like to speak to them confidentially about any opportunities they might have.

If you discover that there is interest, I recommend that you have one or two telephone conversations to establish your credibility, experience, and background and also to investigate the interest level on the part of the employer. I would *not* recommend sending your résumé. You should tell him or her that you will bring a résumé to the interview. Arrange the interview at a neutral site. Do not interview at the office of your competitor, supplier, or customer. If you are recognized by anyone, it will get back to your current employer in a heartbeat.

Being Recruited

When you get a call from a recruiter, one of your competitors, or any organization that is interested in speaking to you about a job (when you're happily employed), you are being recruited. Most people associate being recruited with hiring middle, upper-middle, and upper management types of positions. The truth is that when there is "pain," recruiting a good candidate can be valuable on any level. Our firm has recruited just about every kind of position you can imagine—from hourly welders, chemical compounders, and production people all the way up to presidents and executive vice presidents. Wherever there is "pain" for a particular type of employee with particularly narrow skills, there is a recruiting opportunity.

If you are being recruited by an organization or a third-party recruiter, there are a few things you must keep in mind. First, and most important, if you decide to pursue a new job opportunity that you were called about, when you were not mentally and emotionally looking for a job, you better prepare yourself to interview and possibly change jobs. When an individual is not contemplating changing jobs, and the person is relatively happy with the job he or she has, getting emotionally and mentally prepared to look for a job is a very big hurdle.

When being recruited for a particular job, before you go on an initial interview, you need to emotionally and mentally come to grips with the idea of changing jobs. Having been recruited, if you go to an interviewing situation without at least *acting* like you are interested in the new opportunity, you are not likely to get to first base with the job.

Second, don't let being recruited go to your head. Often, because a candidate really isn't looking for a job, he or she goes into the interviewing situation with all kinds of ridiculous demands on the possible new employer—ones that are totally out of line with reasonable requests. The attitude is, "Well, I'm not really looking for a job, but if I'm going to change, I really have to have a lot of very good reasons to do it—they are going to have to make it worth my while."

The problem with this thinking is that the candidate (unless coached by a good recruiter) may come up with ridiculous demands that are so obviously out of line that he or she could very well not only not get the opportunity, but embarrass him- or herself and destroy any potential future opportunity with similar organizations. So, if you are being recruited and you decide to pursue the opportunity, be realistic about what you can expect in money, title, and responsibilities in order to change jobs. Sell yourself one step at a time. Interview as though you were interested in changing, sell yourself really hard, get a reasonable offer, and then see if it works for you.

A recent candidate of ours went to work for a client that we recruited him for—three years *after* we initially recruited him for the company. He got all the way to receiving an offer back then, but he decided to stay where he was. He sold himself so well, they remembered him. When things changed at his company, we called the client we had recruited him for three years previously. They met for one hour and hired him—at a better job than the one we originally had recruited him for. He was so good at selling himself the first time, it carried over.

Conclusion

Looking for a job when you have a job is much harder than most people imagine. It is like having a second job that you have to perform over, under, and around your current job—while continuing to perform that job to the best of your ability. In addition, you must make sure that your current employer doesn't discover that you're looking for a new job.

Be sure that you are completely committed to the job search and the time and extra effort it will entail, or it's not worth pursuing. Start by closely examining your reasons for wanting to change jobs; make sure they are valid and make sure they are your reasons, not someone else's. Once you have decided to take the plunge, give as much energy and time as possible to the job search. You will be in competition with serious job candidates, so you must be equally serious. You can't simply play job search as a sideline to your existing job. You must arrange as many interviews as you can possibly handle and sell yourself as aggressively as if you have been out of a job for months.

14 : References: The Silent Killer

ONE OF THE FIRST THINGS that a hiring organization is going to do is try to find out everything it can about the candidate—through a supplied list of references and, now, on the Internet. Traditional reference checking has its own challenges, which I'll discuss in a minute. But these days, the biggest "reference check" problems have to do with the permanent nature of the Internet and the intermingling of personal, social interaction, and business information that it encourages.

In this chapter I discuss the problems and questions that surround reference checking, and how best you should handle this aspect of the job search process. But, to begin, let's view the matter in this new age of cyberspace information.

New-Age Reference Checking: Self-Inflicted Wounds

> "They found something on Facebook about me they didn't like. Is that legal?"
> — Geoffrey T., *The Job Search Solution* radio caller

Your prospective employers are going to Google your name, try to find your MySpace, Facebook, Twitter, or any other kind of social/business networking account, and review your LinkedIn profile. Anything they find will be used to either help or hinder your candidacy.

For better or for worse, *everything* you might do, write, or say could show up on the Internet. At least two times a month, one of our candidates who seems like he or she is going to get hired, instead gets eliminated because of what a hiring organization finds out about the candidate just by searching around on the Internet. Sometimes what companies find has nothing to do with our candidate, except they find something under the same or a similar name. Recently, one of our hiring authorities Googled the email address of a candidate and found that someone with a very, very close email address had written a review—of a prostitute. Unbelievable! It wasn't our candidate, but the hiring authority was so taken aback, he simply didn't even want to discuss it. It wasn't exactly the same email address, but close enough to be disturbing.

We've had candidates eliminated because of comments they made on Facebook or comments made about them on Facebook; pictures they posted on their social networking sites like MySpace; off-color public Twitter posts they forgot about; blogs in which they wrote about their views, as well as insulting blogs written about them by ex-spouses, ex-boyfriends, or ex-girlfriends; eight-year-old articles mentioning their names and questionable circumstances; as well as pejorative writings about them by others. These things all show up on the Internet when a name is Googled.

We've had candidates eliminated because their LinkedIn profile did not agree with their résumé, or because they didn't have a very robust profile on LinkedIn. And we can't count the number of times that candidates' identities have been confused with other people with the same name, causing a hiring authority to stop and think. (And don't think that "positive" recommendations on LinkedIn make a big deal of difference. They don't seem to.)

The *New York Times* reported a study done by Microsoft claiming that 75 percent of the executive recruiters and human resources professionals surveyed said they research promising candidates online, using search engines, social networking sites, personal Web sites, blogs, Twitter feeds, and online gaming sites, as well as photo and video-sharing sites. Of the surveyed, 70 percent revealed that information they found online led them to reject a candidate.

The *Times* also reported that a twenty-five-year-old Pennsylvania high school "teacher in training" posted a photo of herself on her MySpace page, in which she wore a pirate hat and held a plastic cup at a party, captioned, "Drunken Pirate." Less than a week before she was scheduled to graduate, the university refused to issue her a teaching degree because the students could find her photo online and get the impression that she was encouraging drunkenness. When she sued, citing her First Amendment rights, the court ruled against her.

The constantly evolving, permanent digital record of our lives means that we've lost, to a large degree, control of our reputations. The possibility of second chances may be lost as well. Most hiring authorities, when they discover anything of a questionable nature regarding a candidate, will simply drop them. Unlike traditional reference checking, which is usually centered on businesspeople, this kind of reference checking has only the limits that the Internet poses. Over the next few years, people may come to their senses and realize that anything they do, personal or public, that might show up anywhere on the Internet is not going to help them.

There are two major issues that candidates need to be aware of regarding this kind of reference checking. First, clean up anything that might be questionable regarding your Internet "presence." And don't complain that personal stuff like this should not be used to make business decisions about hiring you. Companies want to try to assess your character as much as anything else. They're going to check your credit, arrest record, and anything else—including what there might be about you on the Internet.

Second, do your own research on yourself. Be as extensive as you possibly can. If you find anything that you can't do anything about, like articles about people with your same name, be prepared to let a hiring authority know of this problem before they do this type of reference checking.

There are now services that offer to protect an individual's reputation online. These services help their clients deal with negative personal information and enable them to monitor the Web and influence what people see when they search for them online. Some of these services will not only monitor your online presence but also check your formal business references for you.

When these kinds of challenges became a reality a few years ago, many candidates were surprised that companies paid attention to the "social media." Some candidates used to simply blow it off; others get downright mad about it. The bottom line is that it is very serious stuff and it can cost people not just their jobs but also their careers.

Traditional Reference Checking

"I had two great opportunities where I thought I was going to get offers. Then nothing happened. They just stopped. I couldn't figure it out. After I read your chapter on references, it dawned on me. I hadn't done this part very well."
—Michael T., Chicago, Illinois

Providing business references to potential employers is something that everyone takes for granted, yet few people really understand the true implications or possible pitfalls. References can be silent cancers that kill a great opportunity. At least once or twice a month, we have a placement that looks as if it is in the final stages, then it gets sabotaged by a bad reference. A reference doesn't even have to be out-and-out bad to cause problems—hiring authorities will perceive a reference as poor because it is neutral, uninformative, or downright unhelpful.

If you are the kind of candidate who has excellent references from everyone you have ever worked for or with, you probably don't need to read this chapter. It may not hurt to read it, though, because some of the logistical ideas are of value.

You may not think you need any help here, but one of the most shocking surprises you can ever have is when you assume that all your references are excellent, only to find out that one or more of them has cost you a job opportunity. I would estimate that at least 20 to 25 percent of the job-seeking candidates out there have at least one reference challenge in their background—and they have absolutely no idea that it is there.

This may come as a surprise to most readers, but (except in instances of disclosing acts of violence or acts of financial mismanagement) companies are not legally required to provide any kind of references about previous employees. Companies may be subject to a charge of defamation by giving a reference that could be construed as bad, and they have absolutely nothing to gain by giving any kind of a reference, good or bad. So, any kind of reference an organization will provide goes beyond what it *has* to do.

Companies will usually verify dates of employment and earnings and confirm if a person is eligible for rehire in the eyes of the company (but there is nothing that states they have to do any of this). Many companies will not even respond to references that are solicited over the telephone; they require a written request for references and only respond to those requests in writing. Most prospective employers are going to ask you for specific references from the most recent jobs you have had. Even in situations where you know that a previous employer is not going to provide an adequate reference, you are going to be forced to find someone within the company who can speak of your performance, even if it's against the policies of the company. This poses a tremendous difficulty for many candidates.

I know numerous potential employers who will tell a candidate, "Look, I don't care what your previous company's policy is, I need to talk to someone you have worked for before I consider hiring you. If you can't get me someone like that, I can't consider you."

Why References Are So Important

The hiring environment is treacherous these days. As I've said several times in this book, hiring authorities are afraid of making a mistake. They are operating more out of fear of loss than they are vision of gain. They are so afraid of making a mistake that they go to great lengths to be *careful*. They are so leery of what people write on their résumés, so guarded about everything they hear from candidates, that they become extra careful about checking references. They check more of them than they used to, and they check them more carefully. Some hiring authorities insist on checking "back door" references on every candidate and read into what they hear.

Don't Take Them for Granted

Most employers will ask you to give them three or four people as references and specify the relationship you had with those people. Some employers are going to ask you for specific people, like previous supervisors, customers, or maybe peers. Be sure that you're prepared to provide these different kinds of references when asked.

As you begin your job search, it is a good idea to think about who you might give as a reference in just about any interviewing process. I would recommend calling those people to let them know that you are actively looking for a position and asking their permission to use them as a reference. It is rare, but I have seen situations where the people who candidates thought would be references for them refused to do it.

After they give you permission, inform them that you will let them know who might be checking your reference, what kind of position it is, and exactly what in your background they should emphasize when the reference is checked.

When to Provide References

Most potential employers are going to ask you to give them permission to check references. Some ask to do it with a form to sign. Others simply ask it verbally from you before they make an offer. I've encountered a number of companies over the years that ask for references before they even interview the candidate. My advice is to provide your references when you are asked to, not before, no matter how proud you are of them. Employers have their preferred way of asking for and handling references, so you're not going to gain any advantage by handing them in early.

I also have known candidates to put references on their résumés. I don't recommend doing this. You don't want your references contacted unless you are a serious candidate for the opportunity and you are close to getting an offer. I've known situations where a prospective employer used the references on a person's résumé to find other candidates (ones that the candidate provided in the résumé), so that they could have, in essence, more competition for the job. There are few things that will make you feel as stupid as finding out that one of your references got the job for which you were interviewing, simply because you provided the person's name and their number. Bet you never thought that would happen!

Reference Letters and LinkedIn Recommendations

It certainly doesn't hurt to have letters of reference from previous employers that you can use in the interviewing process. These are usually very broad statements regarding your work, but they certainly can't be denied. A hiring authority may likely want to speak personally to the person who wrote the letter, but having a letter certainly can't hurt. Having three or four reference letters ready at the time references are requested is pretty powerful.

Having positive recommendations from previous supervisors, customers, or peers on your LinkedIn profile also can't hurt. A hiring authority will probably view these as nice to have but won't use them in the same way as an actual employment reference.

Treacherous References

Bad, poor, and mediocre references occur all the time—far more often than you probably realize. Let's discuss situations where references can jeopardize your candidacy and give you solutions for each situation.

When a Blatantly Bad Reference Is Given

Few people will admit they might get a bad or poor reference from a previous employer. It happens so often that I need to address it in detail. Remember that 97 percent of the companies in the United States are run by people who are involved in businesses they know well, but these businesspeople are not really people oriented. The owners and managers of many of these organizations simply don't realize the liability they might incur for giving a bad reference.

If you have been fired by a company, the best that you can hope for is to convince the company to provide a neutral reference when it is contacted. A neutral reference is simply the verification of dates of employment, earnings, and the question of being rehired.

There are professional organizations that will actually check a reference for you. I've known candidates who had friends do it or a previous manager whom they could trust. If you suspect that you are going to get a bad reference from anyone in the company, the most effective way to deal with it is not to get mad or angry. The first thing to do is to call the person you think might give a bad reference and discuss the reference that he or she might give. Go over your strengths and weaknesses and ask for the person's suggestions. Most of the time, people will soften and at least provide a neutral reference. Ask the person if he or she would be willing to give you a positive reference in certain situations; tell the person that you will call and inform him or her about who will be calling and what might be asked. If these people won't come to the phone or return your call, you might simply be stuck.

If you are certain someone is giving you a bad reference and you cannot talk to him or her, write a letter to this person explaining that you understand he or she has been giving you a bad reference and you would like it to stop. Send a copy of the letter to the president of the company. Do not threaten. You're trying to get, at least, a neutral job reference. You do not want to threaten legal action unless you have absolutely no other choice. Most of the time, an organization in this situation will get the message loud and clear, and start providing neutral information.

One of the premier labor attorneys in the Southwest, Stephen Key, reminds me from time to time that a previous employer can tell anyone checking a previous employment reference *anything* about a previous employee—as long as what he or she says is the *truth*. The law seems to protect previous employees only from being lied about. Most employers, however, are so afraid of litigation that a gentle threat will usually stop bad references.

If you know that you are going to get a poor reference, even if it is neutralized, especially for the last position you had, it is advisable to line up a number of positive informal references at the organization from which you were fired. To do this, ask a number of peers or supervisors if you can get them to talk off the record to a prospective employer about your work habits. So, the party line of the company might be a poor or, at best, a neutral reference, but it is offset by three or four people at that company who will say very positive things about you.

Another way to counterbalance a bad reference at one particular organization is to provide a number of other glowing references from previous organizations that you've worked for. A third way of counterbalancing a potentially poor reference is to have letters of reference from some of the customers for whom you have done a good job. It is not uncommon for salespeople, when interviewing, to be asked for customer references.

If you are an accountant and you were the interface between your firm and an external auditing or external accounting firm, you might find one of those people with whom you interfaced to write you a letter of reference. No matter what position you were in with the company, think of whether there were any external organizations you worked with where you built rapport with individuals.

When Silence Is Interpreted as a Bad Reference

This is a situation in which a reference is called, usually a previous employer, and he or she refuses to answer any questions at all. He or she ignores the phone calls, refuses to talk with the potential hiring authority, and sends the person checking the reference to the HR department, if the company has one. This kind of response does not normally come from someone whom the candidate has asked to give a reference. It's usually a supervisor or manager whom the candidate has worked for whose name the candidate had to provide during the interviewing process. I've had previous managers or supervisors of my candidates, when contacted about a job reference, simply state, "I'm just not going to discuss it."

When an ex-manager or ex-supervisor will not discuss anything about you as a previous employee, it raises all kinds of red flags for a prospective employer. Unfortunately, people will generally assume a dreadfully bad reference in a situation like this. The silence is then interpreted as a negative reference. You want to offset this kind of poor reference in the same way that you offset a bad reference. Get a plethora of positive references from peers you worked with, customers, or previous employers. If you know silence is going to be the response, you need to forewarn the interviewing, hiring, or reference-checking authorities that they're not going to get any reply from anyone, even when they ask.

When a Bad Reference Is Implied but Not Specified

When the person giving a reference answers only the minimal questions but answers them in such an emphatic, disdainful manner, it communicates nothing but a bad reference. For instance, the person inquiring about a reference asks, "Would this previous employee be considered for rehire?" And the answer comes across something like, "Are you kidding me! Absolutely, unequivocally, undeniably, under no circumstances, over my dead body, not in this lifetime. No!" And it is said with the most animated, hateful tone imaginable. True, all the person giving the reference did was answer the question, but the way he or she answered it communicates a very bad reference.

There is not much you can do about this type of negative response to a simple question. It just happens. But, again, if you have some reason to suspect that this will happen, you can mention your concern to the hiring authority.

When a Reference Is Given by a Poorly Informed Source

When the candidate neglects to brief the person giving the reference on exactly what kind of position the reference check is for, it puts the reference at a disadvantage. It is important for you to call your references who will be checked and inform them what company will be checking the reference, who will be checking the reference, what kind of job you are being considered for, and, most important, what aspects of your history pertain to the job being pursued.

A few years ago, I had an employer check a reference of one of my candidates. My candidate was in the final throes of getting an offer from a company that sold small-ticket products to mid-market organizations (that is, $500 million companies and under, which required a high number of cold calls to generate a high number of small trans-actions). He was an excellent candidate and the opportunity was outstanding. It looked like a great match.

When the hiring authority got one of my candidate's references on the phone, the reference started telling the hiring authority how wonderful my candidate was on large big-ticket sales, how wonderful he was at schmoozing with large, national accounts, how great he was at going after large deals, along with mentioning that he had never seen the candidate make a lot of cold calls or generate a high number of transactions. End of reference. End of being considered for the job.

All my candidate would have had to do was talk to his reference and explain to him the nature of the position for which he was being considered. His reference thought he was helping the candidate get the job, but he wasn't.

Backdoor References

There is nothing more treacherous than backdoor references. These are people who are known by a prospective employer who know people who know people who know you. And, supposedly, these people know something about your personal and profes-sional capabilities. For the most part, backdoor references will hurt you more than they will help you.

Usually these backdoor references are so far removed from knowing the candidate that their opinions are not valid. I guess that the reason most of these kinds of references are negative is this simple fact: If I imply that you should not hire someone, based on a negative reference that I give—and you don't hire that person—you will never know if I'm right or wrong. So the safest thing for distant, backdoor-reference givers to do is to give a less-than-positive reference—even if they don't know what they're talking about—because, if you're not hired, they're right and you're never going to know the difference.

If you find out that a hiring authority is going to try to check backdoor references of people who may or may not know you, you need to be on your guard. One way of overcoming this problem is to provide a number of written references, as well as an extensive list of people for whom you have actually worked, trusting that the hiring authority will focus on them rather than trying to find backdoor references elsewhere.

Reference from Your Current Employer After You Are Hired

Many people think that if they fudge on the dates of employment in their most recent job, they will not be discovered. In other words, a person will put a date of employment, for instance, of April 2009 to Present, when he or she actually left the job recently, but wants to appear currently employed. Candidates often fudge on their current earnings, too, thinking it won't be checked since they are employed.

I really don't have a problem with using "to present" regarding employment dates. Of course, if you left your most recent position nine months ago and you are still putting this phrase on your résumé, you're going to run into big problems. But if it was in the past two or three months, you can probably get away with it, *if you inform* the prospective employer, during the interview process, of when you departed. However, embellishing your earnings will cause you a problem, even after you've been hired.

Many companies will hire you conditionally with the understanding that they may change their mind after they check the reference of your present employer, even after you have started working for them. You would be amazed what these companies find out in checking such a reference. So, if you are lying about anything regarding your present employment, thinking that no one will ever check the reference because you are currently employed, you're likely to get caught. The bigger the lie, the bigger the problem it will cause.

General Guidelines on References

Here are several helpful thoughts about references:

Whom to Ask

A prospective employer is going to be interested in references from people who can tell him or her about your work and your ability to perform on a job. Personal references are nice, but most employers don't really care that much about them. They want to talk with people you've worked with, whether those people really like you or not. In fact, if you provide too many personal references rather than professional ones, you appear to be covering up the professional ones.

Try to find these references before you are asked for them because there is nothing more frustrating than spending two or three days scrambling around trying to find references when a job offer hinges on it. So, locate those people before you need them and know where they are.

Make a list of your references. Start with the people who you are confident will give you a positive reference. Obviously, people you were friendly with and worked well with are better than those you didn't really get along with or with whom you had work-related problems. Choose people with titles as far up the food chain as you can, but you want to use people who actually knew and worked with you. (The president of your former company, whom you met once in five years, may look good as a name and title on the page, but he or she is unlikely to have much of substance to say about you, if anything.) In addition, you should list people who held a specific position that you might be asked about, such as your immediate supervisor or team leader.

How to Ask

Asking someone to be a reference for you is a fairly simple thing to do. You just want be sure that you don't communicate the idea that you are going to be burdening someone. Giving a reference for someone can get old really fast if it is necessary to do more than four or five times. After all, you are asking someone to do something out of the kindness of his or her heart without any compensation.

Here's a basic script of what you should say:

"Hello, ____ [name] ___, this is [your name]. I am in the process of changing jobs and I would like to use you as a reference. Please keep this very confidential, but I have to change positions [or, I lost my job]."

Then explain in a brief manner why you are looking to change or why you lost your last position. Make sure that they are the *exact same reasons* that you are giving to a prospective employer, so that you and your references are consistent with what you say, and make the reasons as positive as possible.

"I would like to ask for your help. I will not take advantage of your kindness and your time. I will have people call you only when I am a serious contender for an opportunity. I will call you before each prospective employer speaks to you and brief you regarding the kind of position and the kind of opportunity I am applying for, so that you can be prepared. Would that be all right?"

Most reasonable people are willing to help you. Assure them that you will inform them about each prospective employer before that employer calls them. You will want to prepare them for the specific opportunity that you might be applying for. As I mentioned above, a poorly informed reference can be a bad reference.

Customizing Your References

This is a simple concept, but most people don't think to take advantage of it. It is the idea of providing different kinds of references to different employers depending on the type of position you are seeking.

Not only should you consider providing different people for references in different positions, but you definitely should call those people and prepare them for giving a reference. It is important that when you prepare a reference, you clearly explain to the reference *exactly* what kind of job you are applying for; the company you are applying to; the person who is going to actually be checking the reference (such as the hiring authority or the HR department); what kinds of questions may be asked; and, most important, what kinds of specific attributes your reference might emphasize to the prospective employer, or what kinds of issues the prospective employer might have concerning your candidacy that the reference might be able to address. You want to set the stage for the prospective employer to not only get a specific work reference but also to become more convinced of your ability to do a specific job.

An example would be something like this:

> "Hello, ____ [name] _____, this is [name]. I am a finalist for a job as an assistant controller for _____ company. The comptroller of company is going to give you a call to check my employment reference with you. I would like to know your availability over the next few days and ask if it would be convenient for this person to give you a call? [pause]
>
> "The company are particularly interested in someone who has had supervisory experience because there are three accountants who are going to be responsible to this person. I would appreciate it if you could relate to the caller the supervisory skills you observed in me. [pause]
>
> "Two of the people that the assistant controller is going to oversee are going to need to be released and two new ones hired. I would like you to pass on to the hiring authority, Mr. or Ms._____, your knowledge of my ability to let people go, as we did when I worked with you, as well as my ability to successfully hire good employees. [pause]
>
> "One of the important aspects of the job is to be able to supervise and be responsible for the filing of SEC reports. The one concern that Mr. or Ms. _____ might have about my candidacy is that I was involved in filing the SEC reports only once, when I worked for you. I would appreciate it if you can emphasize, when he or she calls, the kind of contribution I made in supervising the filing of those reports for the company when I worked for you. Please remind him or her of how independently we worked and how unsupervised I was. [pause]
>
> "The opportunity is a very good one for me. [*Then you might want to describe the job in as much detail as necessary*] I really want the position. Anything you can do to help me would be appreciated. Does this all make sense to you and might you have any questions?"
>
> In this scenario, the reference would not only report on the candidate's work ethic but also address the candidate's specific ability to supervise the filing of an SEC report. This doesn't sound like a really big deal, but people are often hired or not hired for relatively small issues.

If You Burned Some Bridges

Hardly anyone will ever admit to having burned bridges when leaving a job, but it probably happens at least 25 to 30 percent of the time. Few employees or managers would ever want to admit to the embarrassing things that they did as they were going out the door.

Burning bridges can occur in a couple of different fashions. The first can be an overt, obvious action, like a yelling or screaming match with the supervisor or someone in authority in the company. It can also be a relatively passive activity, like just plain not showing up for work. Both types of burning bridges are usually cases of being very emotional at the moment and being so embarrassed afterward that a person doesn't really know how to rectify the mess he or she made.

When this ex-employee later needs a reference from that organization, he or she is really in a predicament. If that is your situation, the only thing you can do when this situation has happened is call your former supervisor or the person you are going to give as a reference and ask for forgiveness. You explain to that person that it was a terribly emotional time in your life for many different reasons and that if you had it to do over again, you wouldn't have done what you did. You would like this person to be a reference for you, speaking of your work habits, the quality of work that you've done, and so forth. Now, unless you physically threatened someone, most people are willing to go out of their way to forgive. Why? Because they want forgiveness from other people themselves.

I would then recommend that you describe the kind of position for which you are applying and handle the call just as you would when you customize a reference. I have known candidates who, when they can't get their previous employer on the phone, write a letter or email the individual. You might not get a phenomenally glowing reference, but if you can neutralize a blatantly negative one, you're better off.

Overworking Your References

You need to be careful not to overwork your references. People don't mind being a reference two or three times. When it gets to be more than three or four times, they may become irritated at having to do it so many times. A bit exasperated, they will put off calling the prospective employer back or be hard to reach. It isn't so much that they won't do it, it's just they feel taken advantage of.

There are two ways to keep this from happening. First, have several different references you can use in different situations. Unless an organization that you are interviewing with asks for more, it is reasonable to give it two or three references. Coming up with two of your previous managers is reasonable.

The second way to deal with the reference that you really need is to be sure that you call the reference *every time* a prospective employer is going to call the person. The personal touch each time a reference is going to be used makes the whole experience more palatable. Once you are employed, if you feel like you have overused a reference or two, you may want to send the individual a gracious thank-you note, along with a gift certificate to dinner or tickets to a play or a movie.

> **Key Point:** References are crucial to your successful job search. Prepare them and use them wisely.

Credit Checks, Lawsuits, Criminal/Arrest Records

All of these issues have become more prevalent in the hiring process than they ever used to be. It is much harder to get real personal references so companies now rely more on objective reports like credit and lawsuit reports, as well as criminal reports. Bruised credit, or a very poor credit report, will disqualify a candidate from being hired in certain businesses. Arrest and conviction records are extremely difficult to overcome in a hiring situation, although I have seen companies discover DWIs on a candidate's record and still hire the person.

Different states have different laws regarding how long arrests and convictions can stay on your record. If you are unfortunate enough to have some of these lingering in your background, check with an attorney about what you can do regarding them. "Ancient history" records that show this kind of misconduct ten or twelve years earlier may be easier to deal with than any issues that have come up in the last two or three years. Just be aware that these issues are going to stand in your way. Some employers are more understanding about these than others.

Credit checks are a bigger problem than most people will admit. The last few years have created a phenomenal number of people with poor credit and housing foreclosures in their background. People with a poor credit report will rarely admit to it until it is checked. If your credit has been badly bruised, or you have a poor credit rating because of being out of work for a long time, you should share that fact with a prospective employer *before* the credit check is done. You can check your own credit reports to see what the results are through the credit bureaus themselves. If there is a problem with your credit report that the company may not like but can tolerate, at least your telling the hiring authority softens the blow.

Some professions like banking won't even begin to consider a candidate who's had anything less than an A+ credit rating. (It is as hard on the banks as the candidates. Recently, it took us two-and-a-half months to find a relatively entry-level computer operator for one of our banking clients. We can find plenty of candidates, and between us and the bank, probably interviewed twenty-three or twenty-four local candidates. Upon doing credit checks for all of them, *not one of them* could pass the credit requirements. Believe it or not, we found a candidate in Washington State who was willing to relocate to Texas at his own expense. He had the qualifications and passed the credit stipulations. The bank interviewed him over the phone and hired him. Credit became the major qualification for getting the job. Go figure.)

Know what your credit situation is. Different types of businesses and companies may respond to different issues different ways. Don't let the issue be a surprise to a hiring authority when your credit is checked. If you are a serious candidate, tell the company beforehand.

15 Even When You Reach the Finals, Take Nothing for Granted

IF YOU'VE REACHED THE FINALS and you've been through numbers of interviews, and you've gotten to third base with a couple of different opportunities, the end is near, right? Wrong! As with many of the parts of the process, the final activities—getting from third base to home plate—are just another series of events that you are going to manage. One of the biggest challenges that you have in all of this job-finding process is to unemotionally, objectively, and mindfully manage the process of finding a job from one step to the next step.

> "They told me they were going to hire me. That was three weeks ago and I haven't heard from them. It's a good thing I read your book and I kept other interviews going." —Sally M., Los Angeles

Most people get to the finals with one—or at most, two—job opportunities and they quit working the process. They think that when they get to third base, it's just a matter of time before they reach home. Big mistake! You cannot afford to count on anything regarding a job opportunity until you actually have an offer and a start date. Even then, I would not recommend that you shut down all the other opportunities that you might have at various stages of the process.

In this chapter I present, first, the ten top mistakes candidates make when they *think* they are going to get a job offer, and then the five big mistakes they make when then believe they *won't* get that offer. Then, I tell you how best to proceed when the offer comes through: how to quality the offer and evaluate it, how to negotiate a better deal, and how to accept the offer and start work.

Coming into the Home Stretch

So what do you do when you reach the finals? Exactly the same thing you did to get there. Keep working the process. Find the employer's "pain," sell yourself as hard as you can, get a commitment from a hiring authority, go to the next interview, do the same thing, go to the next interview, get a commitment, and try to get an offer. The goal of the process is to get an offer—one, two, or as many as you can.

Don't become overly excited, don't get down in the dumps—just keep working the process. Every event in the job-seeking process is just that—an event. Some events will be more beneficial than others. The key to the whole situation is to understand that all events are positive; some are more beneficial positive events and some are less beneficial positive events. But all events are just steps along the way to a positive outcome. If you are juggling enough opportunities in the job-seeking process, you don't have to worry about landing on a more positive event. It's a numbers game.

But first, let's make sure you don't mess things up for yourself.

Top Ten Mistakes Candidates Make When They're Told They're Going to Get an Offer

1. *Thinking that the search is over and they're going to get hired.* An offer is like any other step in the process of getting hired. It is just a step. This whole process really is not over until you not only have been hired but have been in the job for six to nine months.

2. *Assuming that they can quit selling themselves.* Candidates think that because they're getting an offer they don't have to keep selling themselves. I have seen lots of offers become much better simply because candidates realize that until they accept an offer they need to keep selling their ability to do the job and reasons why they ought to be hired.

3. *Thinking that the negotiations at the time of a final offer need to be adversarial.* Candidates get fearful and scared and approach the final offer stages with an attitude of "fear of loss." They need to approach an offer stage with an attitude of, "We're all in this together—let's work something out that's valuable to all of us."

4. *Being too anxious and not listening or asking the right kind of questions so they totally understand the offer.* Oftentimes, candidates are so anxious to get an offer that they don't really listen to all of it. They don't take good notes and take a logical or reasonable step-by-step approach to the offer stage.

5. *Being too cautious about an offer and afraid of making a mistake.* Candidates often are so afraid of making a mistake and accepting a job that they become too cautious about an offer. They start thinking about things to consider and think themselves out of a very good opportunity.

6. *Assuming that since they're getting an offer (that they might take), they can stop other interviewing cycles.* If candidates recognize that offers are simply steps in the process they're more likely to get more than one offer. Never quit getting offers until you have one that you have accepted.

7. *Not taking every offer seriously.* Candidates will often go into receiving an offer pretty convinced that they will not accept it for lots of different reasons. I don't recommend doing this. It is important to go after every offer as though it were the last one on earth. Until you hear everything there is to know about an offer, you really don't know enough about it to know whether you will accept or reject it. Assume nothing until you have the offer and you know everything about it.

8. *Taking too much time to think about an offer.* If a candidate takes more than a day or so to "think about" an offer, any employer in his right mind is going to rescind the offer and hire the no. 2 candidate. Most employers will assume that, if you tell them number-two that you are going to think about an offer for more than one day, you're going to leverage that offer with another company. They won't like it and will be irritated.

9. *Making assumptions about an offer after they have received it.* Because having to accept/reject an offer can be emotionally stressful, candidates will often be embarrassed and not ask further questions after they get an offer. If you don't understand everything there is to know about an offer, act like a good businessperson and call the hiring authority to get a further explanation.

10. *Setting the start date out too far after an offer is accepted.* If an offer is accepted, you want to be sure that you start the new job just as soon as possible. Any time that elapses between the offer and starting the job beyond two weeks opens up too many possibilities for a status change. No company or hiring authority will want to admit that this kind of thing can happen, but I see it regularly. Once you have committed to take the job, start it just as soon as possible. Leave nothing to chance!

Handling the Less-Than-Beneficial Positive Events

These are the events that, in one way or another, do *not* get you a job offer. You are going to experience a much greater number of these events than you are going to experience getting job offers. And as you go through each one of them, *you need to assess what you could have done better.*

Make notes about each opportunity you pursue. Follow up on those notes with a phone call ten days or so after you last had contact with a hiring authority. You will be amazed at the number of opportunities that present themselves to people simply because they were persistent in calling. Oftentimes, a hiring authority zones in on one or two particular candidates, but drags his or her process on so long that the primary candidates are lost and the process must start all over again. And when the hiring authority needs to start over, you want to be the one who is available at that time.

If you do not hear from a hiring authority after you call several times, you need to call or write and ask his or her input as to why you weren't pursued. If you can get the person on the phone, something like the following script works well:

> "Mr. or Ms._____, I really appreciated the interview that we had the other day. Since I did not hear from you at the time that you said you would get back to me, and I called a number of times, I'm assuming that I'm no longer a candidate. I would like to ask your help. Could you please tell me where I might have gone wrong in the interview, what I might have been able to do better and, constructively, why I was not considered beyond the initial interview?"

Don't expect a call back or an email from every initial interview that you follow up like this. If you do not hear from the hiring authority after you've gone to this effort, put this person on the same rotation to call ten days later to remind him or her that you are still available. Remember to keep your cool. Never sound irritated or mad. Do not take it personally!

If you are eliminated as a candidate after a second or third interview, the hiring authority will usually communicate directly with you as to why. If he or she does not, it is a good idea to call—or, as a last resort, write—and ask what happened. Again, remember to keep your cool. You will be amazed at the number of times that the reasons for not being hired have nothing to do with you.

Most people, even hiring authorities, think they are going to interview and hire someone within a two- to three-week period. But the average hiring cycle (even when there is "pain") is more like 90 to 120 days. Many things can happen in that time. Primary candidates can take a different job or turn an offer down. So keep calling and keep yourself on the mind of a hiring authority.

My experience has been that if you make it to a second or third interview with any organization, you are probably qualified to do the job. When a company hires someone else, it is not necessarily based on that person's ability to do the job, but for other kinds of reasons that are intangible. If you have gone beyond the second or third interview, you may still very well be a viable candidate—even though the company is pursuing someone else. So, for goodness' sake, unless you have found a job, keep pursuing this opportunity at least four or five weeks after the new employee has reported to the job.

If you get to the second or third level of the interviewing process and are not hired, it is always a good idea to call and talk to the hiring authority. Let this person know that you were very interested in his or her opportunity and company, and say that you would like to be considered for any other opportunities that may arise.

Tell the hiring authority that you really appreciated him or her and the company and that you would like the individual to keep your résumé or pass it on to any other hiring authority, in or out of the company. You will also want to ask permission to call the person from time to time and ask advice about other opportunities that you may come across. The idea here is to make this hiring authority your friend and mentor.

You would be surprised how often people are hired this way. If they made it that far into the interviewing process, they were obviously well thought of by the hiring authority. Making that authority your friend and calling this person every once in a while to keep your name in front of him or her, especially if you haven't found a job yet, is a great idea.

You cannot keep this kind of disappointment from happening. But if you follow my system, you will be in the cycle of so many other opportunities that may be equally good that your disappointment will be short-lived.

The Top Five Mistakes Candidates Make When They Think They've Been Eliminated After an Interview

1. *Not following up with the interviewing or hiring authority.* No doesn't always mean a "no." Just because you think you have been eliminated from contention doesn't mean you shouldn't follow up with employers, thanking them for their time and expressing interest in them personally and the company for the future.

2. *Not letting the hiring or interviewing authority know that you would still like to be considered for other opportunities in the company.* Most candidates simply stop selling themselves to a prospective employer. They confuse the job they're interviewing for with being hired. I had one of my candidates a few years back stay in contact with the hiring authority even though he had been rejected for the position he was interviewing for. He was hired by the hiring authority—seven years later at a totally different company.

3. *Not asking the interviewing or hiring authority how you could have done better in the interviewing process.* In other words, what made the difference between the people they pursued and you? What could you have done better? Feedback is the breakfast of champions!

4. *Not asking the interviewing or hiring authority who else he or she might know who might need a good employee.* Just because hiring authorities may not hire you doesn't mean they won't like you. If they like you well enough they may not hesitate to refer you to friends of theirs who may need an employee.

5. *Not following up with the interviewing or hiring authority even weeks or months after the interview.* If you haven't found a job, it certainly doesn't hurt to email or call a hiring authority even weeks or months after the interview. Most hiring authorities love persistence and the willingness to work. Keeping in touch this way certainly can't hurt.

Handling the More Beneficial Positive Events

These are all the events that culminate in getting a job offer. Getting a job offer is the most important thing you can do in the job search. You can't accept an offer that you don't have. I must warn you that there are going to be times when you will be expecting an offer and it won't come. In fact, from time to time you are going to hear momentary lies like, "We really want to hire you. We will get back to you in a day or so." Whatever you do, don't celebrate anything at that point. Don't do anything until you have an offer in your hand.

Qualifying Your Job Opportunities

Most people who write books about finding jobs talk about qualifying your opportunities before you really get to the end of the interviewing process. Don't do that. The reason is very simple: Almost everything about a job opportunity can change between the initial search for a candidate and the final offer and acceptance. If there is one thing that I have learned since 1973, it is that what companies normally start out looking for in an employee from the top to the bottom of the organization—the titles that they will give, the duties and responsibilities that are associated with a particular job, and, probably most important, the money that they're willing to pay for it—can change anywhere from a small amount to a drastic amount from the beginning of the job search to the filling of the position.

I've experienced candidates getting starting salaries as much as $60,000 a year *more* than what a company originally wanted to pay. They accomplished this simply because they did not qualify themselves *out* of the opportunity in the initial part of the interviewing process—and they proved value to warrant a larger starting salary. So often, candidates start qualifying opportunities before they establish their value to a prospective employer. I get candidates all of the time that, after an initial interview, make all kinds of assumptions about the job, the company, and the opportunity *before* they really know about everything.

Sell, sell, sell yourself and communicate what you can do for a company to the point that you are the one the organization wants to hire. Then you can talk about what the company can do for you.

The Time to Qualify

Once you are told that you are the person a company would like to hire and it wants to make you an offer, it is your turn to start asking questions and qualify the opportunity. Up until now, your interviewing process has pretty much been a one-way street.

These particular qualifying questions are not, in my opinion, the same things that you might negotiate. We will get to negotiations in a moment. Negotiations center on the things that have inherent flexibility, such as benefits, title, base pay, bonuses, commissions, and so forth. Things like the working environment, employees, peers, subordinates and superiors, customers, market space, and so forth are not negotiable 99 percent of the time. They are real factors and part of the job opportunity that exists, regardless of who takes the job. But now, since you are the finalist, if you have any questions about the opportunity—and I mean down to the minute detail—is the time to get them clarified.

How to Qualify the Opportunity

Keep it simple. Once you are told that you are the candidate the company would like to hire, explain that you would like to have a meeting with the hiring authority and get as much clarification about all the questions you might have before you start negotiating. Unless the hiring authority is out of state, always have this kind of discussion face-to-face. Never do this over the phone, unless you absolutely have to.

Now, when you meet with the hiring authority, he or she may think that you're ready to accept the job, or at least start talking about specifics such as title, money, and so on. However, you may say something along the lines of, "Mr. or Ms. [hiring authority], I'm really excited about this opportunity. However, I have a number of questions about things that I would like to discuss. So, before we get down to the nitty-gritty, I'd like to find out. . . ." You are prepared with a list of questions about the opportunity that you are either unclear on or haven't had a chance to ask before. It is likely that a hiring authority will have covered or explained many of the issues that you might ask about in the interviewing process. However, now is the time to get *clarification*.

Do not hesitate to get detailed in your investigation. And do not hesitate to ask for an audience with anyone who you feel can answer your questions. It is not out of line for you to ask to talk to peers or subordinates or even other managers in the organization. You have to be sure that you have a clear understanding of everything as much as you can before you *consider* accepting the job.

Try to talk to someone who works for the company and has nothing to do with the job for which you are interviewing. Tell the person that you are thinking about going to work for the company and would like his or her candid opinion. Try to find people who have worked for the company before but are no longer there. Take their opinion with a grain of salt, but nonetheless, try to get it. If possible, get the opinions of customers or suppliers of the company with which you are interviewing.

This due diligence may take one or two more meetings with a hiring authority or other people. Do not string it out for more than one or two days at the most. If you come across as hesitant about the opportunity, it's just too easy for a hiring authority to move on to the second candidate. Be interested and proactive, but do it quickly. The purpose is not to overanalyze; it's to have a clear idea of what you know and what you don't know.

Don't be surprised if you find out information that will cause you to stop the interviewing process and, in essence, turn the opportunity down. I cannot tell you the number of things I have seen candidates discover once they got an offer. I've had candidates find out things such as the hiring authority is an alcoholic; there have been four people in your job over the past twelve months; the hiring authority is being sued for sexual harassment; the owner of the company is going through a terrible divorce that is going to jeopardize the company; and all kinds of other drastic issues that nobody wanted to talk about in the hiring process.

Before *accepting* any job offer, you must ask yourself, "Do I understand clearly everything I need to know about this job?" There should be no loose ends or unanswered questions. Sit down and write out everything you think you know about the job that you gathered in the interviewing process. Write down all the questions that are not clear to you. Then start asking.

How to Evaluate an Offer

It's hard for me to recommend to you exactly how to evaluate an offer. A large part of an individual's decision to take a job is *emotional*. No matter how objectively all of us try to evaluate things, no matter what kind of formulas we can come up with, the primary difference between an individual taking a job and not taking a job comes down to how he or she feels about it. Emotions rule most decisions.

There can be, however, reasonable questions that can be asked to go along with or, in some cases, offset a purely emotional decision. I'm not particularly wild about purely emotional job and career decisions. There has to be some logic, common sense, and reason to the decision. After those kinds of evaluations have been done, your "feel" for the opportunity will help make the decision more clear. So, over the years I developed a ten-question formula to help people decide if an opportunity was good for them. These are simple questions with simple yes or no answers:

✓ 1. Do I like the nature of the work that I will have to perform?
       Yes   No

✓ 2. Can I do the job? Is there a good balance of risk/challenge to the job?
       Yes   No

✓   3. Am I well aware of the company's stability or position stability?
       Yes   No

✓   4. Is the chemistry of the people appropriate?
       Yes   No

✓   5. Is the compensation program fair, reasonable, and commensurate with the job?
       Yes   No

✓   6. Is the opportunity for growth in keeping with my personal goals?
       Yes   No

✓   7. Is the location or territory appropriate?
       Yes   No

✓   8. Is the philosophy of doing business compatible with my personal philosophy?
       Yes   No

✓   9. Does this opportunity build on my previous experience?
       Yes   No

✓ 10. Is it likely that this experience would have carryover for my future goals?
       Yes   No

My rule of thumb is this: If you can answer yes to eight of the ten questions, that's about as good as you're going to get. If you can answer yes to five to seven of the questions, the opportunity may very well be a reasonable one, but you need to think about what kind of compromises you may have to make. If you answered yes to fewer than five of the questions, the opportunity is probably a questionable one.

Now, this is about as simple and logical as it can get. The purpose of this approach is to make you think. It is mostly a quantitative exercise and does not take into account the qualitative aspects of how you feel about the entire situation. There is no way to speculate about that for anyone. But I will tell you that if you have only, say, six yes answers to this exercise, and you don't feel emotionally attracted and strong about the opportunity, you should not take the job because you probably won't be very successful. If you have a total of five yes answers to the survey but you feel tremendously passionate, enthusiastic, and have a "failure is not an option" attitude toward the opportunity, you may well be able to make it a good one.

The purpose of these questions is to help you think out on paper (or aloud, with your coach) all aspects of the opportunity. The final decision will be an emotionally driven one, but at least you will have a reasonably logical assessment of the job opportunity's compatibility.

These questions do not take into account things such as how long you've been out of work and how many other opportunities you may have available to you. If you have been out of work for six months, and this is the only offer that you have received, the number of yes answers may not even matter.

Another way to evaluate an offer is the Ben Franklin approach, which means to simply write down the pros and cons, and analyze them. If you have ten or twelve reasons as to why you ought to accept the job and only two or three reasons as to why you shouldn't, the decision is fairly obvious. The idea is to make you think about all aspects of the position. The T format for this Ben Franklin approach is shown in Figure 15-1.

FIGURE 15-1

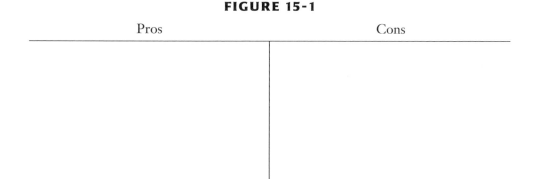

Pros	Cons

Forcing yourself to write out the pros and cons so that you can see all the issues is also a great catharsis. Having your coach helping you out with this exercise is certainly of value. Talking it out with your coach is also of value. Hearing yourself talk about an opportunity and what you think and feel about it will also give you a great perspective.

In the final analysis, I have always stated that if you can get 70 to 75 percent of what you would ideally like in an opportunity, it is about as good as you are going to do. Now, again, this depends on situations to which I am not privy.

At the end of the game, there is always a risk in taking a new job. Do the best you can to analyze all the factors that are involved. Then, follow your gut!

Getting an Offer You Don't Want

If you get an offer that you just don't think you are going to take, it may not hurt to hear the offer out in total. There is a chance that you may have misunderstood many things regarding the job, title, money, or benefits. Again, you have nothing to consider until you have an offer.

If you are certain that you are not going to accept the job, it is best to tell the prospective employer within a reasonably short period of time. Also, I recommend calling the hiring authority to tell the person how much you appreciate the offer, but at this time you are not in a position to accept it.

Always try to leave the door open. If you turn down an opportunity, do it with grace and style. Whatever you do, do not burn bridges by being aloof, condescending, or egotistical. Be very graceful and recognize that you may need an offer from this organization somewhere down the line. I cannot tell you the number of times that I have tried to present a qualified candidate to a good opportunity with a firm that in the past tried to pursue the candidate and he or she had been so rude in dealing with the company that its staff wouldn't consider giving the candidate the time of day. People don't forget when other people are rude to them or treat them in a condescending manner.

If you really want to keep the door open for the future, try this: After you turn down the offer, send the hiring authority a nice note thanking the person for his or her time and effort along with a $10 gift certificate to Starbucks or someplace like it, or maybe a book on the hobby you have in common, like golf or cooking—any small gift that the person will remember you by. This gesture alleviates the irritation that the hiring authority might have over your not taking the job, keeps the door open for future opportunities, and, above all, reinforces the personal relationship that you might have established with the hiring authority.

Getting an Offer You Might Take

Begin by knowing everything there is to know about the opportunity. Get the offer and evaluate it. If you are fortunate enough to be able to compare one offer with another, do it quickly. Another bit of advice is to *never compare an offer in hand with one that you might get in the near future*. A bird in the hand is always more valuable than one in the bush.

Now, if you have a job offer in hand, it is advisable to call any other organizations that you might be considering and tell them you have an offer, and you would like to hear from them by a certain time. You need to put a time limit on this. You don't have much choice, but you might ask the company that has actually given you an offer if you could have a day or so to think about it. However, most organizations won't go beyond a day or so in granting you that time. This is due to fear of losing other candidates who might be viable if you turn the offer down.

By the way, if you are going to discuss other offers with the hiring authority, in order to negotiate and compare, do it only with offers you actually have. And don't hesitate to tell the hiring authority who those offers are with. Most hiring authorities don't believe you when you talk about the proverbial "other opportunities." They consider it to be a bluff.

Some candidates, over the years, have tried to ask the hiring authority for as much as two weeks to make a decision. This screams, "I'm trying to get another offer . . . won't know about it for a week or two. If I don't get it, I might take your job." No smart hiring authority will grant this. I advise my clients to give a candidate one, maybe two days to decide. Even if you are granted more than a day or two, the hiring authority is going to start thinking, "This person is playing this offer against another one. I may lose the next best candidate. I can't afford that." Then he or she will turn around and hire the next best candidate, without your knowledge. Decide, but do it quickly.

Getting an Offer You Would Like to Accept

This is really easy to do. Once you get the offer, tell the hiring authority that you would like to come in and personally discuss the offer face-to-face. The only word of caution I might give you in this situation is to not shut down the interviewing process with any other organization until you are sure of the offer and have it in hand. Even then, I would be sure to try to keep my options open just in case things fall through.

I don't want to jinx anything, but I have experienced numerous instances of candidates being told that they were going to get an offer and then the job never actually materialized. So, when an organization tells you that it would like to make an offer, set a face-to-face meeting to go over the details of the offer and negotiate, if you are going to, but don't tell any other organization that you are in the process or that you are going to accept an offer with someone else.

Negotiating

> "I listened to your radio program over the last two days about how to negotiate. Wow! I had been out of work for four months and as a result of the only interview I had I was getting a job offer. The offer was 20 percent less than what I had earned before and I had to drive 45 minutes to the new job. I felt I needed to take the job because it was the only offer I was even close to. I listened to your strategy on negotiating. . . . I got a signing bonus, a 15 percent increase over what the original offer was, and a review in six months. I would've never known how to do that had I not been listening to you." —Sam, Arlington, Texas

In general, your ability to negotiate an offer depends on the economy and your individual situation. In the late 1990s, it was common, especially for high-tech types of candidates, to be able to look for a job, collect several offers, and literally go to work for the highest bidder. When competition for candidates was very keen, all kinds of things could be negotiated in an offer situation. Much has changed since that time, so you probably won't be selling your services to the highest bidder.

You can get a good sense of the latitude and leverage that you might have in the offering stage by simply paying attention to what you are hearing during the interviewing process. For example, if there are few people in your profession and they are always in high demand, the numbers of opportunities that you are going to have available to you, and your ability to leverage offers, is greater. If, on the other hand, the market is glutted with candidates, your choices and leverage are not very great.

I would never recommend negotiating an offer over the telephone or through email. The only exception to this might be when distance is in issue. Now, the final offer can be discussed and confirmed over the telephone or by email, but if there are going to be any kind of negotiations over specific aspects of the offer, those are always best done face-to-face.

Negotiating an offer, and how it is extended, is done in many different ways by many different organizations, so I can't cover them here. Some companies send offer letters through their corporate office, sometimes from far away. If any negotiation is to be done, it needs to be done before the offer is put into writing. Some companies provide an offer letter, and once that offer letter is in the candidate's hands, the candidate negotiates with the hiring authority. To avoid problems, the candidate—once it is understood that he or she is going to get an offer—should ask the hiring authority how the company would like to proceed with negotiations.

Some companies will make it very clear that there is no negotiation at all in the offer that they will make. Some companies accept the idea that everything is negotiable. Since there is no way of knowing where a company falls between these two poles, you should simply ask for a face-to-face meeting to discuss the offer before it is formally given.

Once you ask for the face-to-face meeting, you should write down every issue that might be covered in the offer discussion. By the way, I do not recommend negotiating an offer with anyone other than the hiring authority. If the HR department insists on making the offer, you have to insist that you need to have a conversation with the hiring authority before you entertain a formal offer. It would be a bad sign if a hiring authority will not discuss a job offer with you before a formal offer is made. In other words, you want to negotiate with the person who has the greatest "pain."

By the time you get to the final stages of an offer, you pretty much know what the parameters of the job opportunity are. It is a good idea, at this offer discussion meeting, to cover each one of these issues to make sure you understand everything that has been discussed and that you and the hiring authority are reading from the same page. Leave absolutely nothing to chance.

The most important issue in your negotiating is for you to know as much as you can about the hiring authority's pain level. You will clearly understand the strength of your negotiating position if you understand as many aspects as possible of what the hiring authority sees and what he or she is experiencing. If you can, you need to find out how many candidates the employer has on the final list. You need to know how long the hiring authority has been looking and whether there are any dates of impending doom—that is, a time when there absolutely must be someone in the job. Has there been a vacancy in the job for a long period of time? Is someone being promoted out of the job within a short period of time? Is there pressure to hire someone, and who is bringing that pressure on? How long has the interviewing process taken?

Step back and put yourself in the shoes of the hiring authority. Try to objectively analyze all the things that have gone on in the interviewing process. Answer this question: "If I were the hiring authority, interviewing me, at this point in the hiring process, how badly do I need and want me?" If your answer is "desperately," then you have a lot of leverage. If your answer is, "Nice to have, but no worries" or "No big deal—if I hire, I hire; if I don't, I don't," then you don't have very much leverage at all.

Some Thoughts on Negotiations

The first rule in negotiation is to never be afraid to walk away. That is a hard concept to understand and difficult to do, especially if you really need a job and this is the only offer you have received in some time. But the hiring authority doesn't know that—and remember, most of negotiating is knowing how to act.

If you sense that the hiring authority is adversarial in the offer discussion meeting, you're off to a poor start. You may not be able to do anything about this, but, I assure you, if the relationship in this conversation doesn't have a "We're all in this together; let's see if we can work it out," tone or attitude to it, you're off to a rocky start and it's not likely to get any better. Most of the time, when a hiring authority comes across in an adversarial way, it's because he or she is scared.

Really Bad Advice

Most of the advice about negotiating a job offer is bad advice. It is usually written by people who never found anyone a job. They come up with crazy theories that can be big mistakes for candidates. One popular book on getting a job advises telling a hiring authority that "I need to negotiate more money because I'm presently underpaid." OMG! Are you kidding me? Say that to most hiring authorities and, *after* they laugh and say, "Well, aren't we all?" they'll probably dismiss you.

If you Google "how to negotiate salary at job offer," you can get some really bad advice, such as:

- "Research the company. If it is booming, go for top salary and benefits."

- "When asked about what you are earning, counter by asking what the pay range is."

- "If you have another offer, leverage it, but don't disclose who it is from."

- "Research Web sites to see what you are worth."

- "Use an offer to get a counteroffer from your company."

- "The person who brings up the salary number first loses the game."

Each one of these statements is either wrong or terribly misleading. For example, "Don't disclose who another offer is with." If a hiring authority asked who the other offer was with and a candidate wouldn't tell them, the hiring authority wouldn't believe there really was another offer. Dumb idea!

The Best Way I've Found to Negotiate

Over the years, I have found that beginning the conversation this way works:

> Mr. or Ms. [hiring authority], I'm really excited about accepting this job and going to work for you and your company. I want you to know I really want this job and I'd like to see it happen for both of us.

This kind of statement lets the prospective employer know that you want the job and you want to try to work something out. Again, the fear of your rejecting them is lessened. (By the way, you still have the right to turn down an offer for whatever reason you wish.) Studies have shown that this kind of "let's all win together" attitude is the best negotiating statement a person can make.

Contrary to what many people might think, most employers are not interested in paying as little as they can get away with paying. Also, most candidates are smart enough to know that if they are grossly overpaid for the service that they render, their employer will catch on and they may be looking for a job, again. Most people are trying to work out as fair a deal as they can for themselves, as well as for the other person.

When you write down all your questions about the opportunity before you get into the final negotiations, you should provide some kind of salary range that you think is reasonable. If you've done your research on this job, you will already know what salary range the hiring authority has in mind. But, if you haven't, you should have some idea about the minimum amount of money that you will consider. If you have been out of work for the past three months or more, you might come up with one figure. If you are currently employed, but anxious to leave your job, you may come up with another one. If you are happily employed, you may come up with a different one. But, remember, compensation is just one aspect of a job. Don't let it be such a focus that you don't take into account other important aspects of the opportunity.

If you are asked about the salary requirement that you seek, answer by saying something along the lines of, "I'm more interested in the whole package—salary, benefits, the company, the future—than I am in one particular salary figure. I'd like to know what you and your company think is fair and to discuss money along with the other benefits of the job. Then I will know what I can and cannot do."

Make sure that you know all the aspects of a job offer before you start negotiating. Here is an elementary list of things that you may want to consider when you look at the total compensation:

- Salary/commissions
- Insurance plans (both health and life)
- Signing bonuses
- Bonuses on specific personal performance
- Overtime pay
- Salary reviews
- Sick leave
- 401(k) investment plans
- Pension plans
- Car and insurance
- Educational reimbursement
- Car allowance
- Children's college tuition plans
- Business expenses
- Day care programs
- Title

- Ability to work from home
- Real-estate assistance
- Membership to a buying club
- Stock options
- Performance bonuses
- Stock purchase plan
- Flextime
- Sabbaticals
- Vacation
- Disability insurance (both short and long term)
- Paid personal days off
- Health club/country club
- Separation package
- Vision/dental/family insurance
- Sales territory realignment

There can be all kinds of other benefits that a company might be able to provide. I have seen benefits such as the personal use of a corporate jet; a deer blind or duck blind lease; entry fees to golf tournaments; ski lodge participation; vacation condo usage; and partial sponsorship for a race car. I once had a candidate, before accepting the job, negotiate time off (with pay, I might add) to train for the World Iron Man contest in Hawaii that he had entered a year in advance.

With healthcare costs in a state of bedlam, you need to be sure about the deductibles, co-pays, and limitations of the insurance program that might be offered. Healthcare and insurance costs have been some of the biggest challenges for 97 percent of the companies in the United States—the ones with fewer than a hundred people. Many of these companies are simply dropping healthcare benefits for their employees. You just need to be sure of exactly what those benefits are, especially in the case of insurance, and who is paying for them.

Candidates often jump the gun and start negotiating money before they hear the whole offer. It is not a good idea to pick out one or two issues about an offer until you have heard and completely understand all of the compensation, benefits program, and any other aspects of an offer. So, even during the face-to-face meeting with a hiring authority, write down all the details of the offer. Most offer letters do not include any of the benefits that I've just mentioned. Some things such as life insurance or health insurance benefits are cast in stone. However, things like base salaries, salary reviews, commissions, and so forth may have a great variable—that may not be known to you.

After you have heard the entire offer and you want to try to negotiate the salary, here is the most successful way to do it. You say:

> "Remember, Mr. or Ms. _____, I do want this job. My employment here will be good for both of us. However, I need to ask, 'Is that the best you can do regarding the salary?'
>
> Then s-h-u-t u-p! If the hiring authority asks something like, "Why do you ask?" Then, you'd better have a good reason, like,
>
> "Well, my last salary was (is) \$XXXXXXXX and I'd like to see if we can get to \$YYYYYYY. What can *we* do to get there?"

This approach does not paint the candidate into a corner. It communicates the idea that "We are all in this together . . . what can *we* do to work this out?" If the hiring authority has done the very best he or she they can and either will not or cannot provide any more money, the candidate has not created an adversarial situation where he or she either begrudgingly accepts the offer or is forced to turn it down. The point is that this kind of negotiation is not confrontational. It communicates, "Let's see if we can work it out—and if we can't, at least we all know that we've done our best."

When my candidates approach negotiating an offer—either the issue of salary, or any other part of the offer—whether the offer changes or stays the same, they always believe that they have asked the hiring authority to do the best they can and the hiring authority usually does. The vast majority of the time, when a candidate asks for reconsideration in such a congenial way, the hiring authority does something to make the offer better. Sometimes it's a lot, sometimes it isn't. But simply asking the hiring authority what he or she can do to make it a better deal for *everyone*—the candidate, the authority and the company—creates an emotional environment where the hiring authority actually wants to make the offer better.

Even if the offer doesn't change, the candidate knows that he or she has done what is possible to get the best offer without creating an adversarial feeling on the part of the hiring authority. It makes it easier for the candidate to accept the offer without feeling as if the individual has "lost a fight." The hiring authority will respect the manner in which the candidate negotiated.

Now, you've got to *practice, practice, practice* these statements. When you do, you will be mystified by how well they work. There is not a week that goes by that I don't get three or four candidates call me, laughing with excitement and saying, "It worked . . . just like you said it would. It really worked. Thanks. I would never have thought to negotiate that way."

Last week one of our candidates got an offer for $95,000. She told us that after discussing every aspect of the job with the hiring authority, she calmly and sincerely said: "This opportunity is great for both of us. I really want this job, but is that the best we can do with the salary?" She said that the hiring authority immediately said with no hesitation, "I think we can make it $110,000; can you start immediately?" An extra $15,000 for one simple question—not bad!

Accepting an Offer

Once you have received an offer, have negotiated every aspect of the offer that you need to, and have a clear understanding that the opportunity is reasonable, you can either come to an agreement at that meeting or explain to the hiring authority that you would like to think it over and/or discuss it with your spouse. Do not postpone letting the hiring authority know your decision for more than one day. When a candidate asks for more than a day to inform the employer, this will usually result in one of two conclusions: The candidate is not very decisive or the candidate is going to use the offer to leverage another opportunity. I've known hiring authorities to rescind an offer on the spot if candidates didn't appear decisive in their acceptance.

Until a candidate has accepted an offer, most hiring authorities feel absolutely no moral obligation to that candidate. Hiring authorities, just like anyone else, want to avoid the fear of loss. It is not uncommon for an employer to make an offer, be told by the candidate that he or she will let the company know in a few days, then the employer gets scared that he or she may be left in the lurch, so the job is offered to the next candidate—without even telling the first candidate.

Getting It in Writing

Contrary to what people may think, a signed written offer, except in very rare instances, is not a legally binding implied contract. Candidates often think that because they have a written and signed offer, signed and accepted by them, that they have some sort of legal document that protects them if they show up for work and the job has been eliminated before they even begin. There is nothing that protects the candidate from that scenario.

According to our labor law attorney, most states are *employment-at-will* states, which means that the employer or the candidate can terminate the employment relationship at any time for just about any reason, except for illegal ones like race or age discrimination. I'm not an attorney and don't want to interpret law. But I do know that unless there is a clear or implied long-term promise of employment—as well as hefty damages that can be proven—if a candidate accepts a job, even if the offer is spelled out in writing, he or she has practically no legal recourse if the job doesn't materialize.

However, there are two major reasons you want to get a written offer with as much detail as possible. The first reason is that, at least 30 percent of the time, the written offer you received will be somewhat different from all the things you talked about with the hiring authority. These usually are not malicious mistakes. Often these letters are standard letters that emanate from an HR department or simply an administrative person whose job it is to write offer letters, among other things. Sometimes things get lost in translation.

The biggest shock in this kind of situation is that often hiring authorities literally overpromise what the company will allow them to do in an offer situation. Now, nobody is ever going to admit to doing that, but it does happen more than you would think. An overzealous hiring authority convinces a candidate to come to work by promising things that the company won't allow such as special stock options, large signing bonuses, or a salary beyond the permissible limits. The hiring authority often waits until the candidate—who has emotionally already bought into the job and emotionally accepted the opportunity—receives the letter and then explains, "Oh, by the way, I wasn't able to get that for you, but I tried." This can cause a great deal of heartburn and pain for a candidate who thinks he or she is accepting a position with one set of terms and then is faced with another set when he or she receives the offer letter.

Along this same line, special arrangements that you might make with the hiring authority in order to take the job may completely change if crazy things happen—such as if the hiring authority leaves the company three or four weeks after you start. So, any kind of special arrangements that are made between you and the hiring authority should be reflected in the offer letter.

The second reason that you want to get an offer in writing is to be sure that your paychecks, when you start getting them, are what you agreed to, including benefits and benefits deductions. It is not uncommon for an earnings agreement, either verbal or actually written, to be handled by a number of people on its way to getting put into the payroll system. These are normally just human errors, but the shock of something like this doesn't make the start of your new job any easier. You don't want any surprises, so have as much written down in the offer letter as is reasonable.

Setting a Start Date

Most people would think that this is an easy thing to do once they have accepted a job. But as I've mentioned before, it ain't over 'til your butt is in the chair—and even then it might not be over. You will want as little time to go by as possible between the time you accept the job and when you actually start the job. Why? Because strange things can happen.

Once you've accepted the offer, you should try to get to the new job as soon as possible. It is rare to have something happen to the job between the time of accepting the offer and actually starting the job, but it can and does happen. I have seen companies sold, head counts frozen, changes in management, and all kinds of other things that may alter the status of the situation just before the candidate shows up for work at the new job.

Personally, I always get a little nervous when the starting date for a candidate is further out than two weeks. If there are extenuating circumstances and a starting date has to be set beyond a two-week period of time (I have seen as much as ninety days), you need to take precautions to be sure that you stay on the mind of the hiring authority. I recommend that if the starting date is more than two weeks away, you should call the hiring authority; take the hiring authority to lunch during that period of time, or take some other action that will keep your interest in the forefront of the hiring authority's mind.

Handling Your Transition Smoothly and Confidently

HERE'S A LETTER I RECEIVED from a candidate whose experience proves the value of my advice:

> Good morning, Tony,
>
> I'm not sure if you remember meeting me in your office, but I wanted to send a quick email to touch base. You may remember I had accepted a position with your client and then declined the next day due to a large counteroffer from my current employer. Well, we had some interesting developments yesterday. It turns out that what you said about a counteroffer was true. It was the biggest mistake of my business career. After giving me a big raise, the board of directors has decided to dissolve the company as of yesterday afternoon. That being said, I'm back out on the market. I've attached my résumé again for your review. If you have anything that you think I might be interested in, please give me a call. Thanks, Tony.
>
> Justin
>
> P.S.: When you tell people about the disasters of accepting a counteroffer and they don't believe you, have them call me.

If you were unemployed and have recently found a job, resigning is not a crucial issue to you. However, if you are currently employed, and especially if you have been for a fairly long period of time (five years or more by today's standards), leaving your job may be harder than you think. You should be prepared for your own trepidation. Even if your resignation ought to be an easy thing to do, it is still emotionally charged, and *doing it the right way* makes a really big difference.

Whether you think resigning is going to be emotionally easy on both you and your employer or not, you need to be prepared to do it the right way so that you don't burn any bridges on the way out.

The Graceful Way to Leave

I've had candidates resign by email. I've known people to just not show up for their job and, three or four days later, call their supervisor to tell the person that they are resigning. In other cases, they simply did not show but never called; after a number of days, it was just assumed that they had left the company. None of these are the right way to do things.

People will often resort to this type of final exit simply because they are nervous, scared, and just don't want to face up to the task of gracefully resigning. Most people mentally and emotionally leave the job a long time before they actually physically leave. They are so mentally and emotionally spent and so sick of the whole thing that they just want to leave as fast as possible.

Where this sort of thing comes back to haunt them is in a reference check. It is common for a previous manager, even though he or she knows better, to tell someone who is checking a reference in a situation like this something along the lines of, "Well, when he or she left here, it was a real mess." A poor reference is implied simply by communicating a veiled aura of negativity surrounding the previous employee's departure from a company.

There are some people who will have a more difficult time than others in resigning. If you fall into any of the following categories that I'm going to mention, be prepared for the process to be a little more difficult than you thought. The kinds of people who have the most difficult time in resigning are:

- *First-Time Job Changers.* You feel guilty about leaving the company that gave you your first chance.

- *Longtime Employees.* You feel like you have grown up with the company; it's hard to say good-bye.

- *Those Who Hint About Leaving All the Time.* You have repeatedly threatened to leave before and now you really are!

- *Single-Reason Leavers.* You may be reluctant to tell the single reason for your wanting to leave or you may be afraid your reason sounds insignificant to others, although it is important to you.

- *Multifaceted/Multitask People.* You're the kind of person who has significant influence in the company; you feel like you are letting everybody down by leaving.

- *Family Members.* You are either immediately or closely related to the people who own or manage the company.

The Resignation Letter

"Leaving my company was emotionally difficult. The way you instructed me in handling the transition made it so much easier." —Marla T., New York

Always resign with a written letter. Be resolute and firm in your commitment to resign. You cannot afford a weak or ambivalent attitude. Here's a sample resignation letter:

Date_____

Dear [direct supervisor's name]:

My resignation from the position of [current title] is effective as of today.

I really appreciate and will always remember my experience in working with you and [your company]. Thank you for what you've taught me over the [a period of time] and for the many contributions that you have made to my personal and professional development. I truly hope that we can stay in touch from time to time in the years ahead.

I will always have positive memories about the professionalism at [your company].

The status of my work is up-to-date and I will turn it over to whomever you designate.

Sincerely,
[Your name]

That's it! Do not make the letter more complicated than this. Do not teach, preach, cajole, or elaborate as to why you're leaving. Many people want to set 'em straight, tell them where they went wrong, tell them where they can get off, explain to them why they have a stupid company, list what they ought to do to fix the company, and so forth. You're wasting your breath. You are leaving and they don't care what you think.

The Face-to-Face Meeting

Be relaxed and easy. Don't be nervous. Take a deep breath. Play a movie in your mind that it's going to go very smoothly. Practice the scenario in a role-play with your coach. You want to be aggressive and prepared. Do not make an appointment to resign. Simply go to your supervisor during a regular, workday moment and say, "May I speak with you a moment?"

You should resign to only one person. Do not convene a group or committee. Doing so creates a one-against-many situation, and the emotional odds are against you. Resign with your direct supervisor. Try to do it in person, unless your supervisor is in a distant city and you must do it by phone.

If you have to resign from a distance, have a telephone conversation before you either send or email the letter. If you think that there is going to be a negative emotional response to your leaving, you want to communicate person-to-person. Begin by thanking your boss for all the opportunities that he or she and the company have given you. Even if you hate the person, the job, and the company, it is hard for a person to have an acrimonious conversation when you are thanking him or her.

Be sure to include in your opening statement that you have already accepted another position and that you are going to be leaving the company. Say something like this:

"Mr. or Ms._____, I have accepted another employment opportunity and I want to give notice today. I'd like to thank you for making a real contribution to my career development. I would like to do everything possible during the next [time frame] to make my transition out of your department and the company a smooth one. What is the easiest way for us to make this transition?"

If the boss tries to engage you in conversation about the new job, or the offer, or says, "How could you do this to me or us?" or even hints at a counteroffer, preempt his or her comments by saying:

"[Name], I think you know I really respect our relationship a lot and I know that this comes as a surprise to you. However, I would really appreciate it if you would not try to make the process of my resignation any more difficult than it has to be. [pause] I have accepted another opportunity, and I appreciate all that you've done but I am resolute about leaving. I have made my decision. I ask for your understanding. Now, what is the easiest way to make this transition?"

You might also add:

"I have taken the liberty of writing up all of the projects I am working on and their current status. If you could take a moment with me to review them in the next day or so, I'd be happy to do anything I can to complete them or hand them over during the next [time frame]."

Do not go into resigning by stating that you are thinking about taking another position, or that you are thinking about changing jobs, or anything that is wishy-washy and spineless. You must go in with the decisive, factual, "I have taken another job" statement. This has to be an absolute fact, not a whim.

Be prepared to preempt a counteroffer. I will discuss counteroffers in a few moments, but even entertaining the idea of a counteroffer is suicide. If you go on and on about how difficult a decision it was or how hard you thought about it, or how you talked it over with your spouse, you not only compromise your position, but you appear weak and pitiful.

Offer two weeks' notice. Even if you know that the company will want you to leave immediately, you still want to be courteous and offer two weeks. *Do not offer more than two weeks!* It is not good for you or your company. You have mentally and emotionally left a long time ago. You're gone—so physically leave as soon as you can.

Remain Graceful

It is best not to gloat about your new job or your new company. It isn't good to brag about the opportunity for which you are leaving. There is a tendency to be proud of your new job and run off at the mouth about the new opportunity, as though to say, "Wow, look at me, guess what I've got!" Simply remember that you are resigning, not competing. Stay away from lecturing or trying to instruct the company on how it ought to change things in the future so people like you wouldn't leave. It will only insult the company.

It is advisable not to discuss your new job, your new company, or all the reasons that you are leaving with any of your peers, subordinates, or anyone else in the company. Your leaving should not be a topic of conversation with you or with anyone else. Even if your parting is amiable, once you quit, the relationship with everyone is strained. Make it simple and easy for everybody.

Counteroffers Rarely Work Out

I don't think that I would say counteroffers are a disaster 100 percent of the time. But I do figure that they don't work at least 98 percent of the time. A counteroffer is when the candidate goes in to resign and the company tries to buy him or her back. The employer tries to do things to patch up the relationship when the person goes in to resign. It hardly ever works out for the candidate.

Interestingly enough, there has been an uptick in these attempts over the last few years. You'd think with the idea that "there are so many people looking for work" employers couldn't care less if someone leaves; he or she would be easy to replace. But the thought of doing that is still difficult and, as you will see, hiring authorities would rather replace someone on their own time table rather than a departing employee's. No matter what the job market, accepting a counteroffer is still a poor idea.

I have seen hundreds of counteroffers over the years where a candidate decides to stay with his or her current employer. However, I know very few who have ever lasted long at all. Most every candidate I've ever known to receive and accept a counteroffer leaves the company within a four- to six-month period of time—either of his or her own volition or because the person is fired. And most of the time, when this happens, it is an adversarial, acrimonious departure. Once a counteroffer is made and accepted, the whole relationship between the employer and the employee who was looking to leave has changed. The emotional strain that it creates results in a distressful, distrustful relationship that becomes irreparable.

More often than not, a candidate who goes to the trouble to go out and look for a job (and actually receives another offer) doesn't really think about a counteroffer. It usually comes as a little bit of a surprise. Don't let that happen!

Here are sixteen reasons why counteroffers rarely work:

1. If your company really recognized your worth, they would've given you the added income, advancement, title, whatever without the necessity of you, in effect, blackmailing your employer by finding another job and threatening to quit.

2. If you accept the counteroffer, you will usually be looked upon as a person who blackmailed management or the company into giving you what you wanted.

3. When the next salary reviews come around, you will already have received your raise and you will be bypassed.

4. The reason that you were made a counteroffer is that, at that moment, they needed you worse than you needed them.

5. In essence, you are firing your company. No one likes to be fired. So, the company is going to do what any fired person would do: hang on until it can rectify the situation—that is, replace you.

6. Good companies (well-managed companies) don't buy people back. The only kind of company that will buy you back is the kind of company that will take advantage of you somewhere down the line.

7. It is cheaper for a company to try to make you a counteroffer than it is to immediately replace you.

8. Money and title are temporary. If the major complaint about your job has to do with money, when the money changes, you'll only be temporarily content.

9. The momentary emotion of suddenly being made to feel special overrides the logical, common sense that forced you to go out and look for a job.

10. The trust relationship that you had with your employer is no longer there.

11. The fact that you can no longer be trusted affects everyone you work with. You held management's feet to the fire, you blackmailed the company, and, what is worse, everyone in the company knows it.

12. You caught management with its pants down. Most likely, the company had no idea this was coming. So, it's going to do whatever it can to keep you so that it can buy time and find a replacement.

13. Your supervisor and your company, at least for a while, are going to put their finger in the dike to keep you around simply because other people are going to have to take up your slack if you leave.

14. Your immediate supervisor is likely to say, "How could you do this now? It couldn't come at a worse time!" Your ego will be stroked and fed simply to buy time for your manager to recover by replacing you.

15. The world is motivated by self-interest. If your leaving makes your supervisor look bad, he or she is going to do anything reasonable to look good by keeping you—then look really good and decisive by firing you with a replacement in the wings.

16. The higher level position that you have, the more likely you are to be presented with a counteroffer by more than one person in the organization. I've had candidates who, once they gave their resignation notice, were literally escorted from manager to manager throughout the company to convince the candidate to stay.

Put your ego aside and follow good common sense. Tell the people making you a counteroffer that you really appreciate their offer, but that you have made up your mind and you are going to leave. *No matter how tempting it is, never accept a counteroffer.*

A New Job

Most people think that once they have started a new job, their job search is over. I am continually amazed at the strange things that can take place even after a person has started a new job.

The first bit of advice is for you to expect that the job is going to be quite a bit different from what you thought it was going to be when you were going through the interviewing process. Things are never the way they appear on the outside looking in.

The second suggestion is to spend the first few weeks or even months simply observing what goes on in the company. The higher the position that you may have, the more you want to quietly observe how the company is run. You really want to get a good idea of what is going on in the company before you start actively showing people what you can do for them.

The best way to find out what really goes on in an organization is to talk to the most senior level administrative personnel (we used to call them secretaries). These people know more about what is going on in the inner workings of the organization than anybody else. Now, these people may not be the decision makers in an organization, but they still know more of what is going on in a company than all the managers combined.

Get to know your supervisor's personality and style. Do this with all the people with whom you might interface. Remember that you are the new kid on the block and that you don't know the character or personality of the people or the part of the organization that you are working with.

Don't hesitate to ask lots and lots of questions regarding procedures and protocols. Nobody expects you to be intuitive about anything. It may not hurt to take notes about what you learn, especially regarding the unofficial procedures. A friend of mine who has been a "work" psychologist for forty years, Frank Lawlis, tells the story that the best advice he got about starting a new job was to "be quiet and walk around for about six months before you start trying to sound off."

Recognize and avoid the negative people who exist within every organization. They can range from the people who always see the glass half empty to the people who are downright negative, gossipy, and in some cases, slanderous. Avoid them like the plague.

The most important thing you can do as a professional when beginning a new job is to be quiet and try not to draw attention to yourself until you really learn about the company and the personalities of the people from the inside. Too often, newly hired professionals try to make an immediate impact to show how good they are by drawing attention to themselves in a number of ways before they really know the so-called lay of the land.

No matter how good you might be, no matter how smart you are, no matter how much you might be able to contribute to the organization, you will have much more impact and be received with much more respect if you learn as much as you can about the organization and its personalities before you start having significant input. There is going to be plenty of time to prove yourself.

Epilogue: The Top Ten Reasons People Have Trouble Finding a Job

TO REINFORCE THE IDEAS I've presented in this book, I've come up with ten gut-level reasons people have a hard time finding a job. Heed these warnings and your chances of finding a job will increase dramatically.

1. *Finding a job is truly a job in itself—but too many people don't treat it as such.* They don't adopt a committed, passionate, failure-is-not-an-option attitude and recognize that finding a job is entirely a numbers game. First, you must explore numerous avenues for seeking interviews, including friends, relatives, previous employers, former colleagues, competitors, and cold-calling on the phone. Then, when it comes to interviews themselves, it's *all* numbers: The more interviews you get, the better your chances of getting called back; the more times you're called back, the better your chances of landing a good job.

2. *People don't make their job search systematic.* A job search system should include everything from documenting goals and intentions, which dictate planned activity, to role-playing of interviews. If your job search is not strategically systematic, you'll stumble around with no intention, direction, or goal. People who do not employ a systematic strategy are very unlikely to get what they want. Either you decide to look for a job, or your job fate will be decided for you.

3. *People unrealistically assess the marketability of their skills.* As a result, some candidates apply for positions for which they are not truly qualified. These candidates are surprised to receive rejections, and the job search can take them much longer than they anticipated. This can lead to disappointment and frustration, which can further distract a candidate from conducting a focused job search.

4. *People focus on minor things that appear to be job-finding activities, but that aren't the activities most likely to be fruitful.* It is worth remembering that "activity" is not the same as "productivity."

5. *People don't go far enough to get interviews.* Getting face-to-face interviews is the only thing that matters. There are all kinds of ways to get face-to-face interviews; the main thing is just to get them. Pulling out all the stops and doing anything you can to get in front of a hiring authority with "pain" (i.e., the need to hire someone) is the key to job search success.

6. *People don't prepare well for interviews.* At the very least, it's important to prepare and practice presentations, to yourself and others, as to why you ought to be hired. Most people don't prepare—and in addition to leaving such important responses to chance, they are also, as a result, lacking the self-confidence that can be helpful on an interview.

7. *People present unhelpful reasons for wanting a job.* This includes reasons they are leaving their current position (or why they left their last one) and why they want a different one. Most people respond to this question from a selfish, me-centered point of view. They criticize and bad-mouth their current or past employers, imagining that a prospective employer is going to identify with them. They're so wrong!

8. *People are afraid to ask questions that risk rejection.* They don't acquire as much useful information as they could, letting opportunities slip away. Ask the cold, hard questions like "How do I stack up against other candidates you've seen?" or "How would you evaluate me as a candidate?"—and the most important question: "What do I need to do to get this job?"

9. *Job candidates tend to imagine that interviews are a "two-way street."* Too many people interview with a "What can *you* do for *me*?" attitude. They believe that the employer is just as responsible for selling them on the company and the job as they are for selling themselves to the employer. What they don't realize is that until the employer has made them an offer, there is nothing they need to consider. Tell employers what *you* can do for *them*. Give employers enough reasons to hire you, and they will come forward with plenty of answers on what they can do for you—to get you to accept their offer.

10. *People don't know how to sell themselves in interviews.* This is true of the vast majority of people in interviewing situations. People routinely neglect everything from dressing properly to focusing on what they can do for a prospective employer. Perhaps worst of all, they don't come right out and ask for the job. And, as with any good salesperson, if you want to make the sale—it helps to ask.

So, now you know what you need to do. Good luck—and God bless you!

Index

initial interview *(continued)*
  follow-ups to, 162–167
  with lower-keyed,
    analytical,
    amiable types,
    154–160
  purpose of, 134
  selling yourself in, 136–137
  with take-charge types,
    137–154
  top mistakes made in,
    134–136
intensity, 21–22
intentions, setting, 24–28
internal recruiters, 46
Internet job searches, 95,
  116–132
  brand building in, 124–128
  company and people
    research in, 118–119
  the HR barrier in, 123–124
  job boards for, 119–121
  responding to postings in,
    121–123
  scams and solicitations
    related to, 116–118
  using social media in,
    128–132
Internet Your Way to a New Job
  (Alison Doyle), 124
interview questions
  about compensation,
    215–218
  about whether they like
    you, 204–207
  about whether you are a
    risk, 207–215
  about your ability to do the
    job, 199–203
  delivery of answers to, 197
  illegal or inappropriate,
    218–220
  subjects of, 198–199
  top mistakes in answering,
    197–198

interviews
  body language in, 196–197
  dressing for, 195–196
  face-to-face, *see* face-to-face
    interviews
  follow-up, *see* follow-up
    interviews
  importance of, 29
  initial, *see* initial interview
  number of, 174–175
  as one-way streets, 100
  reasons for receiving, 16–17
  telephone, *see* telephone
    interviews
  while still employed,
    252–256
  worst places for, 63
  worst times for, 63
introductory emails, 88–91
IT consulting firms, 47

job boards, online, 119–121
job fairs, 36
job function, explaining,
  140–141
Job Interviews for Dummies
  (Joyce Lain Kennedy),
  241
job market
  changes in, 105
  following recessions, 2
  myths and misperceptions
    about, 92–106
  and quality of skills, 101
job offers, *see* offers
job openings, 16
job postings, responding to,
  121–123
job satisfaction, 15, 249–250
job searches
  casual, 103
  reasons for difficulty in,
    306–307
  while still employed,
    see job search while

employed
see also specific topics
job search process, 19–28
  focusing on, 21
  goals and intentions in,
    24–28
  passion, intensity, and
    enthusiasm in, 21–22
  positive attitude in, 23–27
job search programs, 35–36
job search while employed,
  102–103, 246–258
  and calls from recruiters,
    257–258
  and contacts with
    competitors, suppliers,
    or customers, 256
  and dressing for interviews,
    252–253
  giving your reasons for,
    254–255
  and interviewing, 252,
    255–256
  reasons for engaging in,
    248–250
  and selling yourself,
    253–254

Kennedy, Joyce Laine, 126,
  241
Kennedy Information, Inc., 40
key words and phrases
  in online searches, 119, 120
  in résumés, 74–75

laid off, bias against being,
  222–223
lawsuit records, 273
lawyers, as lead source, 37
*Leadership and the One Minute
  Manager* (Kenneth
  Blanchard), 24
lies (on résumés), 85–86
liking you, questions related to,
  204–207

Announcing!

AMACOM's Career Success Titles